Self-study at A level

THE FRENCH REVOLUTION

Lucille Kekewich
Susan Rose

Longman

Acknowledgements

Many thanks are due to Dr Angela Scholar for translating from French the documents on the following pages: 9; 22; 27; 28; 31; 34; 45-7; 48-9; 78-9.

Thanks are also due to Adele Sheffer, who typed the major part of the manuscript, deciphering the authors' handwriting with apparent ease.

ISBN 0 582 037948

First published 1990

© Longman Group UK Ltd

Set in 10 on 12pt Cheltenham

Printed in Great Britain by Longman Group Resources Unit

The Authors

LUCILLE KEKEWICH has taught history in schools, a college of education and the Extra-Mural Department of the University of London. For over a decade she has worked for the Open University in the London Region, where one of her principal concerns has been the design of effective face-to-face and distance tuition techniques.

SUSAN ROSE taught sixth-form history groups in a variety of London schools for some ten years. Since 1977 she has been teaching for the Open University, and since 1987 at Richmond International College. At both these institutions she teaches courses covering the eighteenth century.

Susan Rose and Lucille Kekewich have previously collaborated in the production of *Open London*, the Open University's study guide to London and its history.

Contents

Contents

Introduction

The 1989 bicentenary of the French Revolution prompted the publication of a whole spate of new books and articles in which the 200-year-old historical controversy over its causes, course and significance raged unabated. This, along with the fact that most histories of early modern or modern Europe either finish or commence in the period of the Revolution, demonstrates the importance that modern opinion still attaches to the event. This book seeks to guide you through the political and ideological developments of that period by considering the principal events of 1789 to 1795 and the ideas which affected them. It does so by quoting documentary and pictorial evidence and by incorporating, in Part Two, five special studies. Part Three of the book consists of three Appendices which are designed, in conjunction with the Glossary, as easy-access reference sections covering the important terms, people and events of the Revolution. Information from all these sources can be used to answer the Self-Assessment Questions which are regularly raised and discussed in Part One. These questions provide valuable preparation for tackling the specimen A level examination questions, selected from a broad range of boards and syllabuses, which can be found in Part Three.

Whatever a contemporary historian's aspirations to provide a neutral commentary may be, the shifting interpretations of the past two centuries cannot be ignored. The anti-Jacobin reaction of the years after 1794 was followed by the work of more liberal nineteenth-century historians who made moderates such as Mirabeau and La Fayette their heroes. Twentieth-century thought has been dominated by the reinterpretation of Marxist and socialist historians like Mathiez, Lefebvre and Soboul, who have seen the Revolution primarily as a conflict between the classes and who sympathise with the aims of the Jacobins. Recent years have witnessed the onslaught of the Revisionists who were anticipated by Cobban in England, and whose views are typified in France by Furet. They question the class basis of the revolutionary crises and also, even more radically, whether the Revolution achieved much social or economic improvement for the majority of the French people. Feminist historians can raise the latter question even more acutely from the point of view of 50 per cent of the nation.

This book does not attempt to offer solutions to the problems outlined above, but rather to provide some evidence from which readers may draw their own conclusions. The Self-Assessment Questions are intended to provide models of how such evidence may be evaluated and used to form an opinion.

The authors have adopted three themes for the book around which to organise the large amount of material available and make sense of it. The first theme is predominantly political, concentrating on why and how the Revolution started, and on why it did not end with the promulgation of the Constitution in September 1791. In other words, since the main demands of the deputies who met in the Estates-General in 1789 were grudgingly accepted by the monarchy during the next two years, what explanation can be given for the increasingly extreme and violent final years of the Revolution? The series of crises which occurred both before and after the agreement on a constitution, which limited but did not abolish royal power, will be considered since their nature and outcome may provide a partial answer to this question.

1

The second theme of the book addresses the question of how far the revolutionaries were attempting to achieve a preconceived ideal of good government, and how far they were carried along by events. It is suggested that two major ideological influences were available to supporters of reform and that both were important. The first influence was the examples provided by the English Revolution of 1688 and the recent American Revolution which overthrew British rule. In the latter upheaval the Americans secured for themselves what the English nobility, gentry and, to some extent, middle classes, had enjoyed for a century. This was the rule of an executive (in the case of America, a president rather than a monarch) limited in power by two legislative assemblies which ensured equality before the law and security of property. Linked to these practical examples of political reform was the work of the Enlightenment, more particularly the writings of French philosophers such as Voltaire, d'Holbach, Montesquieu and Diderot. Their rational, scientific, secular approach to social, political and religious institutions encouraged their contemporaries to question and seek to reform what could not be justified by reason. Rousseau is often included with other thinkers of the Enlightenment, but in this book his life and works, deemed to have deviated in important respects from those of the other philosophers, are considered to be an ideological influence which made an impact on only some of the revolutionaries. His belief in the supreme power or sovereignty of the General Will which could justify either democracy or dictatorship and his fervent support of a religion unencumbered by dogma and based on Nature, distinguished his ideas from those of his contemporaries. It is suggested that Rousseau's ideas can be discerned in some policies of the government for a short period during the Jacobin Republic.

Most of the leading figures of the Revolution were affected, to some extent, by all of the influences mentioned above. Purely pragmatic considerations probably determined many of the developments of the period, yet, since it is so often stated that reforming ideologies were a major cause of the Revolution, it is important to trace their impact throughout its course. Maximilien Robespierre, whose career provides the third theme of the book, provided evidence in both his speeches and writings before and during the Revolution that he had been influenced by the thought of the Enlightenment and especially by Rousseau. Of all the revolutionary leaders Robespierre is the most informative for historians, as some evidence of his beliefs and policies survives from the pre-revolutionary period. In the early years of the struggle, his was a minor but important voice. His influence reached its height between 1792 and mid-1794. When the Thermidoreans dismantled Jacobin power during 1794-5, they were reacting against the theories as well as the practice he represented. His career provides an insight into how the ideas and attitudes of many supporters of reform changed during the course of the Revolution. A rising young provincial lawyer, part of a local intellectual élite, he went to Paris as a deputy for the Third Estate in 1789. A combination of his own convictions grounded in the Enlightenment, and the development of events made him increasingly radical until he became the chief apologist for the Terror.

The concentration on political and ideological themes will have repercussions for the treatment of other important areas. Five of these are given detailed consideration by specialists in the Essays which form Part Two of the book. These are:
1. The French Revolution and the Provinces;
2. Ideas of Government in the Early Phase of the Revolution;
3. Images of Revolution;
4. The War and the Revolution;
5. Jacobinism.

Reference will be made to these Essays in Chapters 1-4, especially in the Self-Assessment Questions, which form an integral part of the Chapters.

The type of study technique used in this book is fairly familiar in contemporary education but it may still be helpful to bear some points in mind. The Self-Assessment Questions only assist readers to measure their knowledge of the material and develop a critical approach to it if they are rigorous in observing the instructions. It is essential to have done the work indicated thoroughly before attempting an answer. These answers should take the form of paragraphs, normally one or two for each question, written by the student. If the authors' discussion, which gives their version of an appropriate answer at the end of the questions, is consulted before the work is completed, the results are unlikely to be so helpful. Few historians believe that absolutely right and wrong answers exist to questions posed about the past, so the discussions provided are by no means the only way in which the questions can be tackled. The discussions contain few new ideas or pieces of information (the latter are usually identified by being enclosed between brackets). For those who do not wish to answer the questions, the discussions can provide useful summaries of the preceding section. Indeed this is one of the purposes for which Self-Assessment Questions are designed.

Judicious use of the Glossary, Appendices and Index will supplement the information given in the Chapters and Essays, and assist in the understanding and answering of the questions. The Glossary explains concisely the most important terms encountered in the text. The Who's Who (Appendix 1) gives a brief sketch of the careers of all those mentioned by name. The Chronology (Appendix 3) clarifies the often confusing sequence of events in the Revolution and emphasises those most significant. In the Bibliography a few of the titles are highlighted as being especially accessible, useful and relevant.

This book has been written to prepare students for A level history papers which cover the revolutionary period. It aims to impart the following:
i)   knowledge of the sequence of major events from the revolt of the Notables in 1787 to Napoleon Bonaparte's intervention in *Vendémiaire* 1795;
ii)   an appreciation of the main factors which determined the nature of the crises which occurred;
iii) an understanding of some of the ideas which can be shown to have influenced the reformers;
iv)   experience of selected documents and illustrations which provide evidence for the opinions discussed;
v)   a deeper knowledge of five areas of special concern to contemporary historians;
vi)   an ability to analyse and discuss issues modelled on the technique of the Self-Assessment Questions.

In other words it should be possible to respond to the sombre questions begged by Lefebvre in the conclusion of his great study of the French Revolution:

> 'An episode in the general rise of the bourgeoisie, the French Revolution still remains among all others, the most striking. This was not because of its tragic events alone; it also contained for future generations the germs of conflict.'

> Lefebvre, 1967

PART ONE

CHAPTERS 1-5

Figure 1 France in 1789, showing many of the places mentioned in this book.

Chapter 1

WHY WAS THERE A REVOLUTION?

1.1 France under the *ancien régime*

French society

French society in the middle of the eighteenth century could be pictured in very simple terms, as is shown in Figure 2 below. All burdens eventually fell, or so it is suggested, on the peasantry which was crushed by the demands of the nobility and the Church. Does this representation bear any relation to the true state of affairs?

Figure 2 *Les 3 ordres.* Caricature of the *ancien régime* tax system: a peasant carrying a noble and a clergyman on his back. *(Edimédia, Paris)*

The privileged elements of French society were certainly the clergy – the First Estate – and the nobility – the Second Estate. The remainder of the population, the vast majority, could in some measure be seen as the Third Estate, though this term was in practice usually reserved for those who had at least a bare minimum of property, thus excluding the destitute and those without occupation. The divisions between the Estates were not simply a matter of wealth or social esteem; they were determined by law. But French society was rather more complex than this simplified picture might suggest.

The nobility, once supposed to be the lineal descendants of the Frankish invaders from the days of the fall of the Roman Empire, now consisted of various groups. The *noblesse de l'épée* (military nobles) were the supposed remains of the ancient warrior caste, though in many cases their nobility was of much more recent origin. The *noblesse de la robe* (lawyer nobles) were the families of the Crown's more important office-holders, who in many cases had purchased the inheritance of both their nobility and their office. In many cities wealthy bourgeois had also acquired nobility through participating in town government, again combined with the purchase of office. Apart from differences in origin, the nobility was also divided in a different way: those who endured the splendours – and discomforts – of Versailles, hanging on the King's every whim in hope of gaining favour and advancement (probably between 4,000 and 20,000 out of a total of 400,000) lived a very different kind of life from that of the provincial nobility.

Among the provincial nobility there was little identity of interest either. Some *hoberaux* (despised, poverty-stricken country nobles) in Brittany (see Figure 21, p.106) might have had only the memory of ancient lineage to distinguish them from peasant farmers. Others might have been highly successful wine growers in Bordeaux, or have been involved in the growth of the textile industry in Lyons.

Some factors did make for unity among this disparate group of individuals. They were all exempt from the *taille personnelle* (the direct tax paid on the estimated annual value of one's possessions) but not necessarily from the *taille réelle* (a land tax raised in certain French provinces, originally paid only by non-noble proprietors, but which continued to be exacted if the land passed into noble hands). The *taille personnelle* was by far the most productive of all the direct taxes, so this exemption was of considerable value. Nobles did pay certain small sums due under the *capitation* (poll tax) and the *vingtième* (one-twentieth of the annual value of most income), taxes introduced by Louis XIV and Louis XV in an attempt to get round the manifest inequalities of the *tailles*. The assessment system was, however, manipulated to the nobles' advantage, leaving them paying a smaller percentage than might have been expected.

The nobility and clergy also benefited from the system of seigneurial dues which could bring in quite considerable sums in income to members of the privileged classes. These dues were a complicated system of payments, sometimes in cash, sometimes in kind, which were due to the *seigneur* (feudal lord) of virtually every landholding. This *seigneur* was usually also the landlord in the modern sense, but this was by no means invariably the case. The dues included various customary payments, the most important of which was a percentage of the sale price of a holding. The most annoying was, perhaps, the obligation to use (for a fee) the lord's corn mill, or bread oven, or olive or wine press. Extensive hunting rights enjoyed by the lord could also lead to the destruction of crops by trampling horses and hounds – that is if the yield of grain had not already been severely reduced by the voracious pigeons housed in the lord's dove-cote. In Figure 2 you can see pigeons picking away at the peasant's corn, and rabbits – many *seigneurs* kept warrens – devouring his cabbages. By the second half of the eighteenth century the possession of feudal or seigneurial rights was also considered a form of investment which might in certain cases be purchased by the bourgeoisie.

The nobility also had a monopoly of certain prestigious and lucrative positions in the service of the Crown and of the Church: commissions in the army, ambassadorships, bishoprics and archbishoprics. This stranglehold had been tightened in 1781 by the Ségur ordinance which restricted commissions to those who could prove four generations of nobility.

Self-Assessment Question 1

After reading the document below which describes some of the feudal obligations of the villagers of Les Alleuds to their lord, in this case a monastery, Saint Aubin's at Angers, consider the following questions.

i)   From this evidence do you think that the tenants of Saint Aubin's Abbey were likely to find the system of dues onerous or not?

ii)   What seems to be the attitude of the *seigneur* to the villagers?

Document A ————————————————————————

From Besnard, *Souvenirs d'un Nonagenaire* (1880)

'These dues consisted of 500 bushels of wheat, weighing 30 livres or 100 hectolitres, 648 bushels or 65 hectolitres of rye, 1,025 bushels or 200 hectolitres of oats, 24 bushels or 5 hectolitres of barley, ten journeys by bullock cart from Les Alleuds near Angers, 40 days' labour by gleaners and harvesters, 15 pairs of capons and hens, and 25 francs of quitrent.

Lods et ventes [percentage payments on land sales] raised 250 francs per year, thanks to the custom of discounting a third and even a half of the right of transfer. These two items were reckoned to produce about 3,000 francs and tithes of about the same amount....

As regards these feudal dues, the lord or his tax farmer [agent], having announced during the sermon at parish mass on which days he would collect them (three consecutive days were allotted for the payment of dues at Les Alleuds), the debtors were bound to make payment of dues on the said days, or risk being prosecuted after their expiry. If at the time of the original assessment of dues, properties were held in the name of a single individual and yet with the passage of time had been divided between several owners, as a result of succession or sale, the feudal lord had the right to demand the totality of the rent owed according to this same assessment from the most solvent of the co-debtors, unless he appealed against each of them, which he rarely failed to do and which yielded considerable sums. Moreover, the grain had to be pure and of the best quality and so was sold on the market at a fifth or a sixth above the current price.

As to *lods et ventes*, the acquirer of a property not only had to pay the feudal lord a twelfth of the price of his acquisition, but he had to hand over to him an authentic copy of the deed of acquisition which the feudal lord was entitled to keep for a year and a day, during which time he could decide either to receive these dues or to exercise a withdrawal, that is, to keep the property for himself, at a cost only of reimbursing the acquirer for genuinely incurred expenses. He also had the privilege of handing over his right of withdrawal to anyone he pleased.'

Lough, 1980, pp.99-100

Discussion ————————————————————————

It seems that the system of feudal dues placed a considerable burden on the villagers. Quite large sums of money were demanded as well as payment in kind, and there is no mention of any allowance made for poor seasons or the effects of sickness among the animals. The system seems to be constructed to favour the feudal lord who must, it appears, on no account suffer from any change which might take place in the village.

The right to cancel any property transfers at will could add what we would regard as an unacceptable element of risk to the sale of land. Even though the feudal lord was in this case a monastery, it is hard to find much in the way of consideration for the villagers' position in this document.

The social group immediately below the nobility was the bourgeoisie, the urban middle class, technically part of the Third Estate. Like the nobility, the bourgeoisie was also varied in composition. The richest members of the upper bourgeoisie of wealthy towns like Paris or Bordeaux lived in a manner that was in many ways indistinguishable from that of the nobility. Certainly in Paris the two groups mingled socially and could be found enjoying together the delights of Queen Marie-Antoinette's gaming table or the latest intellectual gossip in the *salon* (drawing-room) of some leader of fashion. An educated élite could be found in most provincial towns of any size comprising, together with some local nobles and clerics, the leading merchants, lawyers, office-holders and in certain cases manufacturers. Maximilien Robespierre, after receiving a law degree from the University of Paris, belonged to this level of society in Arras, the provincial capital of Artois.

Many bourgeois complained of the inefficiencies and arrogance of French government, but equally many had as their ultimate aim the acquisition of noble status, usually via the purchase of a royal office which carried this privilege. These families would invest their surplus capital not in business but in offices or in *rentes* (loans to the King with the interest paid in the form of an annuity; hence *rentier*, the term for one who lived on income from this source), or in land.

Beneath this group there were many gradations of small employers, skilled workmen and day labourers before the mass of the urban proletariat was reached, who lived on the verge of destitution, always at risk from unemployment and a rise in the price of the basic foodstuff, bread.

The peasants formed the bulk of the population in the countryside, but were no more a homogeneous economic group than the bourgeoisie. The condition of the peasantry varied markedly from one area of France to another depending on geographic and climatic conditions, the weight of the local system of seigneurial dues and royal taxes, and the personality of local landlords and magistrates. Another factor which should not be forgotten is that in many parts of rural France, especially in the north and east, peasant families could work at home at some of the processes required in the manufacture of textiles, particularly at spinning and weaving. Outworkers could also be found in the metal trades. Such extra sources of income could markedly improve a family's standard of living when trade was good.

 Self-Assessment Question 2

Compare the following two documents taken from Arthur Young's *Travels in France during the years 1787, 1788, 1789,* and answer the following questions.

i)   What reasons does Young give for the poverty of one area and the flourishing nature of farming in the other?

ii)   Does he seem prejudiced in his judgements?

(For information on Young see Appendix 1.)

Document A _____

'July 30 1787
Going out of Ganges, I was surprised to find by far the greatest exertion in

irrigation which I have yet seen in France; and then pass by some steep mountains highly cultivated in terraces. Much watering at St Laurence. The scenery very interesting to a farmer. From Ganges to the mountain of rough ground which I crossed, the ride has been the most interesting which I have taken in France; the effect of industry the most vigorous; the animation the most lively. An activity has been here that has swept away all difficulties before it and has clothed the very rocks with verdure. It would be a disgrace to common sense to ask the cause; the enjoyment of property must have done it. Give a man the secure possession of a bleak rock, and he will turn it into a garden; give him a nine year lease of a garden and he will convert it into a desert!'

Maxwell (ed.), 1929, p.47

Document B

'Sept. 5 1788
To Montauban. The poor people seem poor indeed; the children terribly ragged, if possible worse clad than if with no clothes at all; as to shoes and stockings they are luxuries. A beautiful girl of six or seven years playing with a stick and sinking under such a bundle of rags as made my heart ache to see her. They did not beg, and when I gave them something seemed more surprised than obliged. One-third of what I have seen of this province seems uncultivated, and nearly all of it in misery. What have kings and ministers and parliaments and States to answer for their prejudices, seeing millions of hands that would be industrious, idle and starving, through the execrable maxims of despotism, or the equally detestable prejudices of a feudal nobility. Sleep at the Lion d'Or, at Montauban, an abominable hole – 30 miles.'

Ibid., p.109

Discussion

Young ascribes both the prosperity of one area and the desolation of the other to external factors such as the terms of ownership and the attitude of the government and nobility, discounting natural advantages. He does not produce much in the way of evidence for his claims especially in the case of Document A, where he asserts that only land owned by the farmer himself could flourish so well. He seems in many ways to have misunderstood the French situation where a peasant could own his own farm and still be subject to feudal dues. He does not identify a concrete cause for the poverty in Montauban though we could deduce from his description of ragged clothing and lack of shoes that distress in the countryside caused a general slowing down of economic activity. Times could be as bad for the clothiers and other craftsmen as for the farmers.

Within the overall group of the peasantry there were further variations. Some of the wealthier peasants, known as *laboureurs,* owned or rented substantial farms and had quite considerable amounts of surplus produce to sell on the open market in good years. Others were *métayers,* operating a system where the landlord provided land, tools, seed and stock and the tenant provided his labour. The landlord took at least 50 per cent of the produce at harvest time, a system which English observers thought at the root of much rural poverty. Other peasants existed at the level of bare subsistence on tiny holdings, relying on employment as day-labourers with *seigneurs* or *laboureurs* to cover taxes and dues etc.; or wove or spun textiles at home; or were very dependent on the produce of a small vineyard. Others had no cultivable land beyond a garden and were in effect landless labourers, the most vulnerable and poverty-stricken of all the rural community.

There is no denying that the burden of taxes and dues was heavy. Apart from the *tailles* already mentioned there were indirect taxes too, including tolls on roads and bridges and internal customs duties, plus the infamous *gabelle* (salt tax). The Church in theory also claimed a tithe (one-tenth) of all produce for itself, though in practice it took a rather smaller percentage. The final obligation was the ballot for recruits to the royal army, which could wrest away the strongest and most economically productive member of a peasant family to follow a military career.

The so-called First Estate consisted of the clergy, all of the Catholic Church, since other denominations enjoyed no legal standing in France after the Revocation of the Edict of Nantes in 1685. Here again economic conditions varied widely. Some bishops and abbots were veritable princes of the Church; some *curés* (parish priests) or *vicaires* (curates) lived in real poverty, their tithes having been alienated in favour of an abbey or cathedral chapter. They received only an allowance from the owner of the tithes which might have been a mere pittance. The Church as a whole owned one-tenth of the surface of France and was exempt from general taxation. The clergy met every five years in an Assembly which granted the so-called *don gratuit* (free gift – in effect a form of self-taxation) to the Crown. This sum was normally raised as a loan from financiers – a system which was not entirely to the detriment of the Crown, since the Church's credit was somewhat better than that of the monarch and could raise loans at a lower rate of interest.

Education in France was almost entirely in Church hands, as was the organisation of hospitals of all kinds, the care of orphans and foundlings, and the relief of destitution. Much of this work had been undertaken in the past by religious orders but by the middle of the eighteenth century many orders were faced with declining numbers and considerable difficulties in attracting new recruits, quite probably as a result of new intellectual enthusiasms in France.

The intellectual atmosphere

During the reign of Louis XIV (1643-1715) French culture had been dominant in Europe. The building and decoration of the Palace of Versailles, the tragedies of Racine and Corneille, the comedies of Molière, the music of the Chapel Royal set a standard which other countries could only admire. In the eighteenth century the influence of the English mathematician and physicist, Isaac Newton, and the philosopher John Locke, was felt in French intellectual circles and produced a new flowering of thought, particularly in the realms of politics, science and philosophy. Above all a rational approach to problems in these fields was advocated, rejecting explanations which seemed to be grounded in theology or superstition (some even began to act as if they thought these were the same thing) and favouring explanations which were based on observation and experiment and were logically consistent.

Voltaire was the most admired of a group soon known as the *philosophes* (philosophers or intellectuals) which became closely identified with the publication of the *Encyclopédie*, a great 17-volume compendium of all knowledge, the first volume of which appeared in 1751. Many of this group, which included Diderot, d'Alembert and Buffon, rejected orthodox religion. Some retained a vestigial belief in a 'First Cause' or 'Benevolent Creator', a system knows as 'deism'. Others were to all intents and purposes atheists. To express such views in public in France could be dangerous. In theory a system of censorship existed which controlled the publication of books, pamphlets and other printed matter;

material that was held to be offensive could be seized and burned in public and its authors imprisoned. The charge of blasphemy could lead to even greater difficulties. The State had draconian powers at its disposal which were occasionally put into effect. In 1765, the Chevalier de la Barre, aged 19, was accused of making obscene remarks about a religious procession. He was charged with sacrilege and condemned to have his tongue cut out and die at the stake with a copy of Voltaire's *Dictionnaire Philosophique (Dictionary of Philosophy)*, which contained the *Letters from England* quoted in Document B below, hung round his neck. The only mercy finally shown him was that the executioner ensured his death before consigning his body to the flames. The *philosophes* themselves only suffered some brief periods of imprisonment or exile from Paris; their theories became the accepted currency of the Paris *salons* where such matters were endlessly debated.

Self-Assessment Question 3

The *philosophes*, especially Montesquieu, had views on the nature of political power as well as on the natural world and religion. Read these extracts from Montesquieu's *De l'Esprit des Lois (The Spirit of Laws)* and from Voltaire's *Lettres Anglaises (Letters from England)*, and answer the following questions.

i)   In what ways could they be considered to be attacking French royal government?

ii) What system seems to be preferred?

(Note: in Document B Voltaire is describing the government of England in the first half of the eighteenth century.)

Document A ─────────────────────

From Montesquieu, *De l'Esprit des Lois (The Spirit of Laws)*, 1748

'3. In what Liberty consists.

It is true that in democracies the people seem to act as they please; but political liberty does not consist in an unlimited freedom. In governments, that is, in societies directed by laws, liberty can consist only in the power of doing what we ought to will, and in not being constrained to do what we ought not to will.

We must have continually present to our minds the difference between independence and liberty. Liberty is a right of doing whatever the laws permit, and if a citizen could do what they forbid he would be no longer possessed of liberty, because all his fellow-citizens would have the same power.

4. The same Subject continued.

Democratic and aristocratic states are not in their own nature free. Political liberty is to be found only in moderate governments; and even in these it is not always found. It is there only when there is no abuse of power. But constant experience shows us that every man invested with power is apt to abuse it, and to carry his authority as far as it will go. Is it not strange, though true, to say that virtue itself has need of limits?

To prevent this abuse, it is necessary from the very nature of things that power should be a check to power. A government may be so constituted, as no man shall be compelled to do things to which the law does not oblige him, nor forced to abstain from things which the law permits.'

Prichard (ed.), 1914, p.133

Document B ————————————————————————————

From Voltaire, *Lettres Anglaises (Letters from England)*, 1733

'All these new peers who compose the Higher House receive nothing but their titles from the king, and very few of them have estates in those places whence they take their titles. One shall be Duke of D_____, though he has not a foot of land in Dorsetshire; and another is Earl of a village, though he scarce knows where it is situated. The peers have power, but it is only in the Parliament House.

There is no such thing here as *haute, moyenne,* and *basse justice* – that is, a power to judge in all matters civil and criminal; nor a right or privilege of hunting in the grounds of a citizen, who at the same time is not permitted to fire a gun in his own field.

No one is exempted in this country from paying certain taxes because he is a nobleman or a priest. All duties and taxes are settled by the House of Commons, whose power is greater than that of the Peers, though inferior to it in dignity. The spiritual as well as temporal Lords have the liberty to reject a Money Bill brought in by the Commons; but they are not allowed to alter anything in it, and must either pass or throw it out without restriction. When the Bill has passed the Lords and is signed by the king, then the whole nation pays, every man in proportion to his revenue or estate, not according to his title, which would be absurd. There is no such thing as an arbitrary subsidy or poll-tax, but a real tax on the lands, of all which an estimate was made in the reign of the famous King William III.'

Morley (ed.), 1889, p.127

Discussion ————————————————————————————

Montesquieu particularly emphasises the rule of law which he implies should apply to all citizens alike, without the existence of specially privileged groups. He also raises the question of the desirability of what he calls a 'moderate government': political liberty can exist only where power is not abused and for this reason he favours a system where 'power should be a check to power', where no one person or institution can make its will prevail but must submit to the scrutiny or approval of another body or individual.

Voltaire is using the description of English government to criticise conditions in France. He lays particular emphasis on all citizens of whatever rank being liable to tax; he also mentions the aggravations of private justice and hunting rights. Montesquieu is also criticising the lack of equality before the law evident in France. Both, particularly Voltaire, seem to be envisaging a constitutional system somewhat on the lines of that of Great Britain.

———

Montesquieu and Voltaire were not, of course, the only political philosophers writing at this time. Rousseau, who based much of his thought on his experience of his home town Geneva, a city republic, put forward a competing theory. This saw the community, which had originated in the so-called Social Contract entered into by individuals, as the source of law and moral values. The General Will or the collective interest of society was the source of political authority. In Rousseau's view this Will could be determined by a sole ruler or an oligarchy. Consulting the whole body of the citizens would probably only occur in small societies like Geneva.

All these ideas had a fairly wide circulation among the educated bourgeoisie throughout France. In provincial towns of all sizes there existed 'academies', clubs for intellectuals, writers and artists, which often put on debates and set essay competitions. Most such academies also had a library. Arras had both a debating society, the Rosati, and an academy, of which Robespierre became director in 1786. Freemasonry enjoyed a certain vogue; even if not the sinister revolutionary secret society of later royalist imaginings, it did provide a forum where new ideas could be discussed. At a lower level, scurrilous pamphlets were also published in great numbers. Some took a line hostile to the privileged orders and the King. Others indulged in wildly obscene fantasies centred on Louis XVI and his unpopular Austrian Queen, Marie-Antoinette – the accusation that the Queen had infected most of the court with syphilis caught from her supposed lovers being a typical example.

Figure 3 Queen Marie-Antoinette and her children. This picture, exhibited in 1787, emphasises Marie-Antoinette's role as a mother, in an attempt to counteract the scandalous rumours current about her. *(Versailles. Cliché des Musées Nationaux – Paris)*

In general the *philosophes*, despite their hatred of despotism, supported the existing form of society and could in no way be considered egalitarian. However, they did succeed in creating a feeling of anti-clericalism which penetrated at least the upper ranks of society, and they were the inspiration of anti-government feeling, even if this often concentrated on dislike of individuals and their policies, rather than being clearly focussed.

The state of the French economy in the 1780s

One final question needs to be addressed before turning to the events of 1787-9: was France prosperous? From our consideration of the peasantry it is clear that it will be hard to give one overall answer. Some areas of the French economy could clearly be doing very well while dearth existed in others.

Virtually all English visitors to France at this period comment on the excellence of many of the roads. Even if they were maintained by the *corvée royale*, a much disliked system of unpaid labour exacted from peasants since the time of Louis XIV, they were an economic boon to the country. Guild restrictions which had hampered the growth of industry in towns (and which had been strongly enforced by Louis XIV and his minister Colbert) seem to have been in gradual decline. In the countryside the rising population (up from around 22 million in 1700 to about 28 million in 1789) led to the subdivision of holdings. At the same time, however, from about 1730 to 1760 prices, rents and production all rose, creating an atmosphere of buoyancy and optimism. Lady Mary Coke going from Bethune to Lille in July 1767 enthused:

> 'This country at this time of the year, from the very great richness
> of the soil and amazing crops of all sorts of grain, is a very fine sight.'

In the 1770s things changed for the worse: a series of poor seasons depressed the peasants' income and standard of living. Of particular importance was the failure of the vintage in 1778, since many relied on the produce of their vineyards to produce the income necessary to pay the taxes.

This growing crisis in agriculture very quickly affected other areas of the economy. Nobles found problems in maintaining their income from rents. Bourgeois who had invested in land found similar difficulties, while those who were manufacturers found that trade was equally bad, leading to the laying off of workmen. All this happened at a time when the poor harvests caused an immediate rise in the cost of bread.

French production of textiles up to this period had not been very much inferior, if at all, to that of Great Britain. French clothiers, however, depended much more on the use of out-workers, weaving or spinning in their own homes, than on the factory system. In 1789 there were some 20,000 spinning jennies in use in Britain, 9,000 of the more advanced mule spinning frames and 200 textile mills on the model of those set up by Richard Arkwright in Derbyshire. Comparative figures for France are 1,000, nought, and 8. Although French manufacturers were in some cases helped by royal subsidies, the loss of overseas markets, particularly in Spain, increased their difficulties.

One area that seemed unaffected by these developments was overseas trade. Marseilles had a near monopoly on trade with the Levant, whilst Bordeaux, Nantes and Le Havre had all grown prosperous on trade with the French West Indian colonies. Merchants from these towns were involved with the slave trade from West Africa to the West Indian islands; also in the import of their produce – cotton, indigo and, most importantly, sugar – to France, and its re-export to all parts of Europe.

Self-Assessment Question 4

Read the three documents below, written by English visitors describing the trade of Marseilles, Bordeaux and Nantes respectively, then answer the following questions.

i)   What aspects seem to have most excited the travellers' admiration?

ii) What areas of trade seem to have been most profitable?

iii) What importance can be attached to Young's remarks about the countryside near Nantes?

Document A _____

From Swinburne, *Journey from Bayonne to Marseilles* (1787)

'The commerce of Marseilles is divided into a multiplicity of branches; a variety of commodities are fabricated here, or brought from the other ports and inland provinces of France to be exported, and numerous articles of traffic are landed here in order to be dispersed in this and other kingdoms. It is presumed that one year with another business is transacted upon this exchange for near fifteen millions sterling. The exports to the Levant amount annually to thirty-one millions of livres; the imports from thence are valued at fifty. Those from the West Indies and Cayenne are calculated at seventeen millions of exports, and twenty-one of imports. About three millions and a half are employed in the East-India trade, six in the corn trade, and about twenty-nine in that with Spain and the rest of Europe. Four millions worth of salt cod and train oil comes from North America; oils from Sicily, & c. to the amount of fourteen millions, exported again in soap to nearly the same value; as also various manufactures to the amount of two millions and an half. Add to this circulation the dealings in insurances and profits upon bullion, and you will have a rough, but comprehensive sketch of the commerce of Marseilles.'

Lough, 1987, p.89

Document B _____

From Young, *Travels in France during the Years 1787, 1788, 1789*

'Much as I had read and heard of the commerce, wealth, and magnificence of this city, they greatly surpassed my expectations. Paris did not answer at all, for it is not to be compared to London; but you must not name Liverpool in comparison with Bourdeaux [*sic*].... The *place royale,* with the statue of Louis XV in the middle, is a fine opening, and the buildings which form it regular and handsome. But the quarter of the *chapeau rouge* is truly magnificent, consisting of noble houses, built, like the rest of the city, of white hewn stone.... The new houses, that are building in all quarters of the town, mark, too clearly to be misunderstood, the prosperity of the place. The skirts are everywhere composed of new streets with still newer ones marked out, and partly built....

All the world knows that an immense commerce is carried on at this city; every part of it exhibits to the traveller's eye unequivocal proofs that it is great; the ships that lye in the river are always too numerous to count easily; I guess there

17

are at present between 3 and 400, besides small craft and barges.... Here are every sign of a great and flourishing trade; crowds of men all employed, busy, and active, and the river much wider than the Thames at London, animated with much commercial motion, will leave no one in doubt.... Shipbuilding is a considerable article of their trade; they have built sixty ships here in one year.... The export of wine alone is reckoned to amount to 8,000 tons, besides which brandy must be an immense article.'

Lough, 1987, pp.95-6

Document C

From Young, *Travels in France during the years 1787, 1788, 1789*

'*Mon Dieu!* cried I to myself, do all the wastes, the deserts, the heath, ling, furz, broom, and bog, that I have passed for 300 miles, lead to this spectacle! What a miracle, that all this splendour and wealth of the cities in France should be so unconnected with the country! There are no gentle transitions from ease to comfort, from comfort to wealth; you pass at once from beggary to profusion – from misery in mud cabins to Mademoiselle Saint-Huberti [an actress of renown] in splendid spectacles at 500 livres a night (21£.17s.6d.)....

The accounts I received here of the trade of the place, made the number of ships in the sugar trade 120, which import to the amount of about 32 millions; 20 are in the slave trade; these are by far the greatest articles of their commerce; they have an export of corn, which is considerable from the provinces washed by the Loire, and are not without minoteries [trade in flour], but vastly inferior to those of the Garonne. Wines and brandy are great articles, and manufactures even from Switzerland, particularly printed linens and cottons, in imitation of Indian, which the Swiss make cheaper than the French fabrics of the same kind, yet they are brought quite across France. They export some of the linens of Bretagne, but not at all compared with S. Maloes, which has been much longer established in that business.'

Lough, 1987, pp.103-04

Discussion

English visitors seem to have been much impressed by the magnificence of the towns themselves. Clearly much building had been undertaken recently, a lot of it on a grand scale and including amenities such as theatres, which presupposed the existence of a fairly large leisured and moneyed class. Trade across the Atlantic seems to have been particularly important, though Marseilles seems to have also traded extensively in the Mediterranean. Goods, whether agricultural or industrial, produced in the immediate neighbourhood of each city formed an important element in the trade through the port, but it should be noted that Young was very struck by the poverty and lack of development to be found in the immediate hinterland of Nantes. His phrase 'There are no gentle transitions... you pass at once from beggary to profusion' makes the point very clearly.

The situation all over France worsened dramatically following the harvest failure of 1788. One can only imagine the deep anxiety which must have been felt among the functionaries of the *Conseil des Dépêches* (the committee of the Royal Council charged with dealing with affairs within France), if not in the Court, when news came from 27 out of 32 of the *généralités* (the administrative districts of pre-revolutionary France, each under the care of an *intendant*) that the harvest had failed completely, leading to an almost immediate steep rise in the price of bread. Even in good times a wage earner spent 50 per cent of his income on bread and a further 16 per cent on other food and drink. A rise in the price of bread left such people with no room for manoeuvre. A 4-pound loaf cost 9 *sous* at the beginning of August 1788; 9.5 *sous* by the 18th; 11 *sous* by 7 September; 12 *sous* in November; 14 *sous* by Christmas and 14.5 *sous* by February 1789. It was rare for an unskilled man to earn more than 20 *sous* per day. To add to the general misery the spring of 1789 was unusually cold with heavy snowfalls and prolonged periods of frost.

Many people held the royal government directly responsible for their desperate situation and rumours began to circulate, as they had done in the bad seasons earlier in the decade, of a secret plot or *pacte de famine* between the King, his ministers, and the suppliers of grain to starve the people into submission. All this increased the political pressures on the government, something which will be examined in the next section.

1.2 Events in France 1787-9

There had been an atmosphere of crisis at Versailles (the centre of French government) in discussions between Louis XVI and his advisers since 20 August 1786 when Calonne, the controller-general of finances, had told the King that the government was facing bankruptcy. The King's income would shortly be insufficient to cover the interest due on loans outstanding, most of which had been raised to pay for French help to the former British colonies in North America during the War of Independence. Moreover the extra tax of a *vingtième* (in theory one-twentieth of the value of most incomes) was to expire in 1787. The way that was suggested to get out of this impasse was that a special and carefully selected Assembly of Notables be summoned to meet the King to devise and approve ways of reforming and improving the royal finances. Calonne himself had suggestions for radical reforms: internal customs duties, the *corvée* (forced labour on the roads) and the *gabelle* (salt tax) would all be either abolished or given a more rational basis. The keystone of his policy was a proposal for a revised land tax. Landowners would pay between 2.5 and 5 per cent of the annual value of their holding, irrespective of the legal status of the land or its owner. The assessment and administration of the new tax would be in the hands of new provincial assemblies where power would be in proportion to the size of landholding, again ignoring all the old distinctions of status. (The issues at stake in Calonne's suggested reforms are fully discussed in Essay 2, pp.114-15.)

Calonne's scheme, whatever might have been its merits as a cure for royal financial difficulties, either threatened or seemed actually to undermine noble and clerical privileges and the power of the regional sovereign courts or *parlements*. These courts had had the sole right until this date to register royal edicts, including those relating to taxes and loans. Unrest began to be evident in the provinces, particularly Brittany. At Versailles divisions among the King's family and his advisers led to a failure to back Calonne, and his replacement in May 1787 by Loménie de Brienne, Archbishop of Toulouse, who had the support of Marie-Antoinette. Brienne dismissed the Notables but in turn was very soon faced by the determined opposition of the Paris *parlement* which not only refused to register the more important of the amended edicts enforcing a somewhat diluted version of the Calonne plan, but declared that it had no power to assent to new taxes. This could only be done by a meeting of the Estates-General, a body which had not met since 1614. On this occasion the King refused to give way; the edicts were registered compulsorily by the ceremony known as a *lit de justice* and the still recalcitrant *parlementaires* were sent into semi-exile in Troyes. Instead of calming the situation an unprecedented clamour arose: in pamphlets and broadsheets the *parlement* was presented as standing for the interests of the Nation (a phrase which began to be heard increasingly), against the despotism of the King and his ministers. By mid-September a compromise was worked out and the *parlement* returned to Paris to widespread acclaim. The discussion of political issues now involved a much wider band of French society, especially in Paris, where the cafés newly opened in the neighbourhood of the *Palais Royal* were the sites of many heated discussions and debates.

Figure 4 The Assembly of Notables, Versailles 1787. This Assembly was an attempt by the King's advisers to find a way out of the financial crisis facing the Crown. *(Bibliothèque Nationale, Paris)*

During the autumn of 1787 Brienne convinced himself that the King's financial situation could be recovered provided that further loans were raised. He was prepared to contemplate the calling of a meeting of the Estates-General in 1792 when, according to his plan, the immediate crisis would have passed and a programme of moderate reform would be under way. But the session of the *parlement* at which the new loans were to be registered was mishandled, leading to further hostility between the King and his ministers on the one hand, and the *parlement* on the other. In the country as a whole it seemed as if virtually all educated people were united by the recognition of the need for reform.

By the spring of 1788 the King, on the advice of Lamoignon, the Chancellor, was rumoured to be about to take decisive action against the *parlements*. On 3 May 1788, in an atmosphere of great excitement, the *parlement* of Paris listed the so-called fundamental laws of the kingdom which were, so they said, unchangeable even by royal decree. They included the statement originally made the year before that taxation must be approved by the Estates-General, and went on to claim that arbitrary arrest and imprisonment were illegal. Louis refused to be intimidated. Edicts were promulgated which removed most of the more important political powers of the *parlement*. A new plenary court was set up with the power to register new laws, thus seemingly circumventing the claims of the *parlement* to act as the guardian of the people's liberties.

Protests erupted again all over France. Pamphlet literature became more and more radical in tone referring ominously to ideas like the General Will and the sovereignty of the people. At the same time the financial situation continued to deteriorate as the government's credit became less and less respected. With an empty treasury, Brienne gave way and announced that the Estates-General would meet on 1 May 1789. Still investors were reluctant to trust the government.

There seemed only one way to avoid a total collapse of the government's finances: Brienne resigned and was replaced by Necker, the Swiss banker, who had been controller-general from 1777 to 1781, and who was widely believed to be a financial genius.

All attention was now focussed on the coming meeting of the Estates-General. Arrangements for the elections of its deputies and the conduct of its affairs predominated over all others. Quickly the May decisions concerning the *parlements* were rescinded: the sovereign courts returned with their powers unchanged. But how was power to be divided between the three Estates? In particular, how would votes be taken, by head or by Estate? The registration by the *parlement* of Paris of a decree with the amendment that the customs of 1614 would be followed, only served to deepen the confusion: it was uncertain what these customs were. A further brief meeting of the Assembly of Notables did not help resolve the question. Finally, on 27 December 1788, Necker and the King accepted that the Third Estate should have twice as many members as the other two, but refused to commit themselves on the manner of voting.

The issues were again argued in large numbers of pamphlets, many pushing the claims of the Third Estate – *le Tiers*, as it was familiarly known. Gradually election arrangements were made throughout France. For the Thirds, an indirect system was used. Males over 25, in individual communities, voted in primary assemblies to elect deputies who would in turn elect the deputies to the Estates-General in provincial assemblies.

In these provincial assemblies *Cahiers de Doléances* (lists of grievances) were drawn up containing all the complaints of each Estate in that region and their accusations against the royal government. At no time do the King and his advisers seem to have made any efforts either to influence the elections or the compilation of the *Cahiers*. It was clear that the Estates would be composed largely of those opposed to the King to a greater or lesser extent.

Meanwhile the dreadful winter of 1788-9 gave way to a spring during which the price of bread weighed ever more heavily on the mass of the population. At this time 89 per cent of a working man's wage in Paris would have gone on bread. In April, while the election of the Paris deputies was still proceeding, there was a sudden explosion of rioting sparked off by a chance remark on reducing wage rates made by a wallpaper manufacturer, Réveillon. His factory was attacked and sacked and troops were called in to keep order but, though the trouble was suppressed, a worry began to haunt Necker and his fellow ministers that perhaps the army could not be relied on to confront fellow citizens.

The deputies therefore began to gather against a background of unrest and unease, preparing to confront a government which seemed to have little policy beyond the meeting of the Estates-General itself. Yet there was still residual loyalty and respect for the monarchy and few would have thought at that stage that they were witnessing the last days of the *'ancien régime'*, the 'old regime' of government.

 Self-Assessment Question 5

Read Document A, taken from the *Cahier* of the three Orders (Estates) convoked at Vesoul (in Franche-Comté), and Document B, from the *Cahier* of the Third Estate of Paris. Both documents date from Spring 1789.

i)   What difference do you detect between these two documents?

ii) Can you establish any reason for this difference?

iii) What kind of solution to the difficulties confronting France might each group seem to favour?

Document A _____

'We the members of the three orders of the bailliage [bailiwick] of Amont... united by the identity of interests established between the three orders by the nobility and clergy's complete and authentic surrender of all pecuniary exemptions in relation to taxes at public charge present and future, have resolved to draw up the *Cahier* of our grievances... together....

3.   In order to preserve the personal safety and liberty of all citizens the deputies will demand that the Estates-General pass a perpetual and irrevocable law preventing the future use of *lettres de cachet* [an order committing an individual to prison without a trial] and preventing any person vested with public authority from having a domiciled citizen arrested without bringing him before the appropriate judge within twenty-four hours....

5.   No general law shall be reputed such in France unless it has either been proposed by the king and accepted by the Estates-General or passed in the Estates-General and sanctioned by the king....

10. The deputies will demand recognition of the right belonging to the nation to give its consent to taxation, to regulate the way in which it will be spent... by means of annually published accounts.'

Hardman (ed.), 1981, pp.77-8

Document B _____

Declaration of Rights (from the *Cahier* of the Third Estate of Paris)

'In every political society every man has equal rights.

All power derives from the nation and may only be exercised to its advantage.

The general will makes the law; and the authorities assure its execution.

... Laws exist only to guarantee for each citizen the ownership of his property and the safety of his person.

All property is inviolable. No citizen may be arrested or taken into custody except lawfully.

... On the site of the Bastille, destroyed and razed to the ground, there shall be established a public square, in the middle of which will stand a column of noble and simple design, bearing this inscription: "To Louis XVI, who restored public liberty."'

Thompson (ed.), 1933, pp.2-17

Discussion

Document A is the result of a joint session of all three Estates and might seem to indicate that it was quite possible to obtain some degree of unity among all ranks of society, particularly as the privileged classes seem to be willing to renounce voluntarily their special status regarding taxes etc. The body of the extract focusses on particular grievances and seems to envisage something not unlike the British system where the raising of taxes and the making of laws were activities for which the co-operation of the representative assembly was essential.

Document B comes from the Third Estate only. The tone seems to be more radical, and heavily influenced by contemporary political thought. Phrases like 'the general will' recall Rousseau. However, the Parisians' attitude to property seems to have been far from radical: private property was to be inviolable and the emphasis is firmly on the rule of law. The final suggestion for the erection of a monument to Louis XVI on the site of the Bastille (this was written well before 14 July 1789), reveals how far the Parisians were at this stage from revolution, despite the phrasing of some of their remarks.

Documents A and B above clearly come from different societies with different levels of sophistication, but the emphasis on the need for the rule of law in both gives a clear idea of what the main objection to Louis's government was at this time: it was arbitrary and unfair and was seen to be such. The desire for change was becoming irresistible, with unpredictable consequences both for Louis XVI and for France.

The events of 1787-9 have recently been given rather more prominence in the consideration of the Revolution as a whole than was previously the case. (Traditionally the meeting of the Estates-General (5 May 1789) was taken to be the beginning of the Revolution.) In the opinion of some historians a close examination of this period seems to undermine the older Marxist view of the Revolution as a conflict between the feudal nobility and the rising bourgeoisie. It has been pointed out that some of the most enthusiastic reformers of the winter of 1788-9 were themselves nobles. A particularly prominent group, almost all of noble origin, was the Society of Thirty which provided the text of model *Cahiers* to many communities, and campaigned very strongly for the rights of the Thirds. It has also been pointed out that the *parlements* were 'not just defending narrow class interests but were also advancing principles which they believed to be essential to the national interest' (Blanning, 1987). If a survey is made of the demands put forward in *Cahiers* it is clear that the demands of the nobles and of the Third Estate converged: both groups wanted 'moderate peaceful change to a modernised constitutional monarchy for their mutual benefit' (ibid.).

No simple explanation can cover the increasingly complex situation which was emerging at this stage. It is as well to remember that in early 1789 'very few had any idea just how radical the Revolution would turn out to be' (ibid.).

Chapter 2

FROM VERSAILLES TO VARENNES: A BOURGEOIS REVOLUTION?

2.1 The meeting of the Estates-General

On 4 May 1789 a procession 'of very great solemnity', in the words of a contemporary reporter, made its way to the church of Notre-Dame at Versailles. The deputies of the three Estates – their social differences made obvious by enforced distinctions in the richness of their clothing – the King and his Court, were on their way to hear Mass celebrated by the Bishop of Nancy, before the opening of the Estates-General. The same reporter criticised the sermon as having 'no plan, no ideas and without style', but few events of the summer of this year would be as orderly and decorous as this service.

Figure 5 Procession of the Estates-General to the church in Versailles for the opening service, 4 May 1789. The procession caused offence since the three Estates were compelled by the King to wear costumes reflecting their respective social status. *(Bibliothèque Nationale, Paris)*

All three Estates together added up to a total of about 1,100 deputies. In the First Estate the bishops formed a small minority, some 51 out of a total of just under 300. The majority were parish priests (*curés*), men of education largely from urban backgrounds who had no love of the wealthy and aristocratic bishops, but who were in some cases equally worried by the anti-religious tone of some reforming literature. A small group of radicals (known as 'patriots') were led by the Abbé Grégoire.

In the Second Estate there were about 90 known liberal nobles; only 22 were *parlementaires* (hereditary noble judges of the *parlements*). The remaining 170 were divided between court and country nobles; there does not seem to be any evidence that this distinction was of any political importance.

The Third Estate contained an overwhelming majority of lawyers. There was also a large group of royal office holders, most of whom came from towns and from the north of France. All would have seen themselves as educated men and would have had at the very least a passing acquaintance with the questions concerning the powers and organisation of the Estates-General which had been so vigorously debated all winter. Among the deputies, of course, were some who had had a large part in this debate: Abbé Sieyès sat for the Third Estate of Paris; Robespierre was a deputy for Arras; the comte de Mirabeau, ever anxious to demonstrate his popular credentials, had also been elected for this Estate, rather than the more obvious Second.

We have already seen some of the demands put forward in the *Cahiers de Doléances* (lists of grievances) produced by each local assembly during the process of choosing deputies (see pp.21-3). Now that the great majority of these deputies had actually gathered at Versailles their initial feelings were largely of frustration: the King's speech at the opening session on 5 May had been bland and non-committal. Necker himself spoke for more than three hours on the state of the nation's finances, a speech which one observer found 'full of repetition, of trivialities, of incomprehensible passages' with no sign of a plan of action. After this unpromising beginning the deputies of the three Estates then became involved in argument over the unexciting chore of verifying their credentials. This apparently purely technical matter in fact concealed the still burning question which had first been raised in the autumn of 1788: how should the Estates-General vote? By head or by Estate? The question was still undecided and on its satisfactory resolution depended any chance of the dominance of the Third Estate now that its total number of deputies outnumbered those of the other two combined.

At this stage the Abbé Sieyès – author of 'What is the Third Estate?', one of the most influential of the flood of pamphlets published in the winter of 1788-9 – was greatly respected. His argument that the Third Estate constituted the nation and could alone act in the national interest had been widely applauded. It was largely due to his prompting that on 17 June the Third Estate voted by 491 votes to 90 to adopt the title of National Assembly, thus giving concrete expression to this belief. The vote challenged the other two Estates to join their supposed inferiors in representing the people of France. The assembly of the First Estate (the clergy) which, as has been said, contained a large majority of deputies from the lower clergy, voted two days later to join this new National Assembly. They were followed by some of the well-known liberal nobles over the next few days. (See Essay 2, pp.118-20.)

At Court the King's more thoughtful advisers, including Necker, could see that the situation threatened to get out of hand. The King himself, never the most forceful of characters, and still suffering from the recent death of his much-loved eldest son, agreed under pressure to hold a Royal Session on 23 June where at last an authoritative reform programme would be presented. While this programme was being put together in the royal council, the Queen and the comte d'Artois, Louis's younger brother, intervened to make it seem more rigid and less attractive to the reformers in the National Assembly than was originally intended. Both the Queen and Louis's two brothers, the Counts of Provence and Artois, were hostile to any measure of reform and were seen as reactionaries by many of the new politicians. This was in contrast to Louis's cousin, the duc d'Orléans, who made a noisy show of support for the most radical would-be reformers.

Figure 6 King Louis XVI. *(Versailles. Cliché des Musées Nationaux – Paris)*

Before this Session could take place some alterations were necessary to the *Salon des Menus Plaisirs,* the meeting place of the National Assembly. The doors were locked and soldiers stationed outside. No one had bothered to warn the deputies of these plans, and on the morning of 20 June they found their access to their accustomed meeting place barred. In a state of great excitement they moved to the nearest suitable alternative hall – the King's Tennis Court – and there swore the oath never to disperse until their work of reforming the constitution was complete (see Figure 27, p.126).

2.2 The Royal Session of 23 June 1789

The King came to address the deputies in this atmosphere of mounting tension and suspicion. His speech contained a number of reform proposals, including the right of the Estates to consent to taxes, and a new and more equitable land tax based on valuations uninfluenced by the social status of the landholder. This might well have been acceptable if put forward by Necker on 5 May, but it had now been overtaken by events. In particular the King's refusal to accept the validity of the vote of 17 June establishing the National Assembly swung opinion against him.

Self-Assessment Question 1

Carefully consider the following questions when you have read Documents A and B below.

i) In what ways does the account of the Oath of the Tennis Court and the circumstances surrounding it help us understand the tension between the King and the National Assembly?

ii) What interpretation would have been put on the articles of the King's speech to the Royal Session of 23 June (Document B) by a majority of the deputies of the National Assembly?

iii) What divergent views are put forward concerning the role of:
   a) the National Assembly;
   b) the King?

Document A _____

Procès-Verbal (i.e. official published minutes of the Session) No. 3
20 June 1789

'M. Mounier put forward a view which was supported by MM. Target, Chapelier and Barnave. He pointed out how strange it was that the hall of the Estates-General should be occupied by armed men; that no alternative accommodation should be offered to the National Assembly; that its president should be informed only by letters from the marquis de Brézé, and the national representatives by placards; and that they should be obliged to meet in the Tennis Court.... He further insisted that, since their dignity and their rights had been thus offended, and since they were only too aware of the full strength of the intriguing and of the ruthless determination with which the King was being persuaded into taking disastrous measures, the nation's representatives had no alternative but to bind themselves by a solemn oath to the cause of public safety and to the nation's interests.

... The National Assembly considering itself summoned to decide the constitution of the kingdom, to effect the re-establishment of public order and to maintain the true principles of monarchy... has decided that all members of this Assembly shall forthwith take an oath.... "We swear never to be separated from the National Assembly, and to meet wherever circumstances shall demand it, until such time as the constitution of the kingdom shall be established and secured on a firm foundation."

The members all took the same oath which was administered by the president.'

Thompson (ed.), 1933, pp.40-41

Document B _____

From the speech of the King to the Third Estate at the Royal Session
23 June 1789

'Art.XV. The King, wishing to ensure, reliably and permanently, the personal liberty of every citizen, invites the Estates-General to seek out and to present to him the surest means of reconciling the abolition of the orders at present known as *lettres de cachet* with the need to maintain public safety, to accommodate in certain cases family honour, to repress with all speed the first stirrings of sedition, or to protect the state from the effects of criminal intelligence links with foreign powers.

Art.XVI. The Estates-General will examine and make known to his majesty the surest means of reconciling the freedom of the press with the respect due to the citizens' religion, customs and honour.'

Wickham Legg (ed.), Vol. 1, 1905, p.150

Discussion ───

The National Assembly clearly felt humiliated by the casual way they considered they had been treated by the King over the closure of their usual meeting place. The hurt to their dignity was perhaps the most important but it is clear that the feeling of resentment was general and the dramatic moment of taking the oath was felt to be a virtual declaration of independence. (One delegate, Martin Dauch from Castelnaudary, in fact did not swear – significantly something passed over in this account.)

The King's Article XV can easily be interpreted as offering a superficial element of consultation to the Estates-General (note the King uses this term) but in fact leaving power to define the circumstances when arbitrary arrest might still be used firmly in royal hands. Similarly press freedom and freedom of speech would be severely limited if the King's suggestions were followed up. Virtually any criticism of current behaviour or policy would be caught by such wide and vague categories as the 'respect due to the citizens' religion, customs and honour'. Certainly the kind of unrestrained comment which had recently found such a ready market in Paris would have been outlawed.

The King saw the Estates-General in matters like this as an advisory body – a channel of communication with his people. The Assembly on the other hand saw itself as establishing a new foundation for the French State, setting out the true principles of monarchy which they, not the King, would further define.

───────────────────────────

After the King's speech at the Royal Session was finished the deputies refused to disperse as requested. Arthur Young, writing from Paris the next day (24 June 1789), says the King's propositions were received 'with universal disgust'. The centre of opposition was now the *Palais Royal*, a collection of cafés, shops and other places of entertainment that had recently been built on the site of the King's former Paris residence by the duc d'Orléans, his unpleasant but apparently liberal-minded cousin. Constant meetings were held there, which, according to Young 'are carried to a degree of licentiousness and fury of liberty that is scarcely credible'. The precarious state of government finances seemed to act as a check on the reactionary policies of the Queen and the comte d'Artois. The news on 27 June that the King had finally accepted the idea of a National Assembly, by ordering the nobility to join the other delegates at their sessions, was received with great joy.

2.3 The Fall of the Bastille

As a matter of deliberate royal policy at this time, the number of troops stationed in the Paris area was increasing rapidly. These were drawn largely from foreign mercenary regiments, as one or two incidents had shown that the loyalty of French regiments was suspect. The English Ambassador on 2 July 1789 reported that artillery batteries had been placed on high ground commanding the city and that the maréchal de Broglié, the new commander in the area, was thought to be absolutely loyal to the King.

On 11 July Necker was abruptly dismissed by the King thus confirming, in the minds of many Parisians, all the rumours which had been circulating concerning the desire of the King to arrest the members of the National Assembly and halt the move to reform. Paris was soon in a turmoil with large crowds thronging the streets, including many of the French Guards who had deserted from their regiments.

Figure 7 The Storming of the Bastille, 14 July 1789. *(The Trustees of the British Museum)*

The excitement was not entirely directionless. As early as 12 July crowds had attacked the hated *barrières*, a wall of customs-posts encircling Paris to ensure the collection of internal customs. By 13 July the old municipal government had been pushed aside and replaced by a committee chosen by the Electors (the elected group charged with selecting the Parisian deputies for the Third Estate), who had continued meeting long after all deputies to the Estates-General had been selected. This committee immediately began to organise a National Guard or militia to restore order in the streets. Arms were needed. Thirty-two thousand muskets were found in the Invalides, but there was a lack of gunpowder. Large quantities of it were thought to be stored in the Bastille, the fortress-prison and symbol of royal authority which lay in the eastern quarter of Paris. De Launay, commander of the Bastille, initially refused to open the fortress gates to the representatives of the people of Paris. Within a short time both sides took up arms. At least 70 of the attackers (not in any way members of a mob, but a mixture of small traders, artisans, and deserters from the royal army) were killed by musket fire from the walls of the Bastille. When some of the former French Guards brought up artillery pieces, de Launay surrendered, abandoning his original threat to blow up the Bastille's magazine and most of the surrounding neighbourhood.

Self-Assessment Question 2

Consider the following questions while reading the documents below.

i)   What seems to have been the motivation for the attack on the Bastille? Why was the commander lynched?

ii) Apart from this incident, how did the atmosphere in Paris during the events of 14-15 July strike these observers?

iii) Can you estimate why this particular event was seen later as having such great significance?

Document A ————————————————————————————

Lord Dorset to the Duke of Leeds
16 July 1789

'The Governor agreed to let in a certain number of them [i.e. the rioters, members of the crowd outside the Bastille] on condition that they should not commit any violence: these terms being acceded to, a detachment of about 40 in number advanced and were admitted, but the drawbridge was immediately drawn up again and the whole party instantly massacred: this breach of honour aggravated by so glaring an act of inhumanity excited a spirit of revenge and tumult such as might naturally be expected: the two pieces of cannon were immediately placed against the Gate and very soon made a breach which, with the disaffection that as is supposed prevailed within, produced a sudden surrender of that Fortress: M. de Launay, the principal gunner, the tailer [*sic*], and two old invalids who had been noticed as being more active than the rest were seized and carried to the Hôtel de Ville where, after a very summary trial before the tribunal there, the inferior objects were put to death and M. de Launay had also his head cut off at the Place de Grève, but with circumstances of barbarity too shocking to relate.... Nothing could exceed the regularity and good order with which all this extraordinary business has been conducted: of this I have myself been a witness upon several occasions during the last three days as I have passed through the streets, nor had I at any moment reason to be alarmed for my personal safety.'

Thompson (ed.), 1938, pp.50-51

Document B ————————————————————————————

From a journal written immediately after the events by Edward Rigby, a doctor from Norwich who, by chance, was visiting Paris in July 1789

'We ran to the end of the Rue St. Honoré. We here soon perceived an immense crowd proceeding towards the Palais Royal with acceleration of an extraordinary kind, but which sufficiently indicated a joyful event, and, as it approached we saw a flag, some large keys, and a paper elevated on a pole above the crowd, in which was inscribed *"La Bastille est prise et les portes sont ouvertes."* ["The Bastille has fallen and the gates are open."] The intelligence of this extraordinary event thus communicated, produced an impression upon the crowd really indescribable. A sudden burst of the most frantic joy instantaneously took place; every possible mode in which the most rapturous feelings of joy could be expressed, were everywhere exhibited. Shouts and shrieks, leaping and embracing, laughter and tears, every sound and every gesture, including even what approached to nervous and hysterical affection, manifested, among the promiscuous crowd, such an instantaneous and unanimous emotion of extreme gladness as I should suppose was never before experienced by human beings....'

Ibid., p.56

Document C ————————————————————————————————

Marquis de Ferrières at Versailles writing to his wife
15 July 1789

'The bourgeoisie have taken up arms, more than thirty thousand of them; they've seized the Invalides and the cannons, muskets and munitions which were stored there. The Bastille is taken; the governor and the King's lieutenant have been killed; Paris is completely out of the King's control. Things are beginning to look serious. However, the bourgeois assembly is maintaining order; they've even disarmed the populace. The government has behaved in the most insane way. We asked for the troops to be dismissed; the new ministers, inept and biased men, refused; and yet they've just withdrawn the regiments in the Champ de Mars. The Court is in a state of terror.

I'll write to you regularly; but the mail is held up and letters aren't getting through; and so don't be anxious, even if you hear no news of me. Paris is like a city at war; you can't leave without a passport and communications are disrupted. The Hôtel de Ville is giving the orders, and it's fortunate that the electors of Paris and the municipality still have enough authority to protect the town from looting.'

Carré (ed.), 1932, p.88

Document D ————————————————————————————————

Letter from an anonymous English writer in Paris
27 July 1789

(Note: this description of the King relates to his visit to Paris three days after the Fall of the Bastille.)

'The Revolution in the French Constitution and Government may now, I think, be looked upon as compleated, beyond all fears of any further attempts being made by the Court Party to defeat it. The entrance of the King into Paris was certainly one of the most humiliating steps that he could possibly take. He was actually led in triumph like a tame bear by the Deputies and the City Militia....

There certainly never was an instance of so astonishing a Revolution operated almost without bloodshed, and without the people being led on by any leader, or by any party, but merely by the general diffusion of reason and philosophy.'

Thompson (ed.), 1938, p.61

Discussion ————————————————————————————————

It seems reasonable to suggest that the Bastille was attacked as much as a symbol of royal authority as a possible source of more arms. The death of de Launay seems to be connected with the belief current in the crowds abroad in Paris on that fateful day that he had not dealt fairly with the representatives of the rioters who had tried to negotiate with him about the opening of the gates of the Bastille.

Concerning events in Paris as a whole the various writers quoted convey rather different impressions of events in the city. Lord Dorset (whose account of the happenings outside the Bastille is not entirely accurate) is on the one hand apparently appalled at the violent end of de Launay and on the other amazed at the lack of general excitement on the streets of the capital. Rigby's description of a crowd hysterical with joy seems to indicate an almost complete lack of control by the authorities.

Writing from Versailles, de Ferrières is extremely nervous about developments in Paris. But notice particularly his mention of the fact that the bourgeois assembly (the commune of Electors) is in control, *not* the populace that is the mob. Also note that one of the major concerns of this body is to protect property. The anonymous English commentator of Document D seems to be taking a very sanguine view of events and it is hard to equate his belief that everything had taken place by the 'general diffusion of reason and philosophy' with Rigby's scenes of hysteria, or Lord Dorset's 'barbarity'. De Ferrières' comment about the ineptitude of the government and the ministers perhaps shows the most understanding of the situation developing in Paris and France as a whole.

None of these commentators, however, has any doubts about the importance of the events described. One explanation for the unbridled joy of the Parisians on this occasion is the fact that until this momentous occasion, the Bastille had loomed over the poorer districts of Paris as a grim reminder of the nature of royal power. Rigby mentions placards with the message "the gates are open." This was a potent symbol of the successful flouting of a previously invincible authority. The fact that a correspondent could think that the Revolution was now over also indicates the finality of the change which seemed to be heralded by the seizure of the Bastille by the people.

The King, faced with events in Paris, had little alternative but to recall Necker as his chief minister. As the latter returned slowly to Paris along the road from the Swiss frontier he was passed by members of the upper nobility, including the King's brother Artois, fleeing in the opposite direction. The King meanwhile visited Paris on 17 July with a deputation from the National Assembly (or the Constituent Assembly, as some historians refer to it from this time on), and seemed briefly to accept the spirit of what was now clearly a revolution. When he appeared at the *Hôtel de Ville* with Bailly, the new Mayor of Paris, and the marquis de La Fayette, hero of the American War of Independence and now Commander-in-Chief of the National Guard, the King wore the new red, white and blue cockade, the symbol of the new spirit abroad in French public affairs.

2.4 The Great Fear

Events in Paris, though dramatic, were not the only important developments during the summer of 1789. Bread prices had been rising continuously ever since August 1788 when it first became clear that the harvest would be disastrous. As usual in times of dearth, the countryside was full of rumours that the *seigneurs* and the grain dealers had ample supplies of corn hoarded for their own use or in expectation of higher prices still. When attempts were made to move grain by road the carts were increasingly likely to be attacked. Riots in markets were also reported from all over France. In this situation many of the poorest drifted to towns to beg or in hope of relief. Wild stories began to circulate of hordes of brigands who were at large in the countryside ready to steal the grain before the farmer could harvest it himself, or attack him and his family in their beds. In one or two places these rumours began to take on a slightly different tone: the brigands were in league with the nobles who were preparing to attack the peasants and reduce them to even more dire poverty. In frontier areas people were prepared to swear that they had seen invading armies, also in league with the nobles, on the march. Whatever the case, many fervently believed that the National Assembly and its work for the people was in great danger.

Figure 8 *Le duc d'Orléans et de la Fayette soutenant Necker.* Necker being carried in triumph by La Fayette and the duc d'Orléans. This is a pictorial representation of what was widely felt to be the political result of the Fall of the Bastille. *(Edimédia, Paris)*

Self-Assessment Question 3

Consider the following questions while reading the documents below, and pages 110-11 of Essay 1.

i) What are the chief differences between the general fear of brigands and the Great Fear of July and August 1789?

ii) To what extent do the extracts from the letters of the marquis de Ferrières to his wife (Documents A and B) back up the conclusions put forward by the historian Lefebvre in Document C?

iii) What were the results of this spasm of panic in the French countryside?

Document A

Marquis de Ferrières at Versailles to his wife at their *château*
28 July 1789

'The revolt against the nobility is universal. There are among the deputies from
the Communes [the former Third Estate] people who hate us, without even
knowing why; and their hatred is all the more powerful and active for having
no fixed object. It doesn't occur to them that they will themselves be the victims
of the hostility which they're unleashing, that the people whom they're stirring
up against us will turn with even more violence on them. This has already
happened at Chartres, Fontainebleau, Saint-Germain, Montfort, and in several
towns in the Paris region.'

Carré (ed.), 1932, pp.99-100

Document B

Marquis de Ferrières at Versailles to his wife at their *château*
28 July 1789

'My dear, you mustn't give in to ill-founded fears and worries; I'm really very
safe here. I'm hoping that the harvest, by depriving the agitators of the pretext
provided by the present high price of corn, will restore order and calm....

Paris remains quiet; but a horde of brigands is at large in the surrounding
countryside. There are said to be up to six thousand of them in Maine and that
they have seized Bonnétable. Everywhere people are taking up arms. The
bourgeois militias are guarding the towns. I hope that these misfortunes won't
spread into our region.'

Ibid., p.103

Document C

'The Great Fear arose from fear of the 'brigand', which can itself be explained
by the economic, social and political circumstances prevailing in France in
1789.

Under the *ancien régime*, begging was one of the scourges of the countryside;
from 1788 onwards, unemployment and rising prices made it worse. Famine
brought countless disturbances which could only increase the general disorder.
In all this, the political crisis played an important part, for the general excitement
it provoked made the people restless and unruly. Every beggar, vagrant and
rioter seemed to be a 'brigand'. There had always been great anxiety at harvest
time: it was a moment the peasants dreaded; local alarms increased daily.

As the harvest started, a new factor came into play. The conflict which set in
opposition the Third Estate and the aristocracy (supported by the royal authority)
and which in several provinces had given a social character to the hunger riots,
suddenly turned into civil war. The uprising in Paris and the security measures
which sought to expel vagrants from the capital and other major cities spread
the fear of brigands far and wide, and at the same time people anxiously waited
for the defeated aristocrats to take their revenge on the Third Estate with the aid
of foreign troops. No one doubted for a moment that they had taken the promised
brigands into their pay and in this way the economic crisis and the political and
social crisis combined their effects so that the same terror spread through

everyone's mind and allowed alarms which began by being purely local to spread swiftly through the country. The fear of brigands was a universal phenomenon, but the Great Fear was not, and it is wrong to confuse the one with the other.

There is no trace of plot or conspiracy at the start of the Great Fear. It was far from foolish to fear the vagrant, but the aristocrat-brigand was a phantom figure. The revolutionaries helped to spread his image, but they acted in good faith. If they spread the rumour of the aristocrats' plot it was because they believed in it. They exaggerated its importance out of all proportion: only the court really considered a *coup de force* against the Third Estate and they showed themselves pathetically incompetent in its execution. The men of the Revolution did not make the mistake of despising their adversaries and as they credited them with their own energy and resolution, they were inclined to fear the worst. Furthermore, they did not need the Great Fear to bring the towns on to their side: the municipal revolution and the arming of the people had already taken place and this was a decisive point in their favour. As for the unfortunate poor who constantly moaned and murmured behind the bourgeoisie in both town and country, they gave great cause for concern; the bourgeoisie had everything to fear from their outbursts of despair and they left their mark deep on the revolution. It was natural for the enemies of the revolution to accuse its supporters of encouraging the poor to overthrow the *ancien régime* so that they could put in its place a new order where the new men would rule – but it was equally natural for the revolutionaries to suspect the aristocracy of fomenting anarchy to keep them out of power. Clearly, the supposed appearance of brigands was an excellent excuse to arm the people against the royal power – and did not the king use the same excuse to mask his plans for attacking the Assembly? And as to the peasants in particular, it was not especially in the bourgeoisie's interest that they should overthrow the seigneurial régime by their jacqueries and the Constituent Assembly was not slow to show its concern in this direction. Even so, the Assembly did not need the Great Fear to help it on its way: the jacqueries had started long before.

But one must by no means conclude that the Great Fear exercised no influence on the course of events, or – to speak in philosophical terms – that it was an epiphenomenon. The panic was instantly followed by a vigorous reaction in which the warlike passion of the revolution was seen for the first time and which provided national unity with an opportunity to appear in its fullest vigour. Then, this reaction, especially in the countryside, turned against the aristocracy: by gathering the peasants together, it allowed them to achieve a full realization of their strength and reinforced the attack already launched against the seigneurial régime. It is not only the strange and picturesque nature of the Great Fear which should hold our attention: it played its part in the preparations for the night of 4 August and on these grounds alone must count as one of the most important episodes in the history of the French nation.'

Lefebvre, 1973, pp.210-11

Discussion

De Ferrières is clearly worried about the situation at home. He seems to find the relatively sudden wave of hatred of the nobility distressing and almost inexplicable. Showing his usual shrewdness, he has grasped the potential danger to all property owners of encouraging this kind of irrational behaviour. It is significant that he does hint that many of the stories of bands of brigands on the loose are exaggerated. Lefebvre's analysis of the summer of 1789 in the French countryside shows how powerful these myths of roving bands of brigands were. He sees the Great Fear as a separate wave of panic whose course can be determined quite precisely, and which links the presence of 'brigands' with an aristocratic plot against the infant Revolution and fears of foreign invasion by the armies of the reactionary powers.

From both writers one can deduce that the most notable result was the arming of the people and the organisation of town militias (similar to the Parisian National Guard) to protect lives and property. Clive Emsley in Essay 1 makes clear the relationship between these developments and later events in both provincial towns and the countryside. In towns the old municipal government was pushed aside, with varying degrees of violence. The new authorities were not necessarily more egalitarian. A franchise limited to property owners ensured that much the same social group remained in charge; but they were usually imbued with revolutionary zeal often following the lead of Paris. In the countryside the *châteaux* of the nobility were attacked with the aim of destroying for ever the records of feudal dues and the system of economic and social oppression which they symbolised.

2.5 Remodelling France

The night of 4 August and the Declaration of the Rights of Man

The members of the Constituent Assembly were well-informed about the spreading tide of insurrection in provincial France. The letters of the marquis de Ferrières, from which we have already quoted above, are full of references to the situation. He writes on 7 August 1789 to his wife sending elaborate directions on how to save their valuable documents and possessions from a possible attack on their *château* at Morsay. For example, money from selling wheat from the new harvest was not to be put as usual in their 'Treasury', ('if they come to Morsay I don't think they'll burn the *château* as it's too well loved in our district but they will burn the *titres de vente et devoirs* [records of sales and obligations]'). He tells her to put the money in the cellar under the great hall in a place where there isn't any wine. From our point of view, however, the most important point is that he states clearly that he hopes the sacrifices of the session of 4 August made by the nobility will restore order.

What had happened in the Assembly on that memorable evening? Was it an emotional reaction to events in the countryside at large? Was it a moment of *ivresse patriotique* (patriotic fervour) or something much more calculated?

One deputy, M. Parisot from Bar-sur-Seine wrote that very night to his Electors – the letter is dated 4 a.m. Wednesday 5 August. He speaks of the 'patriotic fervour' which gripped the deputies of the Assembly, but also mentions the necessity of ensuring that royal (as opposed to seigneurial) dues and taxes be paid if the country was not to face bankruptcy. It seems clear that while many deputies were carried away by emotion, the plan to renounce feudal and seigneurial privileges and dues had actually been formulated in advance, principally by the progressive nobles the vicomte de Noailles and La Fayette's brother-in-law, the duc d'Aiguillon (one of the richest landowners in France) and their supporters, in order to restore order and protect property in the countryside. It was successful at least superficially: resolution after resolution was passed abolishing the privileges of the nobility; the right of hunting over peasant lands; of dispensing justice; of exclusive rights to certain official jobs; of tax privileges. All went, with many others besides. Many privileges of the Church, especially the right to levy tithes, were also abolished as were those of corporations.

The work of dismantling the structure of the *ancien régime* continued throughout August. The resolutions of 4 August were transformed into decrees which in most cases laid down that the seigneurial rights already apparently relinquished either had to be redeemed in cash, or in kind, or had to be paid as in the past until they were. Months later, notably in the spring and summer of 1790, the Assembly was to find that these decrees were very hard to enforce and in fact gave rise to continual disturbances in country districts.

The flame of idealism, however, was not extinct. A Declaration of the Rights of Man was also debated and finally passed between 20 and 26 August.

Self-Assessment Question 4

Consider the following questions and put forward possible answers while reading the documents below. (See also Essay 2, pp.120-1.)

i)   Compare Document A with Document B, the American Declaration of Independence. What are the most striking similarities?

ii) What is the importance of ideas associated with sovereignty and the General Will?

iii) What has Document A to say about:
   a)   equality;
   b)   religious toleration;
   c)   property rights?

iv) What differing views of events in France seem to underlie the opinions of the historians Soboul and Thompson in Documents C and D?
   What are the differing opinions of Soboul and Thompson

Document A _____

The Declaration of the Rights of Man and the Citizen, 1789

'The representatives of the French people, sitting in the National Assembly considering that ignorance of, neglect of, and contempt for the rights of man are the sole causes of public misfortune and the corruption of governments, have resolved to set out in a solemn declaration the natural, inalienable and sacred rights of man, in order that this declaration, constantly before all members of the civic body, will constantly remind them of their rights and duties, in order that acts of legislative and executive power can be frequently compared with the purpose of every political institution, thus making them more respected; in order that the demands of the citizens, henceforth founded on simple and irrefutable principles, will always tend towards the maintenance of the constitution and the happiness of everyone.

Consequently the National Assembly recognises and declares, in the presence of, and under the auspices of, the Supreme Being, the following rights of man and of the citizen:
i)   Men are born and remain free and equal in rights. Social distinctions can only be founded on communal utility.
ii) The purpose of all political associations is the preservation of the natural and imprescriptible rights of man. These rights are liberty, property, security and resistance to oppression.

iii)   The principle of all sovereignty emanates essentially from the nation. No group of men, no individual, can exercise any authority which does not specifically emanate from it.

iv)   Liberty consists in being able to do whatever does not harm others. Hence the exercise of the natural rights of every man is limited only by the need for other members of society to exercise the same rights. These limits can only be determined by the law.

v)   The law only has the right to prohibit actions harmful to society. What is not prohibited by law cannot be forbidden, and nobody can be forced to do what the law does not require.

vi)   The law is the expression of the general will. All citizens have the right to take part personally, or through their representatives, in the making of the law. It should be the same for everyone, whether it protects or punishes. All citizens, being equal in the eyes of the law, are equally admissible to all honours, offices and public employment, according to their capacity and without any distinction other than those of their integrity and talents....

ix)   Every man being presumed innocent until he has been declared guilty, if it is necessary to arrest him, all severity beyond what is necessary to secure his arrest shall be severely punished by law.

x)   No man ought to be uneasy about his opinions, even his religious beliefs, provided that their manifestation does not interfere with the public order established by the law.

xi)   The free communication of thought and opinion is one of the most precious rights of man: every citizen can therefore talk, write and publish freely, except that he is responsible for abuses of this liberty in cases determined by the law....

xiv) All citizens have the right, personally or by means of their representatives, to have demonstrated to them the necessity of public taxes, so that they can consent freely to them, can check how they are used, and can determine the shares to be paid, their assessment, collection and duration.

xv)   The community has the right to hold accountable every public official in its administration.

xvi) Every society which has no assured guarantee of rights, nor a separation of powers, does not possess a constitution.

xvii) Property being a sacred and inviolable right, nobody can be deprived of it, except when the public interest, legally defined, evidently requires it, and then on condition there is just compensation in advance.'

Wright, 1974, pp.107-10

Document B

American Declaration of Independence, 4 July 1776

'We hold these truths to be self-evident, that all men are created equal, that they are endowed by their creator with certain inalienable rights, that among these are Life, Liberty and the Pursuit of Happiness....

That to ensure these rights, Governments are instituted among men, deriving their just powers from the consent of the governed.... That where any form of Government becomes destructive of these ends it is the Right of the People to alter and abolish it.

Nor have we been wanting in attention to our British brethren. We have warned them from time to time of attempts by their legislature to extend an unwarranted jurisdiction over us. We have reminded them of the circumstances of our emigration and settlement here. We have appealed to their native justice and magnanimity and we have conjured them by ties of our common kindred to disavow these usurpations which would inevitably interrupt our connections and correspondence. They too have been deaf to the voice of justice and of consanguinity. We must, therefore, acquiesce in the necessity which demands our Separation....

We, therefore, the Representatives of the USA, in General Congress assembled, appealing to the Supreme Judge of the World for the rectitude of our intentions, do, in the Name, and by the authority of the good People of these colonies solemnly publish and declare that these United Colonies are, and of Right ought to be Free and Independent States, and that all political connection between them and the State of Great Britain is, and ought to be totally dissolved; and that as free and Independent States, they have full Power to levy war, conclude peace, contract Alliances, establish commerce and to do all other Acts and Things which Independent States may of right do. And for the support of this Declaration, with a firm reliance on the Protection of Divine Providence, we mutually pledge to each other our lives, our fortunes and our sacred honour.'

Document C

'The contradictions apparent throughout the work of the Constituent Assembly are proof of its members' realism; they had little concern for principle when it came to defending the interest of their class. Nevertheless the echoes of the ideas enunciated in the year of Revolution, 1789, are still resounding to the present day. The Declaration of the Rights of Man, voted on 26 August, sets forth human and national rights with a feeling for their universality far surpassing the empirical statement of liberties made by the English revolutionaries of the seventeenth century. Similarly the American Declaration of Independence, although couched in the universal language of natural law still contained limitations restricting the application of its principles. The bourgeoisie who formed the Constituent Assembly believed that their work was grounded in universal reason and the Declaration expressed this clearly and forcefully. From now on, they felt, the "desires of the citizens based on simple and incontestable principles" could only lead to "the upholding of the Constitution and the happiness of all" – an optimistic faith in the omnipotence of reason in keeping with the spirit of the Enlightenment but by no means proof against the pressure of class interests.'

Soboul, 1977, p.71

Document D

'It is a Declaration of the rights "de l'homme et du citoyen" (of the man and the *citizen*) – not of men as such, not of men who fail or refuse to share a common life but of men who are also citizens who accept the duties as well as the rights of membership of a community. It is made "in the presence and under the auspices of the Supreme Being"; – a mild concession to religion in the language of Pagan Rome and philosophical Deism....

Like all attempts to catch human nature on the run, the Declaration has notable omissions and is capable of unintended uses. Saying nothing of a right of association or of a right of employment it leaves capital and labour unevenly matched. Speaking only of private property, it affords no comfort to the communist.... The general colour of the Declaration is that of a middle-class individualism.... But it is a double-edged weapon which may later be turned against those who forged it.'

Thompson, 1985, pp.88-9

Discussion ——————————————————————————

The language of the Declaration of the Rights of Man does echo that of the American Declaration of Independence, something particularly clear in Articles i and ii. (In fact Jefferson, a leading campaigner for American independence, later third President of the USA, was in Paris at the time and he helped draft the later document.) Both state that men are born equal, that is with equal rights. The French then go on to make the position even clearer by the qualification: 'social distinctions can only be founded on communal utility.' This implies that differences in rank *are* necessary but should be related to an individual's usefulness to the community. The French also include 'property' among the list of the rights of man, the Americans 'the pursuit of happiness'.

The idea of sovereignty is basic to any view of government. The 1776 American Declaration specifically mentions the need for the consent of the governed. The French Declaration sees the nation as the only source of legitimate political authority. This idea, and that of the General Will (Article vi), are clearly at least partially derived from the ideas of Rousseau, though of course the whole document is heavily influenced by general Enlightenment attitudes to the primacy of rationality and the need for liberty. Even so it is a document of its time: equality seems to consist in equality before the law, and religious toleration is treated in a very guarded manner in ambiguous language (Article x). As already mentioned, private property is thought of as a fundamental feature of society (Articles ii and xvii).

Though Soboul and Thompson have very different standpoints, both see the Declaration of the Rights of Man as essentially a 'middle-class' or 'bourgeois' document. They both consider it as capable of later, perhaps unintended, interpretations. Thompson seems to be implying that it would be used to justify later demands for a truly egalitarian society. Soboul, in accordance with his socialist-Marxist interpretation of the Revolution, claims that despite its universality, it was intended to serve bourgeois class interests.

2.6 The October Days

The impatient deputies faced an impediment to the completion of the work of creating a new France with a new form of government: none of their resolutions or decrees would have any effect unless accepted by the King. As usual Louis seemed to hesitate, being influenced now by the progressive, now by the conservative elements in his Council. The Assembly itself had by the beginning of September moved to the discussion of the King's right to veto laws passed by them in due form. Robespierre, who had played a relatively modest role in the Assembly to this point, began to gain a reputation as a forceful speaker by using Rousseau's theory of the General Will (the expressed desire of the community as a whole, which was the basis of legitimate political power) to deny the King's right to even a suspensive veto or delaying power over such laws; the opinion of one man, even if he was King, could not override the General Will which found its expression in the Assembly. Although this extreme view was rejected, monarchists were dismayed by votes in the Assembly in mid-September in favour of a single-chamber legislature and granting the King only the suspensive veto. The rejection of a second chamber showed how out of favour the English model of constitutional monarchy, lauded by Montesquieu, had become. The idea of a second chamber was decried in the Paris newspapers as 'the refuge of the old aristocracy or the cradle of a new one'. It also ensured that the King and the Assembly would very easily be forced into a position of mutual hostility. The question of the veto or the 'royal sanction' roused a great deal of passion. In this respect the situation in the United States as well as that in Great Britain was discussed. The point was made that a suspensive veto gave time for further consideration of contentious matters and could be for the general benefit. In the words of a moderate journal, it 'prevents the despotism of a single ruler; it prevents factionalism among the representatives'. Following these votes, the 'patriots', or reformers, led by Barnave, Duport and Alexandre de Lameth seemed firmly in charge.

In Paris, however, such arguments began to seem less and less relevant. Although the harvest of 1789 had been relatively abundant, supplies were still short in the capital and prices high. Rumours were again circulating about the King's lack of good faith, and his eventual intention to crush the Assembly and disown its decrees. The arrival of more troops at Versailles, including the Flanders Regiment, seemed ominous and feelings were further inflamed by news of the royal family's presence at a banquet attended by the officers of the regiment where, so it was said, the tricolour cockade of the Revolution had been ground underfoot to be replaced by the old white cockade of the Bourbons or, even more ominously, the black cockade of the Austrians. The many newspapers and pamphlets published by extremist elements in Paris – Marat's *L'Ami du Peuple (People's Friend)*, and *Le Discours de 'la Lanterne' Aux Parisiens (The Lantern's [gibbet's] Tales to the People of Paris)* edited by Camille Desmoulins, for example – did nothing to calm the situation.

The idea of a march to Versailles to confront the King with the people's demands had been discussed earlier in revolutionary circles. At the beginning of October 1789 it again came to the fore. It will probably never be entirely clear to what extent the movement was spontaneous and to what extent it was organised. Many groups in Paris, particularly women on whom fell the difficult task of trying to find bread for their families, did not need much encouragement to feel that the time had now come to place their demands directly before the King. On 5 October a motley crowd, with women in the majority, which had originally gathered outside the *Hôtel de Ville* began to pour out of Paris towards Versailles. Shortly afterwards La Fayette followed with the National Guard.

At Versailles Louis at first understood that the mob of women were demanding bread. He soon learnt that political demands were also involved: that he accept the decrees of 4 August, and the Declaration of the Rights of Man. With the crowd roaming almost unchecked through the Palace, and the Queen herself apparently in danger, Louis eventually agreed to these demands, only to learn that the crowd now demanded that the royal family move permanently to Paris. He seemed to have little alternative but to give way. Some members of his bodyguard had been killed and their heads displayed on pikes before the mob.

On 6 October Louis and his family drove slowly into Paris in the midst of a strange escort of women, National Guardsmen and Conquerors of the Bastille, to the Palace of the Tuileries, a building abandoned as a royal residence over a hundred years before and full of royal pensioners, functionaries and hangers-on of every kind. The discomfort and confusion can well be imagined. Some two weeks later the Assembly followed to meet in equally makeshift premises, at first in the palace of the Archbishop, later in the former royal Riding School, the *Manège*.

Depart des Heroines de Paris pour Versailles le 5 Octobre 1789.

Figure 9 The march of the women of Paris to Versailles on 5 October 1789. Note the fashionably dressed woman on the right apparently being compelled to take part. *(Photo Bulloz)*

To those looking back at the events since May it would seem as if at two significant moments, on 14 July (the Fall of the Bastille) and on 4-6 October (the 'October Days'), direct action by a 'crowd' of Parisians, however constituted, had overcome the frustrations and hesitancies of politicians and the King. Certainly with both the Court and the Assembly now in Paris it might seem as if the centre of political gravity had shifted in favour of this kind of popular action away from the negotiations and arguments of politicians.

Self-Assessment Question 5

Read the documents below, while considering the following questions.

i) What seems to be the attitude of the British Chargé d'Affaires to the situation of the French royal family? Can we deduce from this a change of attitude among foreign observers to events in France?

ii) To what extent is it reasonable to lay emphasis on the role of Paris, and particularly the Paris 'crowd', in the Revolution to this point?

Document A ————————————————————————————————

Lord Robert Fitzgerald (Chargé d'Affaires) to the Duke of Leeds
15 October 1789

'Your Grace may conceive how unpleasant the situation of the Royal Family must be, deprived of their Body Guards and usual attendants, they are now surrounded by the *Milice Nationale* and guarded more like prisoners than Princes. It is now the tenth day since they have been at Paris and his Majesty altho' much accustomed to such exercise and hunting has not been once out into the air, indeed a walk in the garden is deprived them as it is constantly crowded with people and suffered to remain a thoroughfare'.

Thompson (ed.), 1938, p.76

Document B

'Paris had changed too. Its citizens were not likely to forget that October 6th was a victory for the policy of direct action. They would not be backward in reminding either king or assembly that the organs of government were accountable to the sovereign people. A capital which had under its protection both the executive and the legislature was in a position to dictate a policy to the whole country. Military control was passing from the army to the National Guard. Political control was passing from the intellectuals to the demagogues. The general will was contracting to the scale of the personal and party relationships of city life.'

Thompson, 1985, pp.100-01

Document C

'One wonders whether the year 1789 might not have become the first phase of an evolutionary movement, during which the nobles would have gradually come to accept the status of mere citizens... what actually happened is that the necessary decisions were not made in time, that the Court turned to force to protect the aristocracy and that the problem was therefore presented in all its fullness. The Third Estate, driven to the wall, had to choose between resistance and surrender so that in fact insurrection became inevitable, considering that fundamentally the Third was resolved to stand its ground.'

Lefebvre, 1947, p.211

Discussion

Fitzgerald, the British Chargé d'Affaires, certainly seems to regard Louis XVI and his family as objects of pity. He uses the word 'prisoners' to describe their situation and hints at a lack of respect in their treatment. This certainly could indicate a growing belief that events in France were in danger of getting out of hand from the point of view of other monarchies.

To Thompson the events in Paris certainly seem to be of overwhelming importance, but we must not forget the effect of the general peasant insurrection throughout France in the summer of 1789 which perhaps produced more important results in the decrees of 4 August and the succeeding weeks than the symbolic removal of Louis and his family from Versailles to Paris.

Lefebvre sees the Third Estate as apparently faced with a stark choice between resistance (which would probably involve violence) and surrender. It is at least arguable that no such choice in fact existed, that the Court was hesitant and muddled in its reactions to the Revolution but not necessarily irremediably hostile. The Thirds, however, refused to take the risk of trusting royal intentions and it is perhaps this which made insurrection inevitable.

2.7 The work of the Constituent Assembly November 1789 – September 1791

Reform of local government and the law

It is easy to pass over this period as lacking in the dramatic events of May to October 1789 or the later days of the fall of the monarchy and the Terror. However, in many ways this was one of the most fertile periods of the Revolution: a concerted attempt was made to construct a new form of government; the opposing views on this became more clearly articulated; and the consequences of the heady summer days of '89 became plain.

First it must be remembered to what extent the previous system of government, the *ancien régime*, had collapsed (see Essay 1, pp.105-08). During this period there was no let up in the flood of publications, of newspapers and pamphlets being produced. The work of the Constituent Assembly was widely reported, but equally furious local debates went on in political clubs, principally in those associated with the Jacobin Club in Paris (see Essay 5).

The Constituent Assembly itself was not exactly comparable to the assembly more familiar to English readers, the House of Commons. In the fairly small, badly lit, hardly heated Riding School where the deputies met, long rows of seating faced inwards, divided on one side by the President's desk, on the other by the 'tribune' intended for the speakers. There was no Government and Opposition (deputies could not be ministers by a decree of 7 November 1789) though the right–left grouping of deputies of similar opinions could be discerned. A large public gallery (seating about 300) allowed for noisy interventions by a crowd usually committed to the viewpoint of the more radical speakers. An English observer, Lord Mornington, commented in September 1790 on the lack of order in debates:

> 'They have no regular forms of debate on ordinary business... I am certain that I have seen above a hundred in the act of addressing the Assembly together, all persisting to speak, and as many more replying in different parts of the House... then the President claps his hands on both ears and roars orders as if he was calling a coach.'

Set speeches by the leaders of opinion got a better hearing but even so 'the galleries approve and disapprove by groaning and clapping, exactly as if the whole were a spectacle.'

Despite this apparent confusion, new forms of government, originating in committees of the Assembly, were approved. Local government was to be re-established on the basis of a France divided into *départements* (see Figure 22, p.107), each in turn subdivided into districts and communes. Even the smallest division, the commune, would have an elected council. This involved a question of great importance which had already arisen in connection with elections to the National Assembly: what qualifications if any, would be necessary for a man (votes for women were not seriously considered) either to vote or to stand himself for election? Could a distinction be made between 'passive' and 'active' citizens, and if so, on what grounds?

As might have been foreseen, it was decided that the distinction between those who had political rights (active citizens) and those who did not (passive citizens) was to be based on property. Those who paid more than the value of three days' labour in taxes could vote for Electors, themselves made eligible by the payment of the value of more than ten days' labour in taxes. The Electors could in turn vote for deputies, who paid at least a silver mark (52 *livres*) in taxes.

Robespierre was among those on the extreme radical wing of the Constituent Assembly who spoke with passion against this limitation of political power to the propertied classes. When he was speaking on this kind of topic he could be assured of rapt attention from the public gallery. He also demanded, with more success, political rights for Jews on the same basis as Christians.

Despite Robespierre's fears it seems that, particularly in rural areas, the proportion of 'active' citizens was actually quite high. It reached 90 per cent in villages in the Sarthe and 96 per cent in a village near Toulouse. Deputies, however, came from a much more restricted social class and included a large number of lawyers.

Whilst some committees of the Assembly were engaged in reforming local government, others undertook the work of creating a new legal system. The *parlements*, who had once seen themselves as the guardians of the people's rights, were abolished. The system finally included in the constitution of 1791 provided for elected judges, trial by jury, and release within 24 hours if a prisoner was not charged. Torture was outlawed and capital punishment restricted to decapitation – a considerable advance if one thinks of the burning at the stake, the breaking on the wheel and other disgusting modes of executing criminals possible before. An appeal court was also set up to review the system. All of this would seem to a modern observer to be greatly preferable to the confusion of courts and jurisdictions, the inheritance and purchase of judicial office, the arbitrariness and expense not to mention the fickle cruelty which had characterised the old system.

Self-Assessment Question 6

Consider the following questions while reading the documents, from contemporary newspapers, below.

i) What kind of objections are made to the voting system put forward in the Assembly?

ii) What criticisms are made, and on what grounds, of the changes proposed in the operation of the law?

iii) Do these criticisms give us an indication of how political thought was developing in France at this period of the Revolution?

(Note: information on named individuals can be found in Appendix 1.)

Document A ─────────────────────────────────────

From *Fouet National*
Written by Camille Desmoulins
10 November 1789

'Half of our representatives thought that, to qualify [for a vote], one should contribute a sum of money to the value of one mark and should besides be a land-owner. Some of them proposed that to be eligible for election to the National Assembly one should have an income of at least 1200 livres. These, then, are the true principles of the aristocracy: "Be rich and you'll be one of us, for our aim is to crush the poor."'

Wickham Legg (ed.), 1905, p.172

Document B _____

From *Courrier de Provence*
Written by Camille Desmoulins
28-9 October 1789

'I don't intend to go into the reasons which sanction and explain the huge contribution which has to be made in England if one wants to be "eligible". I will only point out that this system leads to serious abuses, and that, with the benefit of hindsight, the English nation today would emphatically not adopt the principle of "eligibility", if it were not already established.

One of these abuses – and it is one which our money law would inevitably introduce here – is the fictitious claim to property. If such and such a man is not a land-owner, or at least if his property is not large enough to confer "eligibility" upon him, what happens? He has protectors among the great land-owners, he enters into a secret arrangement with them and soon finds himself listed among the "eligible" citizens. It's of no interest to enquire the cost of his "eligibility". The very qualification which is supposed to assure the independence of the citizen is in fact proof of his servitude. It's not so much that a piece of land is purchased as that the purchaser is selling himself.'

Ibid., pp.172-3

Document C _____

From *Révolutions de Paris*, a radical newspaper
Written by Loustallot, a lawyer whose leading articles were very influential
December 1789

'This "national high court" is the greatest imaginable folly. The existence of such a tribunal is irreconcilable with public liberty. It's inevitable that it will end up by allying itself with the executive against the legislature, and that together they will usurp this latter. As I've already said, the legislative body is the only possible judge of cases presented by the committee to the "high court"; and it's essential that it retain this area of executive-judicial power in order to provide a counterweight to the power of the executive.'

Ibid., p.188

Document D _____

From *Révolutions de Paris*
Written by Loustallot
December 1789

'Is it lawful to carry out the death penalty on criminals? If it were established that no power on earth has the right to impose death *as a penalty*, it would follow that executioners wouldn't be needed.

But these are not the terms in which this question is being put to the National Assembly – far from it. The proposal, on the contrary, is to decree that those condemned to death should be beheaded by means of a "simple device" [an allusion to Guillotin's proposal].

On what grounds do the sovereigns claim for themselves the right to inflict the death penalty? They simply assume that, as part of the social contract, every man has agreed to give up his life if it should prove expedient for the state for him to do so.

It's pure sophistry on Beccaria's part to argue that, because no man has the right to dispose of his own life, he may not bestow it upon his sovereign; but it is also pure sophistry on the part of J.J. to compare the criminal condemned to death with the soldier who marches into battle.'

Ibid., p.188

Discussion

Both the documents (A and B) concerned with 'eligibility' – the right to stand as a deputy – come from newspapers associated with Camille Desmoulins, known as an extreme radical. His major point, particularly with regard to eligibility, is that any system based on a property qualification is intended to keep power in the hands of the rich. He decries the example of England and instead fastens on the opportunities for corruption in such a system. His final point, 'the purchaser is selling himself', is full of scorn at those who do not come up to the high ideals of the true revolutionary.

The document on capital punishment seems most clearly related to ideas current before the Revolution about sovereignty and basic human rights. Reference is made to both Beccaria, an Italian philosopher whose major work dealt with this very point, and to 'J.J.', that is, Rousseau. The issue of capital punishment was clearly now a matter of intellectual debate, something quite unheard of before this period. The document on the national high court (the Supreme Court) reveals the great suspicion of executive government which existed and the overriding need for ultimate control to be firmly in the hands of the Legislative Assembly, that is, the representatives of the people. Overall the documents, which all come from newspapers of the day, reveal how fiercely the arguments raised were debated. The Assembly seems more concerned with pragmatic considerations than the journalists, who were enthused with the latest political ideas.

Finance and the Church

Clear and decisive action was urgently needed in financial matters by November 1789. Taxes were not being paid and Necker found it impossible to find subscribers for further loans to the King. One source of new wealth was temptingly easily available to the deputies – the possessions of the Church. Few were prepared to defend an institution which had been identified by Voltaire as *infâme* (vile, despicable). Tithes had already been abolished on the night of 4 August. On 2 November a further vote placed all Church property at the disposal of the nation (as *biens nationaux*, national goods). In return the State would undertake the payment of clerical salaries and the Church's duty to care for the destitute. Pending the auction of Church lands the government issued so-called *assignats*, a form of paper money in theory backed by the value of the *biens nationaux*. This seemed to postpone the immediate financial crisis, but in fact it was to stoke up inflation in the future when the value of the *assignats* in circulation began to fall as more and more were printed to meet immediate financial needs. (See Appendix 3, for details of the *assignat's* fall in value.)

47

For the Church itself the loss of its property was not the end of the matter. The auctions of Church lands which began in December created a large group of people from all ranks of society, from the richer peasants to the nobility, who had no wish for the Church to regain its former position. Monastic orders were suppressed and monastic vows declared invalid in February 1790. In July the Assembly produced the Civil Constitution of the Clergy, an attempt to reorganise the Church in France on lines that accorded with those already adopted for local government and the legal system. Dioceses would be reduced in number to coincide with the numbers and boundaries of *départements*. Parish clergy and bishops would be elected by their congregations and would be expected to take an oath to be loyal to the nation, to the law and to the King.

The idea of a national Church – one deriving from the so-called 'Gallican' tradition – was not unfamiliar or unwelcome to many French Catholics. The power of the Pope over the internal affairs of the French Church had been severely limited since the early sixteenth century. Other aspects of the Civil Constitution, however, posed greater problems. The question of elections was controversial since not all those able to vote were necessarily Catholics. The King delayed accepting the decree establishing the clerical oath for as long as possible, hoping perhaps for some clear indication of the Papal attitude. The decision to impose the oath specified in the decree was taken by the Assembly at the end of November 1790. The King accepted this and the Civil Constitution as a whole by 26 December. Almost immediately the Catholic Church was split between those clergy who would and those who would not take the oath.

 ## Self-Assessment Question 7

Consider these questions in the light of the documents below, and pages 111-12 of Essay 1.

i)   Why did the division between *constitutional priests* (who took the oath) and *refractory priests* (who did not) beome so deep and bitter?

ii)   What implications did this have for the future course of the Revolution, in particular, for the position of the King?

Document A ———————————————————————————

Procès-Verbal (i.e. official published minutes) No. 484
27 November 1790

'The bishops, formerly archbishops, and the clergy who have been kept on in their former positions will be obliged, if they have not already done so, to take the oath to which they are committed under article 39 of the decree issued on 24 July last and set out in articles 21 and 38 of the decree of the twelfth of this same month, concerning the civil constitution of the clergy. In accordance with this last decree, they will swear to succour the faithful of the diocese or of the parish which is in their care, to be loyal to the Nation, the law and the King, and to maintain with all their might the constitution decreed by the National Assembly and accepted by the King. That is to say, those who are at present in their dioceses or their parishes, within a week, those who are absent but in France, within a month; and those who are abroad, within two months, starting from the publication date of this present decree.'

Wickham Legg (ed.), 1905, p.288

Document B —————————————————————

From *Mercure de France*, an official, conservative, newspaper
11 December 1790

'Men of good faith, whatever their religion, will always respect scruples
founded on religious persuasion, and on a law twelve centuries old. It is laid
down in the canons and the teaching of the Church that the method of election
of the urban clergy and the parish priests, like the delimitation of dioceses, may
not be changed without the authorization of an ecumenical council or of a
national council or, finally, of the Holy See; and it follows that the present clergy
could no longer consider themselves to be catholic if they swore under oath to
institute forms contrary to the teaching which their sacred office obliges them
to respect. Only the decision of a council, or that of the Pope, can release them
from this obligation.'

Ibid., p.290

Discussion —————————————————————

Although the oath itself seemed in many ways innocuous, requiring the clergy
to swear loyalty to the law, the nation, the King and the Constitution accepted
by the King, all of which could plausibly be presented as the civic duty of any
citizen, the underlying stumbling block was that the Church itself had not been
consulted about or involved in any of the proposed changes. They were imposed
from outside and seemed to deny the fundamental nature of the Church as a
divinely ordained institution. A refusal to swear could easily be seen as a way
of rejecting the whole progress of the Revolution and an attempt to rally
opposition around an issue of great emotional force. A general mood of anti-
clericalism had been fuelled by the writings of many *philosophes*, and the
suspicion of atheism hung over some more advanced thinkers. There is little
doubt that the schism in the Church did indeed provide the issue around which
the forces of counter-revolution could rally. Furthermore, the King's reluctant
and grudging acceptance of the Civil Constitution served only to deepen the
suspicion which already existed concerning his attitudes and motives, thus
further weakening his position.

2.8 The flight to Varennes

Who during this time were the leaders of the Revolution? Authority seems to
have been fragmented, with a constant shifting of attention from one leader to
another. La Fayette, the Commander-in-Chief of the Paris National Guard, was a
popular figure with armed power at his disposal. He however shared power in
Paris with Bailly, the mayor, until November 1791 when Pétion was elected.
Neither could ignore the Commune, the central assembly for Paris, which met at
the *Hôtel de Ville*. This body was also to some extent under the control of the
'Sections' or assemblies in each electoral district, established in July 1790, some
of which (the Faubourg Sainte-Antoine, for example) were noted for revolutionary
zeal and support for extreme policies. The confusion existing in the National
Assembly has already been noted. Many of the so-called 'monarchist' group had
fled the country during or immediately after the October Days. The patriots,
supporters of the Revolution, remained but were not a homogeneous group.
Most power seemed to be in the hands of the so-called Triumvirs, Barnave,
Lameth and Duport. However, the Assembly seemed increasingly conservative
and out of tune with the radical and exciting ideas being put forward in the

Parisian clubs, particularly the Jacobin Club (see Essay 5), and the radical press. At the Jacobin Club Robespierre spoke at every opportunity; Marat, Danton and Desmoulins published pointed criticism of the activities of the King, his ministers and the Assembly. Republican and democratic ideas were perhaps expressed most forcefully and clearly at the Cordeliers club, which was founded in April 1790.

Figure 10 Camille Desmoulins, a leading Jacobin and journalist. *(Mary Evans Picture Library)*

The King was still the source of executive power in the French government. His ministers, including Necker who remained in office till October 1790, still had responsibility for the day-to-day conduct of affairs, but their authority was continuously undermined by the Assembly, the legislative arm of government which, in turn, saw the King and his ministers as blocking the legitimate aspirations of the people. When one reads of the disturbed state of many areas of the French countryside, where the burning of *châteaux* continued and the whole system of royal and seigneurial dues and privileges had virtually collapsed, it is hard to be certain that any form of authority existed except that of force. The King received some guarded support from La Fayette, who was well aware of the dangers of anarchy. There was also the controversial figure of Mirabeau, a nobleman of dubious morals who had achieved popularity in the Assembly as a brilliant and effective orator, and who was in frequent contact with the King offering equally dubious proposals for action. (For a discussion of his views see Essay 2, pp.117-18.) His reputation perhaps prevented enough attention being paid to his reasonable idea that the King should leave Paris for a more stable area of the country. It is also true that the Court never accepted his basic thesis that their aim should be to achieve a constitutional monarchy. Mirabeau's death in April 1791 cut one of the few links between the King and the Assembly, and removed one of the King's few sources of reasonable advice.

The King and the Queen were also in contact with the increasing band of *émigrés*, people of standing, mostly nobles, who had left France from July 1789 onwards and who, from safe refuges over the frontier, urged the King to assert his authority. Their leader was the King's younger brother, the comte d'Artois. Royal letters also went to the King of Spain, Louis's cousin, and to Marie-

Antoinette's brother, the Emperor of Austria. In April 1791 the King and his advisers decided that the royal family should flee from Paris and try to establish a base from which to rally resistance to the Revolution in a more secure and less disturbed area of France. Louis and his family had been forcibly prevented by a vociferous crowd from going to Saint-Cloud to hear an Easter mass said by a refractory priest; their virtual imprisonment in the Tuileries was unmistakable. Flight from Paris seemed the only way out of an intolerable situation. By June all was ready, and on the evening of 20 June the royal family left for the *château* of Thonelle, a half day's journey from the Austrian frontier where the marquis de Bouillé had loyal troops under his command. Their success in getting away from Paris soon proved illusory. Their slow, lumbering coach failed to make contact with the waiting loyal cavalry near Varennes (see Figure 32, p.137). The royal family were recognised by the local postmaster and brought back to their capital in ignominy.

 Self-Assessment Question 8

Read the documents below, then answer the following questions.

i)   Is the British Ambassador, Lord Gower's opinion of Louis's actions in June 1791 justified?

ii) What does the King's declaration on leaving Paris reveal about his attitude to the events of the previous two years?

Document A ————————————————————————————

Lord Gower to Lord Grenville
1 July 1791

'If this country ceases to be a monarchy it will be entirely the fault of Louis XVI. Blunder upon blunder, inconsequence upon inconsequence, a total waste of energy of mind accompanied with personal cowardice have been the destruction of his reign…. It has always been the fate of this unfortunate monarch that whenever the enemies of his Government have begun to suffer the public opinion, he has adopted some measure which has reinstated them.'

Thompson, 1938, p.127

Document B ————————————————————————————

Louis's declaration on leaving Paris
20 June 1791

'The National Assembly never dared check this licence, far removed from true liberty. It has lost its influence and even the force it would have needed to retrace its steps and change what it thought should be corrected…. Frenchmen is that what you wanted when you sent your representatives to the National Assembly? Did you want anarchy and the despotism of the clubs to replace the monarchical form of government under which the nation has prospered for fourteen hundred years? Did you want to see your king heaped with insults and deprived of his liberty while he was exclusively occupied with establishing yours?'

Hardman (ed.), 1981, pp.133-4

Document C

From the manifesto fastened to the door of the meeting place of the Assembly on 22 June 1791 by Tom Paine, the English political writer

'The absence of a king is more desirable than his presence, and he is not only a political superfluity but a grievous burden, pressing hard on the whole nation.... He has abdicated the throne in having fled from his post.'

Thompson, 1938, p.129

Discussion

Louis's action seems to have caused him to lose almost all remaining support. The British Ambassador, Lord Gower's judgement is harsh but seems to be borne out by the reaction to Louis's declaration and flight. (Tom Paine's demand for Louis's removal from the throne was echoed by virtually all the radical press.) Louis's public rejection of the work of the Constituent Assembly, much of which he had previously accepted, made him look even more devious and untrustworthy, and made his claim to be working to obtain the liberty of his subjects appear to be mere window-dressing. His tame return to Paris without resistance (undertaken from the admirable motive of avoiding civil war – Lord Gower is unfair in calling him a coward) made him look weak. (As Lord Gower concluded his despatch: 'How he can extricate himself out of the present difficulty I know not'.)

Events in Paris confirmed the atmosphere of crisis. On 11 July 1791 the reinterment of Voltaire's remains in the new *Panthéon* was made the occasion of a great revolutionary celebration. On 14 July the second anniversary of the Fall of the Bastille was celebrated on the *Champ de Mars* at the 'altar of the nation'. This was not a repeat of the celebrations of 1790. Then the *Fête de la Fédération,* the Festival of Federation, had been the occasion for an outpouring of joy all over France. Wordsworth, the English poet, arrived at Calais during these celebrations and later described them as: 'that great federal day... when joy of one is joy for tens of millions.' The King had been present at the Paris *Fête* on the *Champ de Mars* and had sworn the oath of loyalty. (See Essay 3, pp.130-1.) This time, however, the King was absent, and republican feeling was running high among the members of the clubs.

Two days later a petition demanding Louis's abdication was read out at the great altar of the nation. Its reception was somewhat uncertain but the members of the Cordeliers club persisted in their support for it, drawing a crowd of supporters to the *Champ de Mars* the following day. The Assembly and the municipal authorities reacted swiftly: La Fayette's National Guard attacked the crowd and a small number were killed or injured, an action which came to be known as the Massacre of the *Champ de Mars*. The more radical politicians began to fear for their safety – Robespierre for example moved to a new address. Barnave and his associates left the Jacobin Club to found their own more moderate one, the Feuillants. (See Essay 5, p.143.)

Could this be seen as a reaction in the King's favour? Hardly. The result of these events was to deepen the confusion. The King did give his assent to the constitution of 1791 in mid-September, but the constitution itself was now under a cloud in many minds. Even with recent changes to the qualifications for eligibility (i.e. the right to vote or to stand for election), it still kept power in the hands of property owners and accepted a role for the King. The Constituent

Assembly would cease to exist at the end of the month to be replaced by a newly elected Legislative Assembly in which (by a decree proposed by Robespierre in May) no existing deputy could serve. As de Ferrières observed, 'the great aristocrats and the wild men combined to pass the decree' which at a stroke removed from the new Assembly those with some experience, and therefore with some understanding of the need for a workable system of government.

 # Self-Assessment Question 9

What had been the effect of the Revolution to this point? Attempt an assessment after reading the following documents from twentieth-century historians. (See also Essay 2 for a discussion of the issues at stake in the long deliberations over this new constitution.)

Document A

'A bourgeois constitution was infinitely better than none.... The alliance of the middle and lower classes against tyranny and privilege may have been a *mariage de convenance* rather than a love-match. It did not long outlast their common victory. But its offspring was the liberal-thinking, and liberal-living France of 1875-1939.'

Thompson, 1985, pp.226-7

Document B

'Nevertheless the extraordinary sentiment of national unity at the end of 1789 was something of an illusion. In the first place the Revolution was largely an urban phenomenon.... Even within the cities... the revolutionary condition appealed to certain groups... professional bourgeois and skilled and settled artisans.... There was no assured place within the revolutionary galaxy for large numbers of people with little or no property to defend.'

Sutherland, 1985, pp.439-40

Document C

'The search for stability by Barnave and the moderate Feuillants, on the basis of a revived constitutional monarchy, was doomed to failure. Neither the royalists of the extreme right nor Robespierre, Pétion, and the revolutionary democrats would offer any assistance. Although the king publically accepted the Constitution of 1791 (described by the queen in a private letter as "monstrous"), it had little appeal for the Parisian popular movement, resting as it did on a restricted franchise. Neither did it attract many noble deputies who voted against it with their feet by fleeing to the frontier and joining the earlier *émigrés*.'

Wright, 1974, p.48

Discussion

There seems to be some measure of agreement among these historians that this, the first phase of the Revolution, had been mainly concerned with improving the political position of middle-class property owners. They also seem agreed in drawing attention to the groups who were still excluded from the political process, largely the urban working classes. It could be seen as ominous that after all the work of the previous two years no significant group in society felt much enthusiasm for the results of the Assembly's labours. This is perhaps too pessimistic a view relying too much on knowledge of later events. Many fundamental questions about the organisation of society had been raised in these years and some rational answers had been forthcoming.

To the deputies arriving for the first meeting of the new Legislative Assembly there was no immediate indication that the Revolution was about to enter a more violent phase.

Chapter 3

WAR

3.1 The new Assembly

The Legislative Assembly replaced the Constituent Assembly on 1 October 1791. The King's attempt to leave Paris a few months previously had jeopardised the agreement that his power should be limited but not abolished. Yet the fiction adopted by his Feuillant ministers that he had been kidnapped, and La Fayette's violent suppression of a popular anti-government demonstration in the *Champ de Mars*, seemed to signal that a conservative reaction had started. It should be noted, however, that as early as October 1789 the Assembly had introduced a measure of press censorship, and the death penalty for rebellion; the propertied élite had always feared popular uprisings. The new Assembly was elected by a franchise limited to property owners. None of the experienced deputies who had achieved so many reforms in the previous Assembly were eligible to stand. The question that this chapter addresses is why, in the light of such circumstances, the following year saw the outbreak of war with Austria and Prussia, the fall of the monarchy and the establishment of a regime of unprecedented radicalism.

The deputies of 1789-91 and their supporters in Paris and the provinces had changed so many aspects of French government and society that the repercussions of some of the measures were only becoming fully apparent at the end of their term in office. The supposed abolition of feudal obligations and Church tithes (actually many feudal dues had to be redeemed by cash payments, while tithes would be incorporated into rent agreements), the Civil Constitution of the Clergy and the imposition of an oath of loyalty, gave rise to countless disputes and tended to polarise opinion for and against the Revolution. The pressure on the army and the National Guard both to defend the King and his supporters, and to implement the decrees of the Assembly, often led to unpredictable and apparently capricious military action or inaction. The growth in political consciousness at all levels, including groups hitherto discounted such as artisans and women, could lead to violent and often decisive popular action. The Paris Commune grew progressively more radical and was to be the means by which hostility towards the monarchy was translated into action. The great powers of Europe had initially seen little profit in intervention in the affairs of revolutionary France; but the abortive royal flight, the proselytising and anti-monarchical tone of some deputies, club debates and newspapers, and the growth of reformist groups inside their own borders caused them increasing alarm and hastened the outbreak of war. Another poor harvest in 1791, the continuation of the economic recession which had begun in the 1780s and a 25 per cent fall in the value of *assignats* during the winter and the spring of 1792 increased the threat to the stability of the new constitution.

Some of these destabilising factors are further examined in Self-Assessment Question 1 below.

Self-Assessment Question 1

Read the following three documents and pages 108-11 of Essay 1 and identify some of the causes of increasing social and political disruption.

Document A

'[In the department of the Gard] the more radical and jacobin groups appear to have formed separate popular societies during the winter of 1791-2. Due to confessional differences, however, the distinction was based as much on religious as on political grounds. There were two clubs in Uzes, one frequented by "the aristocrats, nearly all catholics, to oppose the democratic club which was mostly protestant". The catholic and royalist stronghold of Saint-Gilles boasted two clubs at the beginning of 1791: one patriot, the other "a society of aristocrats" which met in a café. [In] Beaucaire, mainly Catholic but also the refuge for émigrés of all political complexions... the distinction between [the] two clubs appears to have been political in origin: the jacobin club, dating from 1791 was described by one royalist as "the source of all the evils which afflict this town".'

Lewis, 1978, p.51

Document B

From the report of the municipality of Caen read to the Legislative Assembly on 11 November 1791

'For some time a crowd of emigrants and former nobles from Caen and the surrounding area had been meeting in public places, patrolling on horse-back, and seemed, judging by their arrogant behaviour and their threatening talk, to have hostile intentions. They had sounded out public opinion and believed that they would easily win over to their side those whom it pleases them to call "worthy" citizens, namely malcontents. But they needed a pretext for action; and so they rallied to the cause of the refractory priests.

On Friday 4th of this month, M. Bunel, former priest of the parish of Saint-Jean arrived to celebrate mass, at about 8 o'clock in the morning. He had, we knew, informed the constitutional priest of his intentions, as well as the majority of the congregation of this parish, which is made up mainly of formerly privileged citizens. And so, at the appointed hour, the church was full. It was alarming to see the sanctuary and the choir filled with former nobles and their servants, whom we suspected of being armed with pistols and positioned so as to stir up trouble. The demeanour of these men provoked the patriots; but they were careful to avoid being drawn into a fight.'

Roberts (ed.), Vol.1, 1966, p.377

Document C

'The beleaguered Legislative Assembly found itself an impotent witness to a spring offensive against the trappings of seigneurialism. In January and February 1792 came reports of fresh outbreaks of château-burning in the South West. As usual the troubled department of the Lot provided the spark. In March the locus of peasant activism shifted to the adjacent department of the Cantal where political agitators incited the rural population to attack châteaux in the neighbourhood of Aurillac. Here as elsewhere, the peasantry used the symbols of the new order – the municipalities and the National Guard – against those of the old. Early in April, just as the Feudal Committee was tabling a draft law to abolish casual dues, further reports arrived of château-burning a little to the south in the department of the Aveyron. The Lot, the Cantal and the Aveyron formed a tight wedge of territory which had long experienced the full panoply of seigneurial excesses.

However, the major arena for agrarian violence during the spring and summer of 1792 lay not in the South West, but in the South East. Disturbances began in the Ardèche in mid-March and spread along the southern flanks of the Massif Central to the Gard. In the first few days of April two dozen châteaux were attacked in this latter department alone. Towers and dovecotes were demolished, armorial bearings disfigured and title-deeds seized for public burning. Intimidation, pillage, forced renunciations and the repayment of fines were routine. Yet the violence overflowed the narrow confines of anti-seigneurialism. The insurgents responded to shortages and spiralling prices by intervening in the market-place to fix the price of grain, they broke down enclosures, invaded the commons, punished usurpers, agitated for the partition of village pastures and wastes and called for the sale of "*biens nationaux*" in small parcels. In short, anti-seigneurialism became a cover under which to advance the socio-economic programme of the poor peasantry. But the risings in the South East also reflected the polarisation of political opinion in the countryside: the image of the seigneur as feudal exploiter was yielding to the image of the seigneur as counter-revolutionary plotter.'

Jones, 1988, pp.120-21

Discussion

In the Gard (see Figure 22, p.107) a particular problem was caused by reaction to the emancipation of the Protestant minority who tended, at least at this stage, to support reform. In the towns they were often prosperous members of the bourgeoisie, in the villages they were peasants who were prepared to come into the towns to support their co-religionists. The aristocrats, although they must have formed a minority in the counter-revolutionary clubs that are mentioned, are identified as the leaders of opinion and as orthodox Catholics. 'Patriots' in Saint-Gilles and Jacobins in Beaucaire represented the other political pole and their existence carried the potential for future political conflict. This had already occurred in Normandy (see Figure 21, p.106), according to the report of the municipality of Caen. Here the existence of priests who would not take the oath of obedience to the State (refractories) was identified as the immediate cause of trouble, especially as they were supported by *émigrés* (who had presumably infiltrated from the Empire), aristocrats and other malcontents. (The report later recounts how the confrontation between M. Bunel and the constitutional priest led to a riot in which several people were wounded.)

By 1791 the peasantry in some areas of France was taking effective political action to secure the benefits of the abolition of feudalism. Despite the tactics of the ex-*seigneurs* this pressure, both legal petitioning and illegal attacks on *châteaux*, was gradually effective in removing the last traces of the old impositions. A new element appeared in areas where the peasantry was committed to the ideas as well as the economic benefits of revolution: *seigneurs* were increasingly accused of plotting to restore the *ancien régime*. Sufficient evidence exists of similar disputes throughout France to indicate that further internal or external disruptions could lead to civil war.

The King and Queen, who were effectively prisoners in the Tuileries Palace, gave what aid and comfort they could to their supporters by rejecting the policies of the Legislative Assembly and their Feuillant ministers. In November 1791 the Assembly decreed that those *émigrés* who failed to return to France by 1 January 1792 would be condemned to death and have their property confiscated. Later it decided that refractory priests were to lose their state stipends, be treated as politically suspect and, in some cases, be imprisoned. Louis used his veto to block both decrees showing unequivocally that his sympathies lay with the *émigrés* and with the refractory priests and their followers. The worst fears concerning his commitment to the new order had been confirmed, but the Assembly could see no alternative but to try to make the constitution work.

3.2 The growth in popular political consciousness

The weakness of the Assembly in face of royal intransigence and the increasing political consciousness of the lower urban bourgeoisie and artisans (*sans-culottes*) gave great importance to alternative means of political expression. The people of Paris had made several decisive interventions in 1789 and retained some influence by formal petitioning and informal disorderly barracking in the Assembly hall, to which the public had open access. Opinion was shaped and further possibilities for reform were aired in a more reasoned fashion by meetings in the 48 Sections and by their representatives in the Commune at the Town Hall, by debates in the clubs and by the views expressed in the many newspapers and journals which circulated in the city.

Figure 11 *The Carmagnole*, a popular revolutionary song and dance, whose words were full of scorn for the *ancien régime*. (Roger-Viollet, Paris)

The Jacobin Club (see Essay 5) had been severely disrupted by the reaction to the Massacre of the *Champ de Mars* (see p.52). Barnave and other moderates had left to form the Feuillants Club and, although most of the provincial clubs retained their affiliation, it took some time to rebuild the membership. Led by orators such as Pétion and Robespierre, the Jacobin Club became more radical in complexion and far more resistant than the Assembly to bribes and pressure by the Court and other counter-revolutionary forces. Meetings had been made open to the public although the membership fee was too high for the poorer classes.

 Self-Assessment Question 2

Read Essay 5 on Jacobinism, especially pages 142-5.

What were the principal factors which contributed to the success of the Jacobin movement?

Discussion

Even before the foundation of the Parisian Jacobin Club and the provincial societies, a network of literary societies, masonic lodges and academies existed. In 1789 many of these simply changed their title to 'Society of the Friends of the People', the official title of all Jacobin Clubs. These kept in touch with each other and the 'mother-society' in Paris to which they were affiliated through the central 'Correspondence Committee'. This maintained links and disseminated ideas and policies not only throughout the country but also kept up communication with sympathetic bodies in other parts of the world. Vetting procedures ensured that only ideologically acceptable societies could be affiliated, and the clubs in the larger provincial cities such as Bordeaux and Strasbourg were responsible for keeping in touch with small town and village societies in their area.

Many women attended the clubs, applauding their favourite speakers, interjecting remarks and presenting petitions, but they were discouraged from taking a more formal part in proceedings. Of the revolutionary leaders, only Condorcet seems seriously to have contemplated the extension of political rights to women.

 Self-Assessment Question 3

Read the following document, a report of the proceedings of the Legislative Assembly, and note what evidence it provides of the attitude of the Assembly towards female political activity.

Document A

1 April 1792
'The former Baronne d'Aelders, a Dutch woman, accompanied by several other women, is admitted to the bar. After a long eulogy of feminine virtues, after having maintained that women equal men in courage and in talent, and almost always surpass them in imagination, she requests that the Assembly take into

consideration the state of degradation to which women find themselves reduced as far as political rights are concerned, and reclaims on their behalf the full enjoyment of the natural rights of which they have been deprived by a protracted repression. To attain this objective, she asks that women be admitted to civilian and military positions and that the education of young people of the feminine sex be set up on the same foundation as that of men. Women have shared the dangers of the Revolution; why shouldn't they participate in its advantages?

The president answers the petitioners that the Assembly will avoid, in the laws it is entrusted with making, everything that might provoke their regrets and their tears, and grants them the honours of the session. (The Assembly sends the petition to the joint Committees on Legislation and Education.)'

Levy, Applewhite, Johnson (eds.), 1979, p.123

Discussion

The women were received politely and their 'long eulogy of feminine virtues' was given a hearing. Did the noble background of d'Aelders, and the fact that she could make an articulate case influence the deputies? Their response was also polite but, perhaps, patronising. The women were assured that the Assembly, which had the sole mandate to make laws, would not cause them regret or tears – could this have been a deliberate reference to supposed female weakness? The grant of the honours of the session was an empty gesture as was the referral of the petition to the joint Committees. The serious content of the petition – the demand for admission to civil and military positions and for equal educational opportunities – was marginalised.

Newspapers were cheap to run. Robespierre, although he no longer received a regular salary, founded a weekly called *The Defender of the Constitution*. Like other politician/journalists such as Marat, Desmoulins and Hébert, he wrote most of the reports and articles himself. These papers provided a valuable means of spreading views, especially for those who were not members of the Assembly. Urban literacy rates were very high, even amongst the *sans-culottes*. The deputies could be sure that their most interesting debates and speeches would be published by major journals such as the *Moniteur*, a paper which was relatively favourable to the government.

3.3 The outbreak of war

There was no compelling reason for France to go to war with Austria and Prussia in 1792. The two latter powers were preoccupied with safeguarding their interests and acquiring territory as the unfortunate kingdom of Poland disintegrated. The Revolution in France had begun, to a large extent, because of the weakness of its economy. The fundamental problems which led to this weakness had by no means been solved and an expensive war would be fatal to any prospects of achieving financial stability. Despite these factors the rulers of Austria and Prussia and a substantial proportion of the French people and their representatives believed, by the end of 1791, that war was inevitable.

Self-Assessment Question 4

Read pages 133-4 of Essay 4, especially the speech delivered by Brissot to the Assembly in December 1791. What were the advantages that the various factions in French politics saw in declaring war on Austria and Prussia?

Discussion

Brissot summarised the views of like-minded deputies from the Gironde (see Figure 22, p.107) and other parts of France (this group is usually referred to as the 'Brissotins' or 'Girondins' although they were never tightly organised). Only war could establish France's security externally and, by quelling the *émigrés*, stop internal counter-revolutionary activity. This would save the enormous expenditure required to suppress such movements and vindicate the commitment of the French people to their Revolution. Nobles such as La Fayette and even members of the Court welcomed the opportunity that they believed the war would bring them to seize control of the government. In other words, the Girondins wanted a war they could win; the Court one they could lose.

The only radical politician of any significance to oppose a declaration of war was Robespierre. His classical education provided sufficient warnings that victorious generals might seize power. Julius Caesar had made himself dictator, and Oliver Cromwell furnished a more recent and alarming example. The philosophers of the Enlightenment tended to reject warfare as immoral. It was hard to see how an ill-financed, badly organised army whose officers kept defecting to the Empire as *émigrés* could conquer the disciplined and experienced forces of France's enemies. Robespierre also feared the machinations of the Court. These issues were debated with the Girondins in the Jacobin Club, to which most radical politicians belonged, and in the press (Brissot also had a newspaper). The debates provided a rehearsal for the great conflict between Brissot's following and the radical Jacobins of the Mountain in later months. La Fayette came in for even sharper censure as a potential Cromwell in the kind of vituperative rhetoric for which Robespierre was becoming increasingly renowned and feared.

The early months of the war, which was declared by the Assembly against Austria on 20 April 1792, bore out the most pessimistic predictions of failure. The King had appointed several ministers with Girondin affiliations, displacing the Feuillants in a half-hearted attempt to placate the bellicose faction in the Assembly, but he had no enthusiasm for conducting the war. Despite her confinement in the Tuileries, the Queen held court and managed to maintain communications with Austria and with counter-revolutionaries within France. So the country was being led by a legislature and executive with diametrically opposed policies. The royal use of the veto made this brutally clear in early June when Louis blocked decrees of the Assembly exiling refractory priests and dissolving the King's Guard. The latter was to be replaced by 20,000 provincial National Guards (*fédérés*) who had converged on Paris to defend it from invasion, and to provide a check to ambitious generals or counter-revolutionary elements in the army. For good measure the King sacked his pro-Girondin ministers and replaced them by pliable nonentities. This belated display of firmness combined with memories of the flight to Varennes and the rumoured intrigues of the Court with France's enemies were probably the factors which finally brought about the fall of the monarchy. A 'dress rehearsal' took place on

20 June when a mob peacefully invaded the Tuileries for a few hours. More interesting than the subsequent fall itself on 10 August is the means by which it happened. The forces that successfully established a Republic, and the attitude of the political factions towards how it should be organised, also determined the ideological complexion of the new government and what its bases of power would be for the next two years. Ultimately, the Girondin failure to give firm leadership in the summer of 1792 contained the germs of their overthrow by the Jacobins of the Mountain, the Paris Commune and *sans-culottes* nearly a year later.

3.4 The fall of the monarchy

Jacques-Louis David's painting of Brutus, which was first exhibited in 1789, records the moment when the decapitated bodies of his two sons were brought home. As a consul of the new Roman Republic in the fifth century BC, Brutus had condemned his sons to death for conspiring to restore the monarchy of the Tarquins. Voltaire had written a very successful play on this theme which was performed frequently during the early years of the Revolution. In one production a tableau of the actors deliberately referred to David's renowned picture. In 1791 Voltaire's body, in a lavish ceremony heavy with classical symbolism, was taken to the *Panthéon* (which, bearing a suitably Deist name, had been dedicated to the reception of the bodies of heroes of the Revolution). Busts of Brutus proliferated and one was installed in the Legislative Assembly. The Jacobin Club, of which David was a member, had already adopted Brutus as their patron. The political force of the imagery was underlined by the radical newspapers and politicians who frequently referred to Louis XVI as 'Tarquin'.

Figure 12 David, *The Lictors bringing back the bodies of the sons of Brutus* (1789). This was often interpreted as praising those who put loyalty to the Republic above loyalty to their own family. *(Louvre, Paris. Lauros-Giraudon)*

Self-Assessment Question 5

Examine David's painting of Brutus (Figure 12), and read Essay 3.

What impact could the picture be expected to make on:

i)   contemporary cultural values;

ii)   contemporary political objectives?

Discussion

It would be misleading to imply that the Revolution initiated the fashion for neo-classical design in art, architecture, furniture, costume etc. The vogue for cultivating antiquity was well under way by 1789 but the historical accuracy and austerity of David's images as well as their support of a prevailing ideology strengthened and hastened the process. The increasing simplicity of costumes and hair-styles during the final decade of the eighteenth century proclaimed more than just a change in fashion. It was the adoption of a more democratic form of appearance in which distinctions of class would progressively become less apparent. By the end of the century the powdered hair and culottes (breeches) of the *ancien régime* had become the preserve of the elderly and of public functionaries.

David's picture provides an example of the way in which the leaders of opinion, inside and outside the Assembly, were trying to replace the Christian moral code with one founded on what they perceived to have been the classical obligation to put the public good, embodied in the State, above personal interests. We should, however, remember that when David produced the picture, in the early stages of the Revolution, he may only have held these views in a very abstract way, as had the philosophers of the Enlightenment who were one source of his inspiration. By 1792 the significance of Brutus had become far more specific: the story of his integrity and devotion to the new Roman Republic could be used to justify the overthrow of the monarchy and even regicide.

In July 1792, the heavy handed manifesto of the commander of the allied armies, the Duke of Brunswick (see Essay 4, p.135), coincided with a groundswell of opinion in the radical Paris Sections, orchestrated by the mayor, Pétion (who had replaced Bailly), that the monarchy should be abolished. *Fédérés* were still arriving in Paris on their way to the front and some, especially those from Marseilles, lingered to give encouragement and support to the republican movement, as the words to this popular song show:

> 'Tremble tyrants – and you, betrayers,
> Who bring disgrace to every side!
> Tremble scheming father-slayers,
> Find at last your just reward.
> The world is up in arms against you;
> And though our brave young heroes die,
> The world will blossom forth anew
> With soldiers ready to defy.

Chorus
Citizens to arms! Close ranks and take your guard!
Forward, forward, let our fields be washed in traitors' blood!'

Marseillaise, Verse 3

Robespierre and the majority of the Jacobin Club had decided that the constitution was no longer worth defending and were colluding with the Commune to overthrow it. As he said to the Club on 11 July:

> 'It is in vain that we make good laws if the executive will not carry them out, if they annul them by treacherous vetoes, if corrupt administrators conspire with the Court to use the constitution to destroy the constitution. It is in vain that armies of brave and patriotic soldiers risk their lives in combat, if they are halted in their march to victory, or if they are sent into battle to be defeated by an enemy of twice their numbers. In moments of such peril, ordinary measures are not enough: Frenchmen, save yourselves!'

On 28 July La Fayette justified the worst allegations that had been made against him by an abortive attempt to save the constitutional monarchy. He demanded that the Assembly suppress the clubs, including the Jacobins, and punish those who had insulted the royal family by (peacefully) invading the Tuileries on 20 June. But he had lost his hold over the National Guard, despite the fact that many battalions were still dominated by prosperous and cautious members of the bourgeoisie. La Fayette returned to his army on the frontier and soon fled from France.

The Girondins who, after the King's humiliating rejection of their measures and their ministers, had eloquently condemned him in the Assembly, belatedly seemed to realise that a violent show-down was likely. They advised him to make conciliatory gestures, and in turn moderated the republicanism of their rhetoric. The King and Queen seem to have believed that only the intervention of Austria and the German princes would save them. They had not trusted either Mirabeau or the Feuillants, so they were certainly not going to co-operate with the Girondins: Louis refused to make any concessions.

 Self-Assessment Question 6

Document A below is taken from a petition voicing Jacobin policy presented to the Assembly by Pétion on 3 August 1792. The two following documents are from sources favourable to the monarchy: Document B is by the aristocrat, Madame du Bourg, and Document C by Gouverneur Morris, the American Ambassador.

When you have read them note what you can learn about the mentalities of radical popular activists and supporters of the monarchy just before it fell.

Document A ————————————————————————————————

'Enemy armies threaten our territory. Two foreign tyrants have issued a manifesto, as insolent as it is absurd, attacking the French nation. Parricidal Frenchmen, led by the king's brothers, his relatives, his allies, are getting ready to tear open the breast of the fatherland. Already the enemy, on every front, lets loose his tormentors against our warriors....

The first link in this chain of counter-revolution is the leader of the executive... Louis XVI is always invoking the Constitution; we, too, invoke it and we demand his removal.

Once this important step has been taken, we demand the election – for it is unlikely that the nation can trust its present royal-house – of solid and reliable ministers. Selected by the National Assembly but independent of it, bound by the constitution and its laws, elected by the vote, loudly proclaimed, of free men: they will carry out the functions of the executive until such time – as soon as national security permits it – as the will of the people, your only sovereign and ours, shall be declared through a national convention.'

Roberts (ed.), Vol. 1, 1966, pp.509-10

Document B _____

Madame du Bourg in Rouen to Gouverneur Morris in Paris
9 August 1792

'I pity you, obliged to stay in that cursed Babylon, where one can but foresee and dread every day some fresh misfortune. I do not, however, believe in dethronement; the Duke of Brunswick's manifesto may well make them pause and reflect, it strikes me as very useful, and wisely conceived for present circumstances; events seem to be rushing on and yet at the same time slowing down, it is said that the Austrians cannot reach the frontier before the 13th, what disasters might not happen between then and now.... I am pleased at my choice of Rouen for my retreat; one is in perfect tranquillity here, all the constituted authorities are animated by the best intentions and the merchant, absorbed in his commerce, does not trouble himself about the revolution; as nobody has any interest in stirring up the people they remain quite calm, and the jacobins are without influence in this town.'

Davenport (ed.), Vol. 2, 1972, p.486

Document C _____

From Gouverneur Morris's diary

'August 8 Monsieur de Monciel [Terrier de Monciel, recently a minister] calls this morning... tells me that things are going on well. The King seems to hold the proper opinions also, which is a desirable thing. I dine with Madame de Stahl [*sic*] [Necker's daughter] and after dinner, the gentlemen desiring to drink, I send for wine and get them preciously drunk. Go to the Louvre and take my friend [his mistress, Madame de Flahaut] to ride; after I set her down I go to Lady Sutherland's and pay her a pretty long visit. She will be at Court tomorrow. The weather is very warm still.'

Ibid., p.489

Discussion _____

Petitions, speeches and newspaper articles demanding the deposition of Louis XVI had proliferated during the summer of 1792. This petition represents a carefully argued case put together by members of the Jacobin Club, *fédéré* leaders, the bourgeois and artisan activists in the Sections and their representatives in the Commune. At this stage they feel able not only to demand Louis's deposition but also to imply that a Republic will be established and to

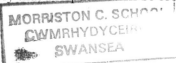

ask that a Convention, a body formed by the agreement of the electorate rather than by royal decree, should be summoned. Note the reference to the 'will of the people' which is 'sovereign'. Is this evidence that the ideas of philosophers like Rousseau had penetrated quite deeply into radical political thought by this stage in the Revolution? Even the more moderate politicians of the Constituent Assembly had, after all, used such phrases (see Chapter 2, pp.38-40).

The confusion, false hopes, intrigues and enjoyment of comfort and pleasures of the royalists du Bourg and Morris contrast with the austere recognition that the Paris petition gives to the realities and dangers of the situation. Madame du Bourg totally mistook the likely impact of the Brunswick manifesto, although she was probably right about the climate of opinion in Rouen, which was later a centre of counter-revolutionary activity. (Chronologically the du Bourg letter is dated a day after Morris's diary entry. It was quoted first because of the time lapse that would have occurred in her reception of news from Paris and the front.)

On 10 August 1792 the radical Parisian leaders, the *fédérés* (especially those from Marseilles) and the National Guards from the more revolutionary Sections moved to overthrow the monarchy by storming the Tuileries Palace. Louis and his family took refuge in the Assembly, leaving the Swiss Guard and gentlemen loyalists to defend the Palace. Both sides were well armed and the casualties were far higher than when the Bastille was taken. The following laconic account, from the American Ambassador Morris's diary, describes the storming of the Tuileries and the suspension of the King.

> 'August 10 this morning Monsieur de Monciel calls and his report is tranquillizing but shortly after he leaves the cannon begin and the musketry mingled with them announce a warm day. The Château, undefended by the Swiss, is carried and the Swiss wherever found are murdered. The King and Queen are in the National Assembly who have decreed the suspension of his authority. Madame de Flahaut sends her son and comes afterwards to take refuge. I have company to dine but many of those who were invited do not come. Mr Huskisson, the Secretary to the English Ambassador, comes in the evening. He gives a bad account of things. The weather continues very warm or rather, extremely hot.'

About a thousand died in this conflict. Most were Swiss Guards and aristocratic defenders of the Tuileries, some were *fédérés* and ordinary citizens of Paris.

Some writers describe the sequence of events which led, by the end of September 1792, to the abolition of the monarchy and the establishment of a Republic as 'a second revolution'. It was certainly better planned and executed than the first one, being the product of the concerted action of popular activists in the Commune and the Sections in alliance with some of the *fédérés*. Their views were voiced by such means as Robespierre's speech of 11 July and the petition of the 48 Sections. August 10 was the successful conclusion of their agitation: the royal family was removed from the protection of the Legislative Assembly and confined in the Temple prison.

Figure 13 Gérard, *The Insurrection of 10 August 1792.* The royal family are cowering behind protective bars near the President's chair, while the *sans-culottes* have invaded the chamber of the Legislative Assembly. *(Louvre. Cliché des Musées Nationaux – Paris)*

3.5 The last days of the Legislative Assembly

To the end the Girondins had not clearly identified themselves with the republican movement and were suspicious of Parisian activists. The deputies were strongly influenced by pressures from their own *départements* which were largely hostile to the establishment of a Republic and especially to the proposal to put the King on trial for his life. The *Chouan* counter-revolutionary resistance in Brittany commenced at this time (see Essay 1, pp.111-12). Many royalist and moderate deputies were unwilling or fearful to attend the Assembly. Its days were, in any case, numbered, as it had agreed on 10 August to give way to a Convention in late September. Browbeaten by the victorious Commune, the remaining deputies agreed to abolish the distinction between 'active' and 'passive' citizens and to dismantle remaining feudal charges without paying compensation. New currency bore the portrait of 'Liberty', modelled on statues of classical goddesses, rather than that of Louis XVI (see Essay 3, p.124). The National Guard in Paris was directly attached to the Sections, greatly increasing their influence. The edict which Louis had vetoed exiling refractory priests was implemented. The disappearance of so many of those who had formerly recorded births, marriages and deaths necessitated the transfer of these functions to the local communes. As Sutherland (1985) says: 'Thus civil existence was defined by the state, no longer by the Church'. The work of creating a new society had started in earnest.

The uncertain leadership and conflicting loyalties of past months had undermined the war effort. Prussians and *émigrés* crossed the frontier into France in mid-August. On 2 September news reached Paris that the great fortress of Verdun had fallen and, remembering Brunswick's threats, many panicked. Danton, an eloquent

Jacobin and the new Minister of Justice enjoying a loyal following in the poorer Sections, roused the courage of the remaining deputies (see Essay 4, pp.135-6). A less inspiring reaction to the emergency and the attendant fear of treason was the massacre in the prisons of Paris of between 1,100 and 1,400 political offenders, monks, priests and ordinary felons. Much ink has been spilt in apportioning blame for these killings which continued for five days. By the time the climate of political opinion had changed sufficiently to condemn them, most of those responsible were either dead or had effectively covered their tracks. The massacres seem to have been a fairly spontaneous reaction to the threat of invasion and internal treachery, encouraged by elements in the Commune and the National Guard. The Assembly and the ministers took no practical measures to halt them. There were similar, smaller-scale atrocities in the provinces. Their long-term significance was three-fold. Firstly, when the news reached other European states it seemed to vindicate all the negative propaganda the *émigrés* had been circulating about the dangers of popular revolution. Secondly, the massacres were combined with Robespierre's original dispute with Brissot over the declaration of war – the origin of the division between the Girondins and the Jacobins – as the former blamed the latter for instigating and encouraging the bloodshed. Thirdly, twice in a month the people of Paris had shown how impotent the constitutional authorities proved to be in the face of violent, politically motivated action. As a result, in the Convention the Girondins were weakened and the influence of their radical opponents, men like Danton and Robespierre, who were popular with insurgent Parisians, was enhanced. The French victory at Valmy on 20 September seemed to vindicate the republican policies of the latter politicians.

In the space of one year, October 1791 to late September 1792, political life in France had been transformed. Prior to this time the achievements of the National Assembly – the limited monarchy, the theoretical abolition of feudalism, the establishment of state control over the Church and equality before the law – had paralleled the gains of the English in 1688 and the American colonists in 1783. They were the kind of moderate measures that philosophers such as Montesquieu had advocated. The writings of these philosophers had contributed to the intellectual climate which had encouraged the reformers amongst the deputies, nobles and bourgeois alike, to persevere against all obstacles. Self-Assessment Question 7 below examines how far the more radical policies of the Legislative Assembly and of external pressure groups also originated in the ideas of the philosophers.

 Self-Assessment Question 7

Document A in Self-Assessment Question 6 (pp.64-5) from the petition of the Paris Sections on 3 August 1792 seemed to recall a central theme of Rousseau's *Social Contract* in its reference to the 'will of the people' which was 'sovereign'. Revise your work on Self-Assessment Question 5 and read the following extracts from Macdonald's *Rousseau and the French Revolution, 1762-1791*. Then write paragraphs on:

i)   the evidence that the philosophers were influential in the radicalisation of the Revolution;

ii) the difficulty of interpreting this evidence.

Document A

'A bust of Rousseau was... installed in the National Assembly in 1790, with copies of *Émile* and the *Social Contract* deposited at its base. The Assembly accepted the presentation of the complete works of Rousseau in 1791. Rousseau's bust was similarly installed in the assembly rooms of many popular societies... including the Jacobins, the Society of Poor People and the Society of the Social Circle of Friends of Truth.... A section of Paris was named "Social Contract", and a street received his name in 1791. Fêtes were held in Rousseau's honour, the most famous of which was held at Montmorency (where he had lived for a time) in September, 1791. The National Assembly decreed the erection of a statue in his honour, and granted a pension to his widow... and... received two petitions demanding the transference of Rousseau's remains from Ermenonville to the Panthéon'.

Macdonald, 1965, pp.156-8

Document B

'Rousseau was neither the first nor the only political philosopher to use the expression [the General Will], Montesquieu, Holbach and Diderot used it in works prior to 1762.... The fact that the expression was used by members of the Parlement of Rouen in 1771 suggests that by this date it already enjoyed a fairly wide currency. It seems unlikely that the parlementaires were students of the *Social Contract* or that they would knowingly utilize a phrase drawn from that work... Sieyès's famous pamphlet *What is the Third Estate?* repeats these phrases constantly ["the national will", "the common wish", "the national interest", "the general interest", "the common interest", the "common will"], but refers only once to the general will. The expression gained a pre-eminent place in revolutionary lore and language, and it was given official recognition by its inclusion in the Declaration of Rights. This may have been because it was regarded as particularly appropriate... the previous use of the expression by political philosophers had endowed it with special weight. As interest in Rousseau's name as a revolutionary symbol gained strength, the expression no doubt received added recommendation because of Rousseau's use of it. There is no evidence, however, that the revolutionaries derived either the phrase itself or their understanding of it from the *Social Contract*'.

Ibid., pp.87-8

Discussion

Section 3.4 and Self-Assessment Question 5 (p.63) discussed the evidence for the use of the classical story of Brutus, including Voltaire's play, to discredit the monarchy and even to justify its destruction. Voltaire's actual writings did not, however, recommend tyrannicide or republicanism, only a fairer society free from the superstitious domination of religion. Rousseau's life and the minor persecutions he suffered were well known. His love of nature and belief that individuals should be absolutely frank about their ideas and personalities responded well to the popular revulsion against the luxury, hypocrisy and artificial manners of the *ancien régime*. Voltaire and Rousseau were consequently adopted by the Assemblies as prophets of the Revolution and both were placed in the *Panthéon;* ironically in life they had detested each other!

The phrase 'the General Will' was one of a number which expressed a view widely held by enlightened thinkers in the late eighteenth century that government should recognise the needs and rights of the whole population of a country, not just of an élite. Confusion arises from the use of the phrase by various other people who had no intention to suggest that society or the sources of authority should be radically altered. The adoption of Rousseau and Voltaire as symbols of change and reform by the various national assemblies certainly identified their ideas with the Revolution, but this in itself provides no evidence of how widely the contents of books such as *The Social Contract* were known.

Most of the philosophers in the course of their careers made various, sometimes mutually contradictory, recommendations on how government should be organised. Taken in isolation extracts from Voltaire, Montesquieu, Diderot, Rousseau etc. could be cited to justify almost any regime. Educated activists such as Brissot and Robespierre selected the parts of the writings which coincided with the political and social changes the current situation seemed to them to require. Brissot, for example, conveniently ignored Voltaire's and Rousseau's hatred of warfare. For the *sans-culottes,* who had probably read little or nothing of the work of the philosophers, the knowledge that their lives and opinions had shown them to be hostile to the excesses of Catholic superstition and a despotic monarchy was sufficient to justify their substitution for the old authority figures in Church and State.

Chapter 4

THE JACOBIN REPUBLIC

4.1 The trial and execution of Louis XVI

As had been agreed on 10 August 1792, the Legislative Assembly was superseded by a Convention, which met on 21 September. The first problem it faced was to decide the fate of the deposed King who, with his family, was being guarded by the Paris Commune in the Temple prison. The argument that raged for the next few months exposed three elements in the Convention: the Girondins, the Jacobin Mountain (who sat on the high benches to the left of the rostrum in the Convention) and the Plain, the majority of the deputies who did not identify with either of the two factions. Together with the Girondins the Plain represented the greater part of the electorate which was unenthusiastic about or hostile to further radical measures. Members of the Jacobin Club were to be found in all parts of the Convention as were a few ex-nobles and many former office-holders and lawyers as well as actors, writers, soldiers, ex-priests and merchants. In other words, there was no obvious class distinction to explain the conflicts which arose. Neither did the elements remain stable. Members of the Plain might join the Girondins or the Mountain – Bertrand Barère and Robert Lindet for example drifted into radicalism. Pétion, on the other hand, who had been one of the popular leaders before 10 August was now identified with the Girondins. One clear distinction between the opposing factions may be made: the Girondins overwhelmingly represented provincial interests and feared the political pressure groups in Paris; many of the Mountain, including their most eloquent and influential deputy, Robespierre, had been elected by Paris. Robespierre's faction drew great strength from the loyalty of the capital's Jacobin Club and its large number of provincial affiliated bodies (see Essay 5). Numerically they never equalled the Girondins, but a combination of their powers of persuasion and the vociferous support they received from the public gallery sometimes led sufficient members of the Plain to vote with them.

Self-Assessment Question 1

Read the contrasting accounts of the Girondin/Jacobin animosity given by the historians Sorel (as reported by Sydenham in Document A), and Soboul (Document B) below.

What are the essential differences between their interpretations?

Document A ————————————————————————

'Ambition and bellicosity were for Sorel equally characteristic of both the Girondins and the Jacobins, he condemned both alike for "mingling the noblest struggles that a people has ever undertaken with the most shabby and atrocious jealousies that have ever divided men". Girondin... love of liberty and their repudiation of raison d'état was the result of policy rather than of principle. Personal rivalry was for Sorel the fundamental cause of the discord, and in the quarrels it caused, the Girondins were distinguished only by political incompetence. Their conduct of the war and their attitude in the trial of the King both demonstrated this incompetence, and their inclination towards federalism was the supreme manifestation of it.'

Sydenham, 1961, p.13

Document B

'The conflict between Girondins and Montagnards [the Mountain] bears the mark of class antagonism, in spite of both groups' bourgeois origin, because of the different political choices that confronted them. As spokesmen of the commercial bourgeoisie, the Girondins strove to defend property and economic liberty against the controls demanded by the Sans-Culottes, regulation of prices and production, requisitioning of essential commodities, a fixed rate of exchange for the assignats. Very sensitive in matters of social rank and status, the Girondins instinctively recoiled from contact with the masses and felt that government should be a monopoly of members of their own social class. In his *Appeal to all the Republicans of France*, written in October 1792, Brissot denounced the Jacobins and Montagnards as "those disorganizers who wish to level everything: property, leisure, the price of provisions, the various services to be rendered to society". Robespierre had already counter-attacked in the first of his *Letters to his Constituents*, 20 September 1792, in which he excoriated the false patriots "who only want the Republic for themselves, and who plan to govern only in the interest of the rich". The Montagnards... sought to endow the concept of nationhood with a positive appeal calculated to win the support of the common people. Speaking on the question of food supplies on 29 November 1792, Saint-Just emphasized the need to "raise the people up from the uncertainty and poverty that are corrupting them. In a single instant you can give the French people a real fatherland," by halting the ravages of inflation, assuring the supply of food, and "intimately linking their welfare and their freedom".'

Soboul, 1977, pp.87-8

Discussion

Sorel writing early in this century, as reported by Sydenham, had little time for either faction and castigated them for their petty squabbles. Their political differences he attributed mainly to self-interest and personality clashes. To these vices the Girondins added the supreme weakness of incompetence. Apart from his disregard for social and economic factors, Sorel is more typical of the previous than the present century of historical thought, in that he made moral judgements on the revolutionary leaders. Adjectives such as 'noblest' and 'atrocious' tend to be used with more restraint by present-day historians.

Soboul was one of the most recent as well as the most eminent of the French socialist historians of the Revolution. He unambiguously saw the Girondin/Jacobin dispute as a struggle between class interests. Instead of using emotive phrases he left the protagonists to speak for themselves and they obligingly proved the point he was making. Yet this passage is not devoid of elephant traps. How do we know that the Girondins were the 'spokesmen of the commercial bourgeoisie'? Soboul does not prove his claim, and most commentators would regard it as a matter for debate rather than assertion. Amongst the Mountain, Robespierre and Saint-Just seem to have been genuinely convinced of the need for some redistribution of food and land to help the poor. (When they were actually in power on the Committee of Public Safety their ability to further this policy proved to be very limited.)

The proposal to execute the former King (he was now given the family name of his ancestors, Capet, instead of a title) for crimes against the nation came from Louis Antoine Saint-Just on 13 November 1792. This able and formidable young man from Picardy (see Figure 21, p.106) joined Robespierre, Danton and Marat in the conflict with the Girondins, which was intensified by the debate about what exactly was to happen to Louis Capet. The resolution of the Plain, the majority of the deputies in the Convention, was stiffened by the discovery of an iron cupboard in the Tuileries which contained a bundle of papers proving the ex-King's counter-revolutionary activities: he had been in communication with Austria. Louis was tried before the whole Convention in late December and his lawyer put up an able defence on his behalf based on the principle of a King's inviolability. This was, however, a political trial in which appeals to precedent carried little weight. Some of the Girondins at this stage, realising the majority in the Convention would find Louis guilty, suggested that the whole electorate should be asked to vote on his fate. This infuriated their Mountain opponents and alarmed the more moderate majority who felt that their responsibility as representatives would be evaded by such a manoeuvre. Between 14 and 19 January 1793 four votes took place in the Convention. Louis was found guilty by a large majority and the plebiscite was rejected. A bare majority voted for his execution, about the same number choosing either condemnation with reprieve, exile or imprisonment. Since this was insufficiently decisive a further vote was taken in which a majority of 70 voted for death without reprieve. Even a majority of the moderates recognised that the time for prevarication had run out. Louis was guillotined on 21 January 1793.

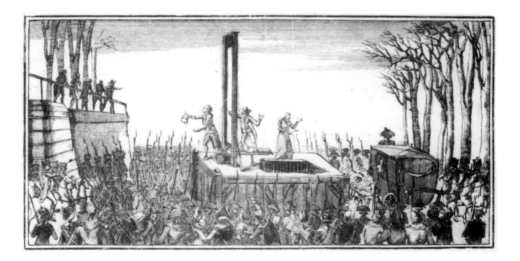

Figure 14 The execution of Louis XVI, 21 January 1793. *(The Trustees of the British Museum)*

Self-Assessment Question 2

The deputies were allowed to give reasons as they voted on the punishment of the King. Read the following extracts from a report in *The Times* and its subsequent account of the King's death.

i)   What information does it provide about the attitudes of some of the deputies?

ii) What was the impact of the execution likely to be on other European governments?

Document A _____

23 January 1793
'Roberspierre – [*sic*, foreign correspondents seldom spelt his name correctly]
"Because you have established yourselves the judges of Louis, without the usual
forms, are you less his judges? You cannot separate your quality of Judge from
that of Legislator. These two qualities are indivisible. You have acknowledged
the crimes of the tyrant. It is your duty to punish them. No consideration should
make you hesitate... I vote for the punishment of death."
Danton – "I am a Republican, and do not hesitate concerning the choice of that
punishment reserved for Louis the last. You ought to strike terror into tyrants.
I vote for the punishment of death."
Robert – "I vote for death, and if any regret remains, it is, that my competence
does not extend to all tyrants. I would condemn them all to death."
Fréron – "Were it possible that a majority should determine upon him
imprisonment, I would move that a veil might be thrown over the bust of Brutus.
I vote for death."
Barrere [*sic*] – "The tree of liberty does not flourish, unless moistened with the
blood of kings. I vote for death."
Anarcharsis [*sic*] Cloots [a German idealist] – "In the name of the Human Race,
I vote for the death of Louis."
Thomas Paine [an English radical] – "I vote for the provisional confinement of
Louis, and for his expulsion after the war."
Brissot – "It would have been desirable that the punishment to be inflicted on
Louis should have been pronounced by the whole nation. It would have been
the best method of carrying along with us the sentiments of neighbouring
nations, and of defeating the projects of the tyrants of Europe, who desire the
punishment of Louis, in order more successfully to excite indignation and
hatred against the National Convention... the only way of avoiding the dangers
which threaten us, is to pronounce the punishment of death against Louis, and
defer its execution to the moment when the people shall have sanctioned the
Constitution which we shall present them."

Ascherson (ed.), 1975, pp.84-5

Document B _____

25 January 1793
'About half past nine, the King arrived at the place of execution, which was in
the *Place de Louis XV*, between the pedestal which formerly supported the
statue of his grandfather, and the promenade of the Elysian Fields. Louis
mounted the scaffold with composure, and that modest intrepidity peculiar to
oppressed innocence, the trumpets sounding and the drums beating all the time.
He made a sign wishing to harangue the multitude when the drums ceased, and
Louis spoke these words. "I die innocent; I pardon my enemies; I only
sanctioned upon compulsion the civil constitution of the Clergy." He was
proceeding, but the beating of the drums drowned his voice. His executioners
then laid hold of him, and an instant after, his head was separated from his body;
this was about quarter past ten o'clock.... Unquestionably the blood of this
unfortunate Monarch will invoke vengeance on his murderers. This is not the
cause of Monarchs only, it is the cause of every nation on the face of the earth.
All potentates owe it to their individual honour but still more strongly to the
happiness of their people collectively to crush these savage regicides in their
dens, who aim at the ruin of all nations, and the destruction of all Governments....
Armed with fire and sword, we must penetrate into the recesses of this land of
blood and carnage. Louis might still have been living, had neighbouring Princes
acted with that energy and expedition, which the case required.'

Ibid., pp.88-9

Discussion

Robespierre and Brissot take the opportunity to make some more general political points as well as to vote for execution. The former is characteristically logical and resolute, the latter pusillanimous and unlikely to attract even the support of moderate deputies. Danton, Barère and Fréron are putting up bench marks as leaders of radical opinion. Foreign-born deputies had been welcomed to the Convention in the name of international fraternity. Cloots, who dreamed of a world-wide Jacobin Republic and was prepared to sacrifice the King's life for it, was from Germany and Paine from England.

The account of the execution in *The Times*, although probably reasonably accurate, is presented in a manner calculated to evoke maximum sympathy for the King – notice the emotive phrases such as 'oppressed innocence'. The exhortation to take up arms to punish the regicides makes the purpose of the report very clear. Austria and the German princes were already at war with France. England, Holland and Spain were soon to follow suit. The rhetorical condemnations in the Convention, not only of Louis XVI but of all tyrants, is demonstrated in the verdicts of Danton and Robert (Document A). The haven offered by the Republic to foreign radicals such as Cloots and Paine seemed to present a very real threat of an international revolutionary conspiracy against European governments.

4.2 A new constitution?

The overthrow of the monarchy and the prison massacres of the summer of 1792 had taken place against a background of a national emergency. The decision to try and execute the King was made at a time when the French armies were winning on all fronts (see Essay 4). There was no reason to postpone the logical sequel to the removal of the traditional executive power: the establishment of a new constitution. Ever since the Convention had met, a constitutional committee consisting of Sieyès, Paine (who could not speak French adequately), Danton, Barère and five Girondins including Condorcet had been at work. Condorcet was a distinguished philosopher who had associated with many of the great thinkers of the Enlightenment before the Revolution. He guided the committee which attempted to reconcile the need to institute a democratic form of government with the danger that an over-powerful executive could present. The animosity that the prevailing Girondin character of the committee aroused amongst the deputies of the Mountain meant that the project was unlikely to succeed.

In March 1793 the new war campaigning season got under way and the French successes of previous months were reversed by an Austrian victory at Neerwinden in the Austrian Netherlands. The losing French general, Dumouriez, who had been the victor at Valmy in September of the previous year was closely associated with the Girondins, so their standing was affected by his loss of prestige. The Girondins had other problems too. The renewed war effort required large supplies of soldiers, and compulsory levies of men sparked off a royalist revolt in La Vendée (see Essay 1, pp.111-12). There was also continuing *Chouan* activity in Brittany to contend with. At last the *émigrés*, who had been waiting hopefully on the borders of France since 1789, had active partisans with whom they could co-operate to wage civil war. The refractory priests and their followers provided centres for the recruitment and support of the rebels. The constant suspicion and animosity displayed by the radical revolutionaries towards *émigrés* and refractories had thus become a self-fulfilling prophecy. Furthermore the Parisian poor were restive as supplies of corn and other foodstuffs were scarce and several riots occurred.

Figure 15 Danton. Although fond of good living and probably corrupt, Danton's drive and energy helped inspire the new Republic in the dangerous days before the French victory at Valmy (20 September 1792). *(Hulton-Deutsch Collection)*

Weak ministers and a Convention whose deputies were meant to express a single, united will but who constantly harassed each other with abuse, could not provide decisive leadership. In early April General Dumouriez, having failed to persuade his armies to follow him in imposing his own solution (making peace immediately) to the crisis of the Convention, went over to the Austrians. Yet again the Mountain's distrust of the ambition of generals was vindicated. The best the Girondins could do was to impeach the populist deputy, and editor of the *People's Friend*, Marat, who had made many virulent attacks on them. This broke the principle that members of the Convention should be immune from prosecution for political views. He was tried before the newly created Revolutionary Tribunal, a much quicker process than in the traditional courts, in front of a sympathetic Parisian crowd. He was triumphantly cleared of the charges of incitement to murder, pillage and attack the Convention.

Throughout the spring of 1793 the Girondins ineffectually attempted to enforce measures which would limit the power of the Paris Commune and bring National Guards from the provinces to protect the Convention against the *sans-culottes*. These policies and their equally futile persecution of Marat only hardened the opposition of Robespierre and the rest of the Mountain and its allies in the Commune, the Sections and the radical clubs. The stalemate between the factions meant that no firm policies were formulated to deal with the military emergency. Between 31 May and 2 June thousands of *sans-culottes*, supported by the more radical parts of the National Guard, besieged the Convention. Many deputies at first resisted this pressure, but eventually the lack of a constitutional alternative means of changing Girondin policy forced their acquiescence to the removal of some of the most prominent members of that faction. Twenty-nine Girondin deputies, including Brissot and Pétion, were expelled from the Convention and placed under house arrest. Seventy-five deputies signed a protest against this and were immediately associated with the Girondins by the Mountain and the insurgents. It was the last time for over a year that the Convention was to show any inclination to defy the Mountain minority. Modern forms of parliamentary democracy had not yet been developed to cope with legitimate differences in policy. It was thought discreditable for deputies to combine together in parties – the Girondins had often been criticised for doing so. Denunciation and the guillotine and, later, exile and the firing squad were the only means available to the republicans, and later Napoleon, to quell political opposition.

The new constitution produced by Condorcet's committee with its 368 articles had been discussed inconclusively over the past months. On 11 June the Mountain produced a modified, shortened version and a new Declaration of the Rights of Man. All adult males, including foreigners, had the right to vote and to take a more direct form of political action.

> 'When the government violates the rights of the people insurrection
> is for the people as a whole, and for any portion of it, the most sacred
> of its rights and the most indispensable of its duties.' (Article 35)

By this means popular insurrection was given a constitutional status. The Executive Council, on the other hand, which took the place of the King and his ministers, was to be a weak body subservient to the Assembly. Early in 1794 a national plebiscite accepted the constitution by a majority of 1,801,918, to 11,610. In practice though, it had been set aside by a decree introduced by Saint-Just during the military crisis early in the previous autumn: 'The government of France is revolutionary until the restoration of peace'.

Self-Assessment Question 3

Re-read Essay 3, and study the engraving of Robespierre with the new constitution (Figure 16) below. This was one of a series of pictures of prominent deputies designed by Bernard to celebrate the introduction of the constitution in June 1793. Assess the intended propaganda impact of such pictures.

Discussion _____

It was a priority for the revolutionary government to substitute strong, patriotic images for the holy pictures and royal portraits which had represented authority to the French people for centuries. The whole composition is heavy with symbolism: a plain monolith displays the sacred words of liberty inscribed in the constitution. It is surmounted by the French national animal, the cockerel, who manages to clasp a sceptre, an orb and the scales of justice in his claws (these were all symbols of good government). These are wreathed with oak leaves, the natural and democratic tributes used, instead of gold, to crown revolutionary heroes. The fasces, the axe and rods, a classical sign of legal authority, the cap of liberty and Robespierre himself, are enfolded by great, billowing tricolours. He does not look like a revolutionary, no shaggy moustache or striped trousers, a paper rather than a sabre in his hand. It has often been observed that, apart from personal inclination, his powdered hair, culottes and immaculate cravats reassured the petty bourgeoisie who supported the Jacobins in Paris and the provinces. Even peasants might not be too alarmed by an image not dissimilar to that of Louis XVI.

Figure 16 A contemporary print showing Robespierre with the constitution of 1793, the embodiment of his ideas on government. *(Bibliothèque Nationale, Paris)*

4.3 The great Committees

From the fall of the Girondins in June 1793 the revolutionary government was effectively conducted by the Committees of Public Safety and the Committee of General Security which were composed of deputies elected by the Convention. Their work was supplemented by a number of other committees, councils and commissions and by representatives who toured the provinces and were attached to the armies of the Republic.

 Self-Assessment Question 4

Read the decree by which the Committee of Public Safety was established in April 1793 (Document A, below). Assess the extent of the powers given to the Committee by the Convention.

Document A ———————————————————————

'The National Convention decrees as follows:

Article 1. – A Committee of Public Safety, made up of nine [soon raised to twelve] members of the National Convention, will be selected by nomination. Article 2. – This Committee will meet in private. It will be responsible for supervising and facilitating the execution of measures taken by the provisional Executive Council, whose orders it may suspend, if it believes them contrary to the national interest, provided that it informs the National Convention of this without delay.

Article 3. – The Committee is authorized, in the case of an emergency, to take such measures as are deemed necessary for the defence, both internal and external, of the nation; and its orders, signed by a majority of the members present, who may not be fewer than two-thirds of the total membership, will be carried out without delay by the provisional Executive Council. It may not under any circumstances issue summons or warrants for arrest, except against executive agents and on condition that it reports without delay to the Convention.

Article 4. – The National Treasury will hold funds of up to 100,000 livres for secret disposal by the Committee of Public Safety; authorizations of payment will be issued by the Committee and signed according to the same procedure used for orders.

Article 5. – The Committee will make each week both a general and a written report of its operations and of the state of the Republic.

Article 6. – All its deliberations will be recorded.

Article 7. – This Committee is established for one month only.

Article 8. – The National Treasury will remain independent of the Executive Committee and will report directly to the National Convention following the procedure set out in its decrees.'

Hardman (ed.), Vol.2, 1973, p.90

Discussion

The secrecy of the meetings of the Committee together with the unlimited mandate for 'supervising', 'facilitating' and 'suspending' the activities of the Executive Council gave it enormous power. Although the Convention kept control of national finances, the large amount of secret service money at the disposal of the Committee increased its freedom of action. The provision that the personnel could be changed once a month might appear to safeguard the control of the Convention. (In fact, until 27 July 1794 (9 *Thermidor*), the majority on the Committee determined its own composition.)

The Committee of Public Safety concerned itself with the conduct of war both outside and inside France, and with maintaining supplies to the army and the civilian population. This last function was the speciality of Lindet. Lazare Carnot, an ex-officer, saw to military affairs, although they also concerned Saint-Just, an arrangement which was later to cause conflict between them. Jeanbon Saint-André, formerly a Protestant pastor, had the difficult task of reorganising France's dilapidated naval defences. Robespierre (who joined the Committee in July), Couthon and Barère were mainly concerned with internal security, propaganda and explaining and justifying the Committee's policy to the Convention. The other deputies who were members of the Committee carried out various combinations of the functions described above and all, with the exception of Barère and Robespierre, left Paris periodically on missions to the provinces and the armies. This readiness to experience difficulties and dangers at first hand, to encourage the work of the Revolution and to punish opponents was one of the great strengths of the Committee of Public Safety.

The Committee of General Security was responsible for policing the Revolution. Its members included the painter David, Vadier and Fouché, two Jacobins committed to the ruthless pursuit of counter-revolutionaries and the destruction of all forms of religion. When the Convention decreed that terror was the 'order of the day' in September 1793, this Committee was primarily responsible for making arrests and sending the accused to the Revolutionary Tribunal. The concern that both the great Committees had for internal security was to be a future cause of conflict, as were clashes between policies and personalities.

During the summer of 1793 preoccupation with the dangerous situation on the frontiers and within France transcended ideological or personal disputes. In large areas of the south and west of France a strange alliance of royalists, moderate revolutionaries and Catholics revolted against the political domination and Jacobin extremism of Paris (see Essay 1). This Federalist rebellion should not be confused with the royalist Vendéan and *Chouan* revolts which were continuing simultaneously. It was called 'Federalist' because it was essentially an affirmation of the needs and aspirations of the provinces, which were seen as irreconcilable with those of Paris. The war was still going badly with the fall of Valenciennes, and yet another general, Custine, was suspected of intriguing with the enemy. In August the Convention decreed mass conscription and Custine was guillotined. This combination of involving hundreds of thousands of soldiers in repelling France's enemies, and of pursuing a ruthless campaign through the Terror against all kinds of counter-revolutionaries was to prove very effective. The murder on 13 July of Marat by Charlotte Corday, a Girondin sympathiser, had presented the government with a justification for intensifying the campaign against its opponents. Marat's funeral provided an opportunity for a massive public spectacle, and the government attempted to channel popular sorrow and admiration for this martyr in the same way that the Church had formerly promoted cults of the saints (see Essay 3). In October, as the Terror continued, a number of the Girondin deputies as well as Marie-Antoinette went to the guillotine.

4.4 The people's Republic

Parisian *sans-culottes* from the 48 Sections in alliance with the Commune and the radical elements in the National Guard had destroyed the Girondins. It was to those radical pressure groups that the Jacobins of the Mountain owed their new power base in the great Committees and their ascendancy over the majority of more moderate deputies of the Plain. Hébert, after the death of Marat, was the most influential journalist to voice the interests of the *sans-culottes*. His paper *Le Père Duchesne* was written in a racy, vituperative style and it often voiced demands for radical measures. This gave him and his associates considerable political importance as their demands seemed to pose a threat to the authority of the Committees and the Convention. The constitution of 1793 had made popular insurrection a civic virtue and on 5 September the *sans-culottes* invaded the Convention to demand recognition of their grievances. The deputies yielded, agreeing to prosecute vigorously suspected counter-revolutionaries and food hoarders. Collot d'Herbois and Billaud-Varenne, two Jacobin activists who were popular with the *sans-culottes*, were elected on to the Committee of Public Safety as a further sign that the people's demands were being taken seriously. Later in the month a new Law of the General Maximum was passed. Several previous measures to control the price of essential foodstuffs had proved ineffective. This law limited the cost of grain and other commodities to one-third of what they had been in 1790; wages were not to exceed one-half, although the Commune of Paris ignored this stipulation. The first part of the legislation was to be enforced by People's Armies, forces of politically active *sans-culottes* who would be armed, paid and put under a military style of command. They would be raised in Paris and the provinces with the purpose of enforcing the Maximum and discouraging the hoarding of food. During the autumn and winter of 1793 fervent revolutionaries from Paris played a supporting role in suppressing the Federalist Revolt in Lyons; in Brittany a local People's Army helped to combat the *Chouans,* and in many places the People's Armies imposed de-Christianisation on 'superstitious' communities.

Figure 17 David, *To Marat* (1793). Marat is shown as a dead hero. The pose of the figure is deliberately modelled on that familiar from paintings of the deposition of Jesus Christ from the cross. *(The Mansell Collection)*

 # Self-Assessment Question 5

Read the following accounts of the activities of the People's Armies and assess the impact they were likely to have on the resident population.

Document A

Proceedings of the commune of Mions, 23 November 1793 (3 *Frimaire*, Year II)

'After having outlined his powers, the civil commissioner [Marcellin] attached to the Parisian Army sent to Lyons told us that he had come with a detachment of cavalry... and we were required to lodge and feed these 20 cavaliers and their horses... citizen Marcelin [*sic*] also told us that in every commune, foodstuffs like butter, eggs, vegetables etc. were no longer getting to the markets of the large towns as in the past, and he attributed this falling off to the ill will of many farmers who did not wish to sell at prices laid down by the Maximum; and that he was determined to see the laws executed and he warned those who were accustomed to taking these foodstuffs to the markets, that they did so under pain of being treated as suspects according to the law, and finally he told us to write to him at the headquarters in Ville-Affranchie [Lyons] stating the result of the present requisition, warning us that just as he acted fraternally at this moment, so he would act severely if he was forced to return'.

Cobb, 1987, pp.278-9

Document B ──────────────────────────────────

Memorial of a Citizen of Auxerre

'The first units arrived in Auxerre on 11 November (21 *Brumaire*), the feast of St Martin, with mounted cannon, wagons, flags, banners and drums. They were met at the Saint-Siméon gate by a patrol from the Auxerre guard, lodged and their expenses met largely by the citizens of the town, and they left the following morning. The second force arrived at Auxerre on the 13th, and were greeted in like manner. This detachment had committed along the way all kinds of frenzied excesses against religious objects, battering down church doors, smashing altars, flinging down statues and images of saints. When they arrived at the chapel of Sainte-Marguérite, they carried out similar horrors, seizing a copper crucifix from the altar and one of them, mounted on a cart, derisively holding it upside-down for passers-by to spit upon. At some distance from the chapel they encountered a quarryman... and forced him to spit on the crucifix. On his refusal, one of the soldiers cut off part of his nose with a blow of his sabre; he had to be cared for in the Hôtel-Dieu'.

Ibid., pp.460-61

Discussion ──────────────────────────────────

The reporting in Document A is relatively neutral in style, as is perhaps to be expected in an official document. The account in Document B by the anonymous citizen of Auxerre is very hostile. We can deduce from Document A that communities experienced several problems with the enforcement of regular food supplies and of the Maximum. There was a danger that so much would be sent to the towns and the armies that they would have insufficient for their own needs. Another grievance felt by farmers would, of course, have been that the prices they were permitted to charge might cause them to sell at a loss. The need to support the men of the armies and their horses, sometimes for weeks on end, must have been very burdensome. These factors heightened the animosity which already existed in many areas between the *sans-culottes* from the towns and the rural peasantry. Document B illustrates that forced de-Christianisation was an even more bitter grievance in many areas. Until this time the experience of the Revolution for many people had been positive, with the disappearance of feudal impositions, unfair taxes and haughty nobles, and the opportunity to purchase *biens nationaux*. Despite the Civil Constitution of the Clergy, many parishes had managed to sustain a refractory priest and the old forms of religion. Now trusted clergy, cherished monuments and images were swept away. Even those who were not particularly religious were shocked at the vandalism and needless destruction of valuable objects.

In Chapter 3 the demands of a few well-born women that their sex should be given political rights were considered, as was the polite but negative reponse by the Legislative Assembly. By the middle of 1793 the social origins of feminists had widened to include some of the female *sans-culottes* who had played so prominent a role in urban agitation and insurrection since the beginning of the Revolution.

Figure 18 Le Sueur, *The Patriotic Women's Club.* A pressure group promoting the participation of women in social and civic affairs. *(Musée Carnavalet, Paris. Lauros-Giraudon)*

 Self-Assessment Question 6

The extracts in Document A below are taken from an account of a meeting of the Society of Revolutionary Republican Women in the autumn of 1793 just before it was suppressed. The writer was a Frenchman, Pierre Roussel, who was accompanied by the English peer, Lord Bedford.
Discuss:

i)   the tone of the account;

ii) the nature of the demands voiced by the women;

iii) the men's view of the legitimacy of the women's aspirations.

Document A _____

'Session of the Society of Women, Meeting in the Ossuary of the Church of Saint-Eustache. Presidency of Citoyenne Lacombe.

After the reading of the minutes and of the correspondence, the president recalled that the order of the day concerned the utility of women in a republican government, and she invited the sisters who had worked on this subject to share their research with the Society.... [A woman gave many historical examples of female influence on government.] Nothing seemed more comical to us than to hear passages of history declaimed by a woman who murdered the language with an assurance difficult to describe. The applause was followed by a long period of murmuring through which one could make out a few words and proposals, each one more ridiculous than the last. One called for the raising of an army of 30,000 women to go into battle against enemies, with all prostitutes being forced to march. Another proposed that women be admitted into all branches of administration. Finally, after a half hour of debate, all proposals were condensed into a petition to present to the Convention, calling for a decree obliging women to wear the national cockade....

The Englishman said to me: Confess that these extravagances are very amusing.
Roussel: I confess, but when I think about it, the delirium of these women frightens me. If their brains are overheated, you know the obstinacy of this sex; they are capable of committing certain excesses.
Bedford: ... Among the follies we have just heard, one can find nothing based in reason. It is, of course, certain that our customs give women much influence over the state. It cannot be denied that they are the most active force in society, the common centre to which all the passions of men are attracted.... It is thus a manifest contradiction not to count them for anything in our code of laws.
Roussel: I grant this contradiction; but you will also admit that it is fully justified by the universal and consequently dangerous ascendancy that you recognize in the sex.
Bedford: That is true. However it seems to me that instead of forgetting women in their households, one could use them. For example, if they were made the reward of great actions, I do not think there would be any effort men would not make to merit their esteem and their favours.
Roussel: I think as you do... we forget them in our new land only because... habit, stronger than reason, makes innovations too difficult in this delicate area. Besides, who is the man bold enough to innovate in this matter?'

Levy, Applewhite and Johnson (eds.), 1979, pp.166-70

Discussion

The account is generally hostile and derisive. The tone is one that might be adopted to describe a visit to the zoo. There is, therefore, no way of knowing whether this whole report, the most extensive that exists for the proceedings of the Society, was distorted to make the women appear ridiculous. Yet some interesting objective evidence does emerge, such as the fact that the women called each other sisters.

The President of the Society, Claire Lacombe, started by setting the agenda for a discussion of the historical role of women in government. This was standard revolutionary practice; classical heroes such as Brutus gave respectability to all manner of radical programmes. The result of the ensuing debate which involved the (to us) reasonable demand that women should be admitted to all parts of the government, was a petition to the Convention that all women should be obliged to wear the tricolour cockade. (This was actually accepted and implemented.)

Despite their determination to find the activists ridiculous, both men seem to have been attracted by their case. They accused the women of violating reason in their debate and yet themselves did not draw coherent or logical conclusions. On the one hand they agreed that women had sufficient importance in society to merit some legal status, whilst on the other they proposed to implement this by giving women as rewards to men who distinguished themselves, a form of state prostitution. Their predominant reaction to the meeting seems to have been fear of feminine political activity and of appearing foolish before other men if they were to support it.

By no means all female *sans-culottes* supported extreme measures or the political aspirations of women. The market women of Paris were a formidable force and they disliked the restraint on profit imposed by the laws of the Maximum. The Convention and the Committees had yielded to popular pressure on 5 September 1793 but they were now looking for an excuse to reassert their authority and reassure the moderate bourgeoisie that the *sans-culottes* were not taking control. Some of the *enragés* (revolutionaries who wished to introduce extreme measures to help the poor) were arrested, and on 30 October the Society of Revolutionary Republican Women and all other women's societies were suppressed. Increasingly the Committee of Public Safety discouraged the continuation of popular societies both in Paris and the provinces. The powers these societies had developed to dominate their communities by denouncing suspects and co-operating with National Guards and the People's Armies were curtailed. Progressively local government, which had been devolved by the measures of 1789-90, was brought back under central control by 'national agents' appointed by the government and responsible to it. Even debates in the Jacobin Club tended to echo the policy of the government rather than suggest new initiatives. Partly in reaction to the pressures of war, partly through what Saint-Just called 'the force of circumstances', the Committees were becoming increasingly authoritarian. An improvement in the military situation on the frontiers dating from the battle of Wattignies in October, the suppression of the Federalist Revolt and the gradual victory of the Republic in Brittany and La Vendée strengthened the government in dealing with its political opponents.

 # Self-Assessment Question 7

Read Essay 4 (pp.136-8). What factors determined the successes of the Jacobin government in the foreign and civil wars?

Discussion _____

The mass conscription of August 1793 gave the Republic a great advantage over its adversaries: a vast, cheap source of manpower which was forever being replenished as new groups reached military age. Many of the soldiers did fight with greater determination and conviction than the mercenaries and unfree Austrians and Prussians. The ruthless efficiency of the Committee of Public Safety, and of Carnot in particular, ensured essential supplies and the punishment of dilatory or disloyal generals. The close control exercised by the central government through its representatives-on-mission meant that weaknesses were quickly identified. The repression that was practised against the *Chouans* and Vendéans was brutal but effective. Although there were sporadic outbursts of defiance in both areas neither was to present a real threat to the stability of the Republic.

The maintenance of adequate supplies continued to be a problem but the good harvest of 1793 and the ability of the victorious soldiers to live off the lands they invaded stabilised the situation. The government could therefore address another issue which had existed since 1789 and which was to reveal a fundamental ideological conflict amongst the Jacobins: religion. This also was a subject upon which Rousseau took a different view from most of the philosophers and it was to divide Robespierre, Rousseau's most important revolutionary disciple, from Jacobins like Fouché and Hébert who wanted an entirely secular society. Rousseau in *The Confession of Faith of a Savoyard Vicar* had advocated a very positive and moral natural religion allied to a toleration for all genuine expressions of faith. In the *Social Contract* he reaffirmed his support for toleration but modified it by suggesting some basic principles of State religion which it would be compulsory for all citizens to recognise. Voltaire and Diderot on the other hand had disliked outward forms of religious expression, did not accept that they could or should be linked to a moral code and felt that the only use of a Church would be to serve the purposes of the State. These opposing views now took political form.

Self-Assessment Question 5 gave an example of the impact of de-Christianisation, and this sort of incident was repeated countless times throughout the autumn and winter of 1793. In Paris Hébert's faction organised an atheistical Feast of Liberty and Reason in the former cathedral of Notre-Dame, in which a scantily clad actress participated. The dangerous effects of such extravagances on the majority of the French, who were still Catholics, was anticipated by the Convention and the Committees. The former condemned acts of vandalism (such as those perpetrated at Auxerre) and the latter began to phase out the People's Armies with the Law of 14 *Frimaire* (4 December) 1793, although the Parisian army, which could still be useful, was retained for a few more months.

The deputies of the Mountain, most of them members of the bourgeoisie, had promoted the political activities of the *sans-culottes* in Paris and the other cities and towns of France. Some of them believed that great inequalities of wealth should be discouraged. Saint-Just, for example, introduced laws in March 1794 stating that the goods of *émigrés* and suspects should be given to the poor. The realities of government, however, prevented any real sharing of power or property with the *sans-culottes*, peasants or indigent poor. The need to placate farmers, merchants and other taxpayers, to terminate the social disruption of de-Christianisation and to exercise firm control over the generals and their armies from the centre was paramount. The democratic constitution of 1793 remained in abeyance and all the most vital channels of *sans-culotte* political activity – the People's Armies, the popular societies and local patriotic committees were discouraged or repressed. The redistribution of renegades' property and the enforcement of the laws of the Maximum were either done without enthusiasm or ignored. The fiery, revolutionary rhetoric of Robespierre or Barère could not disguise the reality from the *sans-culottes*, that they were no longer closely involved in the government of the Republic.

4.5 The destruction of the factions

Relieved of the desperate military and economic pressures of the previous year and with the *sans-culottes* again under control, it was only too predictable that the Jacobins would relapse into internal strife. In the Committee of Public Safety Robespierre, Saint-Just and Couthon, later referred to as 'the Triumvirate' by their enemies, held the balance between extremists such as Collot d'Herbois and Billaud-Varenne and moderates like Lindet and Barère. During the early months of 1794 they all co-operated, presenting a united front in restraining popular political activity and de-Christianisation, and in repressing corruption and 'indulgence'. These last two revolutionary vices were identified in a group which centred on Danton. The evidence is ambiguous as to whether he was actually involved in bribery and illegal financial speculation, although associates such as Fabre d'Eglantine and Chabot certainly were. Danton and Desmoulins, through a newspaper called *The Old Cordelier*, increasingly supported a more tolerant, relaxed political attitude and a scaling down of the Terror. They were described by their opponents as the 'Indulgents'.

Self-Assessment Question 8

Read the following extracts from Camille Desmoulins's *Old Cordelier,* and from a speech Robespierre made to the Convention on 5 February 1794 on 'the Principles of Political Morality which should guide the Convention'. Discuss:

i)   the differences in approach;

ii) the fundamental issues that were now dividing these former friends and political allies.

Document A

The Old Cordelier, No. 4
20 December 1793 (30 *Frimaire*, Year II)

'Some people have disapproved of my no.3 [the third issue of *The Old Cordelier*] where they say I took pleasure in making reproaches that tend to cast disfavour on the Revolution and on the patriots: they ought rather to speak on the excesses of the Revolution, and of professional patriots.... These people apparently think that Liberty, like childhood, has to pass through crying and tears in order to reach maturity.... A people is free the moment it wants to be such (you may recall that this was La Fayette's saying): "it entered into the fullness of its rights, from 14 July." Liberty has neither age or youth. It has only one age, that of strength and vigour.... I think quite differently from those who tell you that terror must remain the order of the day. I am sure, on the contrary, that liberty would be strengthened, and Europe conquered, if you had a committee of clemency.

At this expression, committee of clemency, what patriot would not feel deeply moved? For patriotism is the plenitude of all the virtues, and consequently cannot exist where there is neither humanity, nor philanthropy, but instead a spirit barren and parched by its own egoism. Oh! my dear Robespierre! It is to you that I address these words.... Oh my old college comrade, you whose eloquent speeches will be read by posterity remember well these lessons of history and philosophy: that love is stronger and more lasting than fear; that admiration and religion are born from good deeds'.

Gilchrist and Murray, 1971, pp.293-5

Document B

Robespierre's speech to the Convention
5 February 1794

'What is our ultimate aim? The peaceful enjoyment of liberty and equality; the reign of eternal justice, whose laws are engraved, not on marble or stone, but in the hearts of all men.... We desire to see an order of things where all base and cruel feelings... are suppressed, and where the law encourages beneficent and generous feelings where social distinctions emerge from conditions of equality... where all men's spirits are uplifted by the continual sharing of republican sentiments... where commerce is a source of public wealth, not only of the monstrous affluence of a few families. In our country we wish to substitute morality for egoism, honesty for mere love of honour, principles for customs, duties for convention, the reign of reason for the tyranny of fashion... good men for mere good company, merit for intrigue, genius for slickness, truth for brilliance, the appeal of happiness for the boredom of sensuality, the grandeur of man for the pettiness of great men: a happy, powerful and magnanimous people for one that is amiable, frivolous and discontented. That is to say, we wish to replace the vices and follies of the monarchy by the virtues and miraculous achievements of the Republic.'

Wright, 1974, pp.129-30

Discussion

There is bound to be a difference between the style of a popular newspaper and a speech delivered by a leading member of the government. Even when the contrasting occasions have been recognised, however, the approaches vary considerably. Desmoulins was emotional, dramatic, personal, whilst Robespierre was balanced, logical and impersonal. The former was tactless in quoting La Fayette, a hated and discredited leader, and in implying that Robespierre was inhumane, barren and egotistical one minute and flattering him the next. Robespierre, perhaps, revealed the increasingly authoritarian nature of government policy and the puritanism which informed his own approach by his use of verbs, despite their occurrence amid sentiments that are moral and benevolent, such as: 'suppressed', 'substitute' and 'the law encourages'.

Desmoulins pleaded for liberty and rejection of the Terror. Virtue and patriotism, which were synonymous, would flourish in a gentler, freer environment which would be produced by the creation of a committee of clemency. (Ironically Robespierre had supported the introduction of such a committee but had been overruled.) Love or philanthropy was a better foundation for the exercise of political authority than fear.

The basis of Robespierre's case was that the carefully reasoned programme of national regeneration he described was not yet available. The Revolution was still striving to attain virtue and shake off the burdensome vices of the *ancien régime*. It was implicit in all that he said that more sacrifices would have to be made before the goal was reached. Some of the vices – 'the tyranny of fashion', 'mere good company', 'intrigue', 'slickness', 'brilliance' and 'the boredom of sensuality' – could be found not only amongst *émigrés* and rebels. They were cultivated by philosophers such as Voltaire and were rife amongst corrupt speculators such as Fabre and Chabot and Indulgents like Danton and Desmoulins. Here again the disciple of Rousseau was in conflict with the sophistication and hedonism of most Enlightenment thinkers.

The Indulgents were not the only threat to the authority of the government, and it would prove difficult to discredit Danton for he was popular in the Convention and in Paris. The corrupt politicians and speculators amongst his associates were involved in affairs of such complexity that it would have taken the Committee of General Security a considerable time to produce some credible accusations. A more immediate danger was presented by extremists such as Hébert and the leaders of the Parisian People's Army. Collot d'Herbois, who was more sympathetic towards them than were the other members of the Committee of Public Safety, tried to patch up a reconciliation, but Hébert was better at vituperation than accommodation. On March 13 1794 (23 *Ventôse*), Saint-Just read a report to the Convention in which he denounced both extremists and Indulgents. At the same time an obscure deputy reported the details of a most unlikely plot by the extremists to massacre members of the Convention and the Jacobin Club, to liberate prisoners and proclaim a dictatorship. A decree was immediately passed condemning to death anyone who attacked the safety or dignity of the Convention. Hébert and his associates were arrested and were sent to the guillotine before the end of the month. The Parisian People's Army was disbanded.

The Committees were now ready to deal with the Indulgents, whose criticism of the government might become even more dangerous once their Hébertist rivals were removed. Danton, Desmoulins and several others were arrested on 30 March (10 *Germinal*) and were discredited by being associated with the speculators Fabre and Chabot and various sinister foreigners. The force of Danton's oratory and the unconvincing charges made against him threatened for a while to turn his trial into a victory for his views. There was, after all, a precedent from the previous year in the popular acquittal of Marat. The Committees were warned that a plot was being hatched in the prisons to rescue the accused and murder members of the government, so they asked the Convention to decree a faster trial for those who interfered with the course of justice. The Indulgents were silenced, condemned and executed on 5 April (16 *Germinal*). Their destruction created a dangerous situation for the government because, despite the complacence of the Convention, many deputies had identified with the easy-going, moderate views of Danton and Desmoulins. No member of the Committees could show any inclination to restrain the Terror without the risk of being branded as an Indulgent. Only rabid revolutionaries such as Vadier, Fouché, Billaud-Varenne and Collot d'Herbois could flourish in such a situation. Few members realised the degree to which the majority in the Convention, the Plain, inclined towards moderation.

4.6 The end of the Jacobin ascendancy

May and June 1794 were indeed 'the best of times and the worst of times' (Dickens, *A Tale of Two Cities*) for the people of France. Barère introduced comprehensive measures for the relief of the poor which included pensions for the aged infirm and free medical treatment at home. He later presented a report on popular elementary education. The Convention accepted a report by Robespierre which confirmed that 'the French people recognise the existence of the Supreme Being and the immortality of the soul'. This was celebrated by a great festival in Paris on 8 June (20 *Prairial*) which was designed by the artist David. Robespierre, elected President of the Convention for the occasion, officiated over what he clearly saw as the symbolic national regeneration anticipated (see Essay 3, pp.131-2) in his speech of 5 February (Self-Assessment Question 8). Two weeks later the armies of the Republic, in the presence of Saint-Just, defeated the Austrians at Fleurus. They could consequently go on the offensive in their campaigns. Within France the efficient administration by the Committees of the war effort against the rebels in Brittany and La Vendée, and the sanctions of the Terror, had practically suppressed the risings. And the weather, as Gouverneur Morris (the American Ambassador) was accustomed to remark, was particularly fine.

Figure 19 The Battle of Fleurus, 26 June 1794. On this occasion General Jourdan and the armies of the French Republic defeated the forces of the Emperor of Austria. Note the use by the French of a balloon for observation. *(Bibliothèque Nationale, Paris)*

'The worst of times' saw the Great Terror which was promoted by the Law of *Prairial* introduced by Couthon on 10 June. This speeded up and simplified the system of trying and condemning those brought before the Revolutionary Tribunal. Assassination attempts against Collot d'Herbois and Robespierre a few days previously were probably the reason for the law. The attempts also heightened the atmosphere of suspicion and fear which predominated in Paris. Difficulties with supplies and the ever falling value of the *assignat* caused discontent amongst the *sans-culottes*. This was increased when the second part of the Law of the General Maximum, governing the control of wages, was implemented. Since the fall of the Hébertists the Paris Commune had been taken over by a follower of Robespierre, so it would be Robespierre who would be associated with that unpopular policy. Some artisans saw their incomes drop by as much as half. Many were already disillusioned by the government's suppression of the People's Armies and popular societies and by the punishment of some of their leaders. They had no sympathisers in the Convention apart from the Jacobins, but they might no longer have been prepared to fight for a radical vision of the Republic as they had done in the past.

Self-Assessment Question 9

The following three tables give you some evidence about the Terror from the records of the death sentences given and followed by execution by Courts and Tribunals administering Revolutionary Justice from spring 1793 to autumn 1794. The totals vary between the tables because the record of executions is not always matched by surviving indictments.
Study them carefully and then discuss the significance of:

i)   the frequency of the type of crimes for which the accused were condemned;

ii)   the distribution of the condemned by region and social class.

Note: Greer, the compiler of the tables, remarks on the difficulty of sorting out the indictments since several charges were often made against one person. He

90

Table 1 Death sentences which were followed by execution, 1793-4

Region	Death Sentences	Per Cent
Paris	2,639	16
Parisian region	27	Negligible
North	551	3.5
East	243	1.5
South-east (including Lyons)	3,158	19
South	434	2.5
Centre	124	0.75
South-west	476	3
West (including Brittany & La Vendée)	8,674	52
North-west	268	1.5
Total number of death sentences	16,594	100

Table 2 The social incidence of indictments

Department	Ex-Nobles	Noblesse de Robe	Upper Middle Class	Lower Middle Class	Clergy	Working Class	Peasants	No status given	Totals
Seine (Paris)	490	176	746	357	246	493	94	37	2,639
Parisian region	2	0	1	0	5	4	0	3	15
North	39	6	145	91	63	147	53	7	551
East	8	0	23	15	30	42	62	14	194
South-east (including Lyons)	141	55	600	679	260	571	111	33	2,450
South	7	3	88	37	46	63	69	34	347
Centre	14	2	8	7	27	16	18	4	96
South-west	67	33	121	55	78	56	35	18	463
West (including Brittany & La Vendée)	104	5	227	234	151	2,879	3,413	44	7,057
North-west	6	0	5	13	14	118	106	6	268
Totals	878	280	1,964	1,488	920	4,389	3,961	200	14,080
Per Cent	6.25	2	14	10.5	6.5	31.25	28	1.5	100

Table 3 Indictments

	Emigration	Intelligence with enemy	Sedition including armed revolt	Treason	Federalism	Conspiracy	Damaging or insulting Trees of Liberty	Counter revolutionary opinions	Refractory clergy	Concealment of refractory clergy	Hoarding	Traffic in *assignats*	Corruption	False witness	Counterfeiting	Miscellaneous	Totals
Quiet Departments	40	1	23	1	0	3	2	26	30	4	1	0	0	0	25	2	158
Frontier Departments	57	139	28	0	0	5	2	231	72	3	2	4	3	0	13	64	623
Troubled Departments	49	25	10,291	0	371	19	1	57	162	20	7	0	1	8	20	46	11,077
Paris	66	292	114	95	56	676	7	988	29	5	11	36	100	3	0	161	2,639
Totals	212	457	10,456	96	427	703	12	1,302	293	32	21	40	104	11	58	273	14,497
Per Cent	1.5	3.25	72.25	0.75	3	4.75	-	9	2	0.25	-	0.25	0.75	-	0.25	1.75	100

had to decide which was the most serious or put rather vague charges into one of his categories. Additionally since the people formulating the indictments varied from area to area and month to month what one man meant by 'Treason' could be another man's 'Sedition' or 'Conspiracy'. Also the statistics from 'Quiet Departments' could be slightly misleading since those in the vicinity of Paris often sent their accused to the capital for trial.

Discussion

Whilst we must approach the statistics with caution, they clearly show that the predominant crime mentioned in the indictments was 'Sedition'. If we add to this indictments for 'Intelligence with the enemy', 'Federalism', 'Treason' and 'Conspiracy', no less than 84 per cent of the crimes for which people were executed were either armed rebellion, supporting rebels or seeking to overturn the elected government of France. A mere 1.25 per cent of victims were actually executed for economic crimes, such as 'Hoarding', despite the violent rhetoric with which Jacobin politicians and *sans-culottes* condemned these practices.

With respect to the regional and social distribution of the condemned, ex-nobles may only have been 6.25 per cent and the clergy 6.5 per cent of those executed but, in relation to the other classes, their total numbers were small (and many evaded arrest by emigration). The middle classes accounted for about a quarter of the victims and the peasantry and artisans about 60 per cent. (Note that Greer was writing too early in this century to have a category called '*sans-culottes*', a term which has only gained currency for the purposes of social measurement amongst historians since the Second World War. Even if he had they would have been impossible to quantify in his tables as some were lower middle class and some working class.) The distribution of indictments by region is very enlightening. In Paris, the centre of government, not only were local radical extremists and counter-revolutionaries punished, but many accused were sent in from the provinces too. Bearing this in mind, the Parisian total of 2,639 over an 18-month period of warfare and rebellion may not seem unduly high. The greatest incidence of executions occurred in the west: over 6,000 peasants and workers led by ex-nobles and priests died for their Church and King in La Vendée and Brittany. This was followed by the south-east, especially Lyons, but here it was the middle classes, followed by the working class, who were punished for rejecting the local Jacobins in favour of Federalism. (These figures may perhaps do something to rectify the version of the Terror in Baroness Orczy's romantic novel, *The Scarlet Pimpernel* (1905), where it is portrayed as belonging exclusively to Paris, its tumbrils stuffed with beautiful and noble aristocrats.)

When the crisis within the Jacobin government broke there was no overall plan or direction as there had been on 10 August 1792, or 30 May – 2 June 1793. Robespierre's opponents in the Convention, the Committees and the moderate Sections, could only agree that he should be destroyed, not on the purpose of his destruction. The moderate majority in the Convention, the Plain, had been cowed into submission to the will of the Jacobin executive Committees for over a year. The efficient suppression of popular political activity, however, meant that there was little danger of another insurrection to browbeat them. The deputies who had been sent to the guillotine over the past months went there as a result of accusations by members of the Committees. By July 1794 Robespierre and Couthon had antagonised most of the members of the two Committees. The Committee of General Security resented Robespierre's interference, through his Committee's police bureau, in their sphere of power. He had deplored the violence of Fouché's terrorism when on a mission to punish the Federalists at

Lyons, where large numbers of captives were executed, without a proper trial, by gun-fire and cannonades, and eventually had him expelled from the Jacobin Club. Under the Terror this was often a prelude to denunciation, arrest and conviction. Within the Committee of Public Safety there were tensions: Saint-Just, for example, quarrelled with Carnot about military policy. Some of the more placid specialists were often absent on missions. Robespierre blamed Collot d'Herbois for his co-operation with Fouché in operating the Terror in Lyons. Collot was supported by his fellow extremist, Billaud-Varenne. On occasion the windows of the Committee Room had to be shut so the public would not hear their quarrels.

On 26 July (8 *Thermidor*) Robespierre made a long speech to the Convention. He gave no sign that the Committee intended to end the Terror – indeed he personally condemned in general terms some 'traitors' who should be punished. There was a resigned, discouraged tone to the discourse in which he justified his conduct in the government, but perhaps recognised that he was better fitted for opposition than power: 'I am made to fight crime, not to govern over it.' The speech was received unenthusiastically. Many of the deputies were wondering if they were amongst the 'traitors' who had been mentioned. In the evening Robespierre repeated the speech before a rapturous audience at the Jacobin Club, which emphasised its loyalty by expelling Collot d'Herbois and Billaud-Varenne. There are some signs that during the night Saint-Just, who was due to report to the Convention on behalf of the Committee the next day, attempted a reconciliation. If he did, Robespierre, for once misreading the political signs, would have none of it, or perhaps he preferred the risk of destruction rather than further to compromise his beliefs.

The next day Collot d'Herbois used his position as President of the Convention to prevent Saint-Just from reading his report, and Robespierre from speaking. Several former friends of Danton launched the attack against them. Gradually gathering courage, the Plain asserted itself and eventually sent them both, together with Couthon, Robespierre's younger brother and a follower, Lebas, for trial. They were rescued from custody by the Commune, which was dominated by supporters of Robespierre, and taken to the Town Hall. The more prosperous, bourgeois Sections sent their National Guards to the assistance of the Convention; some Guards from the *sans-culottes* Sections went to the Town Hall but, when no one gave them any directions, they faded away during the night. The Council of the Commune, Robespierre and his associates could not agree on a formula to justify a call to arms which could have led to bloody urban warfare, even to another civil war. The soldiers of the Convention arrested them without resistance early on the morning of 28 July (10 *Thermidor*). Lebas shot himself, Robespierre and his brother were badly injured in suicide attempts. Together with Saint-Just, Couthon and 18 members of the Commune and other supporters, they were guillotined later in the day. More sympathisers of Robespierre were subsequently executed.

During the remainder of republican rule many of the policies of Robespierre and his associates, were either ignored or disowned. Was this because, as was alleged at the time, they were bloodthirsty tyrants who had taken their fanatical beliefs much too far by the institution of the Terror? Or was the explanation for the failure of the Jacobin experiment to be found in a complex of issues such as conflicting class interests, ideological differences, economic pressures and personality clashes?

Figure 20 Sloane, *The Arrest of Robespierre*, by the National Guard during the night of 9-10 *Thermidor* (27-8 July) 1794. This picture clearly shows that he made a suicide attempt; another account claims that his jaw was shattered by a *gendarme's* (a policeman's) bullet. (*Bibliothèque Nationale, Paris*)

4.7 The resurgence of the moderates

Many historians consider that the Revolution continued until 1799 and the dictatorship of Napoleon, although this study only takes it to the end of 1795. These years certainly have a common characteristic in that the moderates, those who were reasonably satisfied with a government that voiced the interests of officials and property owners but excluded royalists and the *sans-culottes*, tried to hold out against the political extremes. 'Neither anarchy nor monarchy' was their motto. In the war, whilst the British navy dominated the seas, on land things went extremely well for the Republic, with the conquest of the Netherlands and northern Italy. The damage that constant fighting inflicted on the economy was to some extent counterbalanced by the spoils of victory which began to reach France. Immediately after the coup of *Thermidor* 1794 the Convention started to dismantle the Jacobin policies without giving undue encouragement to the royalists. The *sans-culottes* in the towns were cowed by the reverses of the previous months and weakened by the constant drain, caused by conscription, of their strongest and bravest young men.

In early August 1794, many of the thousands of suspects arrested under the Terror were released. Executions continued but their number decreased considerably, and exile to Guyana in South America was frequently substituted. The Law of 22 *Prairial* was repealed. Later in the month the executive was reorganised and the powers of the Great Committees were dispersed amongst 16 committees. The Convention no longer allowed the same people to remain in position for long periods and the surviving Jacobins found themselves in an embattled minority amongst deputies who were now determined to avenge past grievances and dispose of laws to which they had unwillingly consented.

A new force replaced the militant *sans-culottes* operating outside the law in Paris and other cities and towns: the 'gilded youth' or '*Muscadins*' (perfumed people) were young men who rejected the austere republicanism of the Jacobins. Some were relations of victims of the Terror, some had dodged conscription. One observer claimed that they had delicate hands more like those of painters of miniatures than blacksmiths. They tended to wear fashionable clothes with high cravats. They even had their own song, *The Awakening of the People*. They were amongst the leaders of the 'White Terror' which affected parts of the country sporadically during the following year, during which several hundred Jacobins were killed and many more were beaten or had their goods seized or destroyed. It became dangerous to wear a red cap or to own portraits of Marat or the other Jacobin heroes. The culmination of the reaction in Paris came with several attacks by the 'gilded youth' on the Jacobin Club. The authorities seized on the disorders involved as an excuse to close the Club down on 12 November (22 *Brumaire*). Its affiliated regional societies, which had been such a force in raising popular political consciousness during previous years, were also disbanded.

The new political climate was defined more clearly by the reception of 73 deputies, who had signed a resolution in support of the Girondins in June 1793, back into the Convention. They were later joined by the few Girondin survivors who had been condemned but had managed to evade arrest. The extent of the reaction led to investigations into the Terrorist activities of ex-members of the Great Committees such as Vadier, Barère, Billaud-Varenne and Collot d'Herbois. None of these measures, however, alleviated the great economic hardships of the winter of 1794. Indeed the desire for the end of controls led to the virtual abolition of the laws of the Maximum by the end of the year. This compounded the problems of the poor who were already suffering from the effects of a particularly bad harvest. The value of the *assignat* reflected the state of the economy: by May 1795 it was down to 7.5 per cent of its original value. The Paris Commune and the 48 Sections were no longer a focus for popular discontent; they had been cowed by the executions after 27 July (9 *Thermidor*). During the course of 1795 the Commune was abolished and the sectional committees of supervision were reduced to 12, dominated by moderate members of the propertied bourgeoisie.

Despite the disappearance of the Maximum, the Convention had attempted to maintain subsidised supplies of bread to Paris, knowing all too well the dangerous consequences of popular discontent. By 1 April 1795 (12 *Germinal*) food was scarce in many parts of the capital and the Convention was invaded by *sans-culottes* demanding 'Bread and the Constitution of 1793'. They were eventually chased out by the National Guard and pursued the next day to their Sections, where leading agitators were arrested. This confirmation of the Convention's strength gave it courage to take other anti-Jacobin steps: Collot d'Herbois, Billaud-Varenne and other former Terrorists were deported and a commission was set up to revise the constitution. Another popular uprising from 20 to 24 May (1-5 *Prairial*) was suppressed and more popular leaders and Jacobin deputies were punished. This coincided with the height of the 'White Terror' in the provinces, and many royalists began to think that the monarchy could be restored.

In June 1795, the *dauphin*, the ten-year-old son of Louis XVI and only direct heir to the throne, died in the Temple prison. This gave his uncle, the comte de Provence or 'Louis XVIII' as royalists now called him, even greater encouragement to attempt a restoration. He made it clear in his Verona Declaration that if he was restored he would execute regicides and nullify all the achievements of the

Revolution. In the mean time his younger brother, the comte d'Artois, with British help attempted to invade Brittany to link up with *Chouan* royalist rebels. This led to a bloody fiasco when the brilliant general, Hoche, pushed the invaders and the *Chouans* into the little Quiberon peninsula. Over 700 of those who survived the fighting were executed. In the course of the year Prussia, Holland and Spain made peace with the Republic, leaving only Britain and Austria to sustain the hopes of the royalists.

The Convention was determined that the new constitution would safeguard the interests of the moderate majority.

Self-Assessment Question 10

Read the extracts from the speech below in which Boissy d'Anglas (see Appendix 1) presented the new constitution to the Convention on 23 June (5 *Messidor*) 1795.

i)   What form of government was likely to emerge from such a programme?

ii) How does the ideology of the speech differ from Jacobin beliefs?

Document A

'Civil equality offers all that the reasonable man could wish for.... We should be governed by the best among us; the best are the most highly educated, and those with the greatest interest in upholding the laws; save for the rarest exceptions, you will only find such men amongst those who, by reason of their owning property, are devoted to the land in which it is situated, to the laws that protect it, to the public peace that maintains it....

If you were to grant unlimited rights to men without property, and if they were ever to take their place in the legislative assembly, they would provoke disturbances, or cause them to be provoked, without fear of the consequences; they would levy or permit the levying of taxes fatal to trade and agriculture, since they would neither have foreseen nor apprehended the atrocious effects of such taxes.... A country ruled by property owners exists in a social state; one ruled by the propertyless is in a state of nature.'

Soboul, 1977, pp.128-9

Discussion

According to this speech power would clearly be confined to the upper classes, highly educated officials on good salaries and property owners. There would be no future prospect of economic laws that protected the interests of the poor rather than of merchants and landowners. 'Civil equality' does at least promise equality before the law to all, one of the great achievements of 1789.

It should be noticed that 'a state of nature' is used as an abusive phrase. Rousseau, the inspiration of Jacobins such as Robespierre, had believed that man could only be truly virtuous and happy in a state of nature where all were equal. After the experiences of June 1793 to July 1794, the surviving deputies wanted none of it. Boissy d'Anglas was very pragmatic in his proposals but, if any ideology can be identified, it would stem from Voltaire, Montesquieu and experience of the English property owners' revolutions of the previous century.

The new constitution proclaimed on 23 September (1 *Vendémiaire*) was extremely complicated and arranged to keep the maximum number of deputies from the Convention in power. All taxpayers could vote in primary elections for electoral colleges but the property qualification for membership of the colleges was high. So the crucial power of choosing the personnel of the two legislative assemblies, the Council of the Ancients and the Council of the Five Hundred, was limited to the upper classes, approximately 30,000–40,000 altogether, who owned substantial amounts of property. To safeguard their continuation in government, the members of the Convention provided that two-thirds of the new deputies be chosen from amongst the existing members. This recognised that the majority of the electorate, if free, would choose very moderate or counter-revolutionary deputies. The executive power was exercised by five Directors, known as the Directory, chosen by the Council of the Five Hundred.

The frustration felt by royalists and other critics of the Revolution at the continuation of the rule of Convention deputies broke out in Paris on 4 and 5 October (12-13 *Vendémiaire*). The Convention was attacked by insurgents from the more prosperous Sections, but it enjoyed the protection of the army. General Napoleon Bonaparte, still under a cloud for his friendship with Robespierre's younger brother, helped to put down the insurrection. He turned his cannon on the protesters and they soon dispersed. A few weeks later he was rewarded by being made Commander-in-Chief of the Army of the Interior. The Directory had started as it continued, depending on the support of the armies in time of internal political crisis. This brought closer the danger of the military dictatorship that the Jacobins had always feared.

Chapter 5

THE END OF THE REVOLUTION?

If the beginning and the end of the eighteenth century in France are compared, it is apparent that the country had changed almost beyond measure. Louis XIV died at Versailles in 1715 surrounded by the glory which was largely his own creation, able to comment 'we grow old like ordinary men, and we shall end like them' without anyone finding it strange. In sharp contrast Louis XVI died in 1793 on the guillotine in the midst of his capital city. Abbé Edgeworth, his confessor, described the scene:

> 'They dragged him under the guillotine which with one blow severed his head from his body. All this passed in a moment. The youngest of the guards, who seemed about 18, immediately seized the head and showed it to the people as he walked round the scaffold.... At first an awful silence prevailed, at length some cries of "vive la République".'

In his *Social Interpretation of the French Revolution* (1964), Cobban provided an explanation: the dramatic fall of the monarchy, the Revolution, was 'in essence a triumph for the conservative, propertied, land-owning classes large and small.' By making use of the discontents of the peasants who rioted in the countryside and of the small craftsmen and artisans who were involved in the great revolutionary 'days' in Paris and other cities, the Third Estate, particularly its land-owning sections, was able to out-manoeuvre the privileged classes and ensure that the upheaval in French society was for its benefit.

Can such an interpretation be justified, or should we look elsewhere? It has already been pointed out (see Chapter 1) that the interests of nobles and bourgeois did not necessarily conflict, that their demands were in many respects identical. Should one, therefore, place greater emphasis on possible economic causes of the Revolution? In the countryside conditions varied so widely from one area to another, as Jones has demonstrated in *The Peasantry in the French Revolution* (1988), that it is hard to draw firm conclusions. But Jones does show that the near famine conditions of the miserable winter of 1788-9 greatly encouraged the development of the 'spirit of revolt'. He further suggests that this 'spirit' gained strength and direction from the 'experience of drawing up the *Cahiers*'. Once written down, grievances long endured seemed increasingly insupportable and the 'disturbances acquired an explicitly anti-feudal character' and an awareness by the summer of 1789 'that the entire social order was crumbling and [there was] an opportunistic desire to strike while the iron was hot' (ibid.).

In cities like Paris a similar opportunistic spirit can also be discerned when one considers the emergence of new revolutionary municipal governments and the raising of militias (see Essay 1, pp.107-08). None of this, however, really attacks the central problem: why did events become so serious that the 'entire social order' crumbled? After all, neither rural nor urban disturbances were previously unheard of in France. It might be possible to turn to the interplay of events and personalities for an explanation. It could be argued that if Louis XVI had been more decisive and had more competent ministers, the summer of 1789 would have seen not the Fall of the Bastille, but the emergence of modernised constitutional monarchy in France. This was what most of the leaders of French opinion and society wanted at this stage.

Hampson, in his *Prelude to Terror: The Constituent Assembly and the Failure of Consensus* (1988), has drawn attention to the fact that in early 1789, despite the general acceptance of this as the desired outcome of recent events, virtually no one had considered in a pragmatic way how to achieve this limited monarchy. The result was that discussion focussed on abstract theories of law, society and government current at the time. Disagreement could soon be discerned between those whose attitudes owed much to Montesquieu, that is who defined liberty in a negative way as freedom from interference by the State, and those who looked rather to Rousseau and derived individual liberty from participation in a free society.

It is certainly true that once the excitements of July and August 1789 had passed and the Constituent Assembly began in earnest its work of reconstructing French government, the arguments in the Assembly and the clubs became increasingly ideological. The idea of popular sovereignty – that the sanction for political authority came from the people – was attractive to all levels of society. If, however, it was combined with Rousseau's idea of the General Will – that the best interests of the people were the only moral grounds for political action – the situation could become very dangerous. The General Will could only too easily be identified with the desires of the dominant group in the Assembly, the clubs or, later, the Committee of Public Safety. Opposition could not be countenanced; it was illogical, unjustifiable and immoral, an expression of faction. As Hampson (1988) says, 'success was proof that one actually reflected and indeed embodied the will of the nation: failure was a sign of faction'.

In debates like this the role of the King seemed increasingly irrelevant. The Feuillants, who adopted the position derived from Montesquieu that government should, in effect, be a compromise between the necessarily divergent interests of the various groups in society, came under fierce attack. An attempt to compromise with the King and the Court in late 1791 could seem like treason to the Revolution. The Feuillants' admiration for English models of government was also unfortunate in a society as fiercely nationalistic as revolutionary France. It seems at least possible to argue that single-minded politicians like Robespierre built their interpretations of Rousseau's theories into a powerful justification for revolution on their own terms. Disturbances in the countryside, riots in the cities, pressure from foreign rulers, the existence of opposition in Paris, all of which might have had many different causes and explanations, could be used to bolster the extreme radicals' position, with its attractive simplicity. There was no tradition of public debate ending in compromise to set against it. The Kings of France had never shown any understanding of the idea of a 'loyal opposition'. The Revolution had, perhaps, begun because a wide range of difficulties for the French King – famine, a financial crisis, demands for structural reforms, weak ministers – had coincided. It continued on its increasingly radical path because a group of ideologically-inspired reformers came to the fore, who had a clear vision of the new society they wished, or even felt compelled, to create.

From the beginning of the Revolution a new element had entered the polite discussion between the educated nobles and bourgeoisie about the best form of government: from time to time the people, both the rural peasantry and the urban *sans-culottes,* took decisive and often violent action. The peasantry was very anxious that feudal impositions and the inequalities in taxation should be removed and, by the summer of 1789, was prepared to break the law to achieve its objectives. As owners or tenants of property, however, with a limited and parochial view of the outside world and its possibilities, most of them had no wish to reform all social relationships and destroy religion.

The *sans-culottes* were mostly small tradesmen and artisans, as Gwynne Lewis shows in Essay 5, and as the Revolution progressed their political consciousness increased, often through the membership of popular societies or even of the originally exclusive Jacobin clubs. As early as 1789 the *sans-culottes* were capable of reacting effectively to royal intransigence, at the Fall of the Bastille and the March to Versailles. In 1792 they again showed their power by destroying the monarchy in the assault on the Tuileries. And they did the same to the Girondins the following June. For six months the Jacobin government passed measures such as the Law of the General Maximum, to please them. Increasingly, however, it realised that it was doing so at the cost of alienating the moderate or secretly royalist majority of the nation. De-Christianisation, limited redistribution of property, and total price control – these aspirations of most *sans-culottes* were never finally achieved.

Those who benefited from the coup of *Thermidor* 1794 seem mainly to have been members of the *ancien régime* who had managed to survive with their property intact, and the prosperous bourgeoisie and office-holders whose aspirations had led them to support the Revolution in 1789. The moderate majority of the Plain, after a year of impotence, asserted themselves and, as Rudé (1988) says, proceeded to 'dismantle the machinery of the Terror (now obsolete), put the *sans-culottes* back to work, return to a more liberal economy and carry the war to a successful conclusion.' The constitution of 1795 shunned any appearance of being an embodiment of the General Will. Elected on a narrow franchise, the government of two assemblies and five Directors had complex powers and inter-relationships; it marked a reversion to the balanced constitution favoured by Montesquieu and adopted by the Americans.

One of the themes of this book has been the interaction between the experience of constitutional reform, the political ideas of the philosophers and the thinking of revolutionary activists. The problems in reaching firm conclusions have been demonstrated. The philosophers themselves were not always consistent and none had written with a situation comparable to France in 1789 in mind. Mirabeau, La Fayette, the Feuillants, Girondins and Jacobins also changed their views of the best forms of government and society as events developed. Yet there remain several areas where a difference of approach can be distinguished between the more moderate politicians of 1789-92 and after *Thermidor* 1794, and those who ruled during the years of the Jacobin ascendancy. These areas are: the role of the common people in the constitution; social justice including education and welfare; religion and civic morality or 'virtue'. On all these issues Rousseau had views which diverged considerably both from other philosophers and from practice in relatively liberal countries such as Britain, Switzerland, and the USA. His belief in a form of government which would implement the General Will, in the importance of measures that would enable the natural dignity of all free men to emerge, and in the need to enforce a natural religion which would promote civic virtue had great influence on the Jacobins and especially on Robespierre.

Historians nowadays are not in the business of handing out praise and blame to the political groups who figured in the Revolution (though the difficulties experienced by the French government over the most acceptable way to celebrate the 1989 bicentenary, illustrate that the Revolution still has the power to arouse controversy). The big question which arises over Robespierre's desire for a Republic founded on his version of Rousseau's ideal state is: could it ever have worked? The complex power relationships of the summer of 1794 have now been analysed sufficiently for us to have a clear idea of why Robespierre and his supporters were overthrown. But what if the Commune's insurrection had succeeded? Either Robespierre or Saint-Just could have become a dictator embodying in himself the General Will. Neither probably had the least desire for such an outcome, which would have violated all their strongest beliefs.

Robespierre, always as much of a realist as an idealogue, answered the big question himself in his personal notebook, probably in 1793, with a sad little catechism:

> 'What obstacle is there to the enlightenment of the people?
> Its misery.
> When, then, will the people be enlightened?
> When it will have bread and the rich and the government stop using hired pens and perfidious language to deceive it; when the interests of the rich and the government shall be confounded [identified] with those of the people.
> And when will their interests be confounded with those of the people?
> Never.'

When the Directory and two assemblies composed of a majority of deputies who had sat in the Convention took office in the autumn of 1795, too many were regicides for there to be any chance of making a settlement with the royalists. Did this mark the end of the Revolution? Claims could also be made for 1799 when Napoleon became dictator, 1804 when the Republic formally became an empire and 1815 when the Bourbons were securely restored. Sutherland (1985) is in favour of the last date, if only because counter-revolutionary forces were active up to that time. Napoleon could be seen as the shadowy 'military dictator' with whom the Jacobins had always frightened their audiences. Yet he was the creation of the Revolution and the war. He had no choice but to perpetuate many of the earlier reforms and continue the war in order to remain in power. Perhaps his great tomb in Les Invalides, Paris, should be seen as a monument not only to his glory but to the million Frenchmen who died or were mutilated in the wars waged in pursuit of his ambition.

Were all the consequences of the Revolution negative rather than positive? As we have seen the economy of France in 1789 was less advanced than that of England, which was already well engaged in her Industrial Revolution. The enormous cost of 20 years of war, even when partially covered by foreign tribute, further retarded national prosperity. On the positive side, after the initial setback caused by the horror of the example of the French Revolution, English political life was influenced by many of the arguments put forward by the French reformers in favour of a more liberal system of government. The franchise, for example, was widened by the end of the nineteenth century to include a majority of the male working class. In many other areas of Europe political freedom had to wait for the twentieth century.

The Jacobins paradoxically can be seen as being most positively influential in areas which contemporaries saw as their worst excesses. The deism of the Cult of the Supreme Being may well have helped spread a climate of toleration among the Christian Churches. Execution for blasphemy would no longer be acceptable. Both the Girondins and the Jacobins indulged in strident patriotic rhetoric but this may well have helped spread feelings of national pride and identity which helped nations like the Italians claim their independence from foreign rulers. The French Republic also preached, even if it did not always practise, racial equality for Jews and Blacks. The rights of women received some consideration.

Many ideals were formulated in 1793 and 1794 which are now seen as desirable and beneficial: manhood suffrage, universal education, relief for the destitute. Not all were attained at that time, but that does not negate the importance of the systematic promulgation of such ideas 200 years ago. Before the Revolution those who tentatively toyed with such an agenda were often thought to be mad or at least wildly eccentric. The Jacobins paid a high price with their own and other people's lives to show that such ideals could become practical policies, something for future generations to aim for.

PART TWO

ESSAYS 1-5

Essay 1

THE FRENCH REVOLUTION AND THE PROVINCES

Clive Emsley
Professor of History
The Open University

Many histories of the French Revolution tend to concentrate on the political events which unfolded in Paris. There is much justification for this: Paris was the capital city and the seat of government; and it was in Paris between 1789 and 1799 that successive regimes were established and overthrown. But of the 28 million or so people living in revolutionary France only some 600,000-700,000 lived in Paris. Furthermore, while events in Paris, and the policies of governments based in Paris, did affect people in the provinces, provincial notables did not simply obey the dictates of revolutionary leaders in Paris. In some instances they deliberately defied them – and events in the provinces could then influence affairs in Paris. The aim of this essay is to introduce you to some of the complexities of provincial France, and to give you some idea of the broad movement and the sweep of events in the provinces during the revolutionary period.

I The complexities of revolutionary France

There were enormous differences and divisions between the different provinces of France on the eve of the Revolution. In many of the provinces, especially in rural districts some distance from Paris, languages other than French predominated. In much of the south people spoke distinctive languages quite different from Parisian French – hence for example the name 'Languedoc', the language of Oc. Angevins, Bretons and Gascons each spoke their own tongue; the people of Lorraine, only united with France some 50 years before the Revolution, spoke a form of German. A linguistic enquiry mounted in the first year of the Revolution concluded, probably over-optimistically, that while three-quarters of the population knew some French, only three million could speak it properly.

There were significant economic differences in the country too. Some large-scale farming was developing especially in the north and north-east, but much of the south and west was still farmed by peasant occupiers in a very primitive fashion. Internal customs barriers and the notorious *gabelle* (a salt tax which varied in different parts of the kingdom) reinforced the divisions. Different provincial weights and measures added to the confusion.

The provinces were divided into both *gouvernements* and *généralités*. The former were supervised by governors appointed by the King. The post of governor was essentially a military one going back to the Middle Ages; increasingly it was seen as honorific and it was generally given to one of the leading nobles in a province. But superimposed on top of the *gouvernements*, though without the boundaries always overlapping, were the more recent *généralités*. These were supervised by *intendants*, also appointed by the King. *Intendants* were state functionaries who had risen in the royal bureaucracy partly through patronage and connections, but also through administrative ability and skills. Some provinces were intensely proud of their independent origins, especially where there were local, provincial *parlements* (law courts) or estates which could provide a focus for provincial identity, at least among the local nobility. Brittany and Languedoc were especially notable in this respect and on the eve of the Revolution their estates had wrested many of the administrative powers from the *intendants*. Nestled within the provinces were towns and cities with their own local administrations. Many of the municipalities had systems of local government in which the principal administrative posts were in the hands of wealthy men who had purchased them.

Key

1	Brittany	12	Orléanais	23	Aunis
2	Normandy	13	Nivernais	24	Gascony and Guyenne
3	Picardy	14	Burgundy	25	Limousin
4	Artois	15	Lorraine	26	Auvergne
5	Flanders and Hainaut	16	Alsace	27	Languedoc
6	Champagne	17	Franche-Comté	28	Dauphiné
7	Ile-de-France	18	Lyonnais	29	Comtat Venaissin
8	Maine	19	Bourbonnais	30	Provence
9	Anjou	20	Berry	31	Roussillon
10	Poitou	21	Marche	32	Foix
11	Touraine	22	Saintonge and Angoumois	33	Béarn

Figure 21 The provincial boundaries and major administrative centres in France in 1789. (Note: the boundaries did not always exactly correspond to the *généralités*.) *(P. Jones, The Peasantry in the French Revolution, Cambridge University Press)*

Inspired by ideas of the Enlightenment, the men of the early revolutionary assemblies were determined to sweep away these complexities and to establish an administrative system based upon reason and rationality. While many of the key documents of the early stages of the Revolution were translated into other languages of France – *les droits de l'homme* (the rights of man) for example, around Bordeaux became *lous dreyts de l'ome* – there were those who wanted to impose one language on the country, believing that diversity endangered liberty and that provincialism undermined national spirit. The internal customs divisions were abolished. A rational, uniform system of weights and measures was established. *Gouvernements* and *généralités* were swept away and a rational division of the country into roughly equal *départements* was made with each *département* subdivided into districts and cantons. These new *départements* were, initially, run by locally elected assemblies. Locally elected assemblies also took over in the towns and cities, but the legislation authorising the latter was passed after many revolutionary committees had usurped the powers of the old municipalities. In some instances, for example Rheims, they shared control with the old council; in others, for example Troyes, where the old municipality strongly resisted change, a new municipal committee seized power. In most instances the new men who took over local government appear to have been eminently respectable, usually urban-based professionals such as lawyers, merchants, and some wealthy artisans and shopkeepers. Most municipalities saw changes in personnel during the turbulent decade of the 1790s, but the same kinds of men, often the very same men, recur on the municipalities following successive upheavals and/or elections. The militants who rose, often through the local Jacobin Club, to brief dominance in Year II (see Appendix 2) were often drawn from men of a slightly lower social standing, but they were never recruited from the masses of wage labourers.

Figure 22 The *départements* of France in 1790. (D. M. G. Sutherland, France 1789–1815: Revolution and Counter-revolution, Collins)

The municipalities tended to be rather more radical than the departmental assemblies, a fact which contributed to the urban/rural divisions which plagued the Revolution. But the most striking thing about the structure of local government established by the Constituent Assembly was the initial lack of central direction. The Assembly never intended to cut local government off from relations with Paris, as many of its declarations reveal; however the Assembly never got round to creating the machinery for the necessary links. Furthermore, it should be noted that in the ideological ferment of the early years of the Revolution several leading radicals, drawing on the ideas of Rousseau and others, urged a federal structure for France – a kind of nation of small states.

The independence achieved by local government in 1789 and 1790 was gradually undermined as the Revolution wore on. As regimes in Paris took economic and religious measures which upset and offended them, many provincial electors seem to have begun to lose interest in politics, both national and local. At the same time in some localities, especially during the Terror, the new assemblies were reluctant to act, and some even ceased to meet, fearful that they might be compromised for backing the 'wrong' side as the Revolution developed. More important, however, the needs of war as perceived by the Jacobin dictatorship militated against local independence: centralisation was increasingly imposed from Paris by the Jacobin dictatorship and then by the Directory. Finally, Napoleon's 1800 institution of Prefects to administer the *départements* on behalf of the central government completed the virtual elimination of local government from rural France, though many vestiges remained in the municipalities.

II Bordeaux, Lyons and Marseilles

Though Paris was by far the largest city in France at the close of the eighteenth century, there were other cities and towns jealous of their independence and proud of their heritage and tradition. Three in particular stand out for their size and significance. Bordeaux, on the Atlantic seaboard, was a booming commercial centre whose prosperity was rooted in wine and West Indian trade. Its population appears to have doubled to about 110,000 in the 75 years before the Revolution. Lyons' population was over 140,000 in 1789. Lyons was an industrial city. About three-sevenths of its inhabitants depended in some way on the manufacture and sale of a single luxury commodity: silk cloth. While the production of the cloth was largely carried out in small family workshops, the city was riven with friction between the silk weavers, known as the *canuts*, and the silk merchants. Due south of Lyons, where the Rhône flows into the Mediterranean, was Marseilles, with a population only slightly less than that of Bordeaux. Like Bordeaux, Marseilles was a booming seaport and commercial centre.

All three cities suffered upheavals during the Revolution. In many instances the violence, the slogans and the political positions of the Revolution were superimposed on existing divisions and exacerbated them. Of the three cities Bordeaux suffered the least violence. Wealthy merchants and professional men seized the opportunity offered by 1789 and established their political dominance over the city. Though temporarily displaced in the aftermath of the Federalist Revolt, this dominance continued into the nineteenth century. In Lyons too it was the merchant élite which profited from 1789, but the class divisions apparent in the silk industry took on a new dimension as a result of the Revolution. At the review of the city's National Guard in 1790 units from the more prosperous districts fell in behind the new tricolour, while those from workers' districts paraded behind the old white flag of the Bourbon monarchy. In the summer of 1793 the city witnessed a Jacobin coup followed by a Girondin counter-coup as a prelude to its role in the Federalist Revolt; again the revolutionary factions drew on existing class divisions and hostilities. In the new revolutionary municipality of Marseilles merchants became dominant and they tried to maintain a balance between rival social groups in the city. But from early on 'the patriots' in Marseilles developed a reputation for revolutionary zeal. Two weeks after the storming of the Bastille several hundred Marseillais marched on the city of Aix and released some 70 men imprisoned for rioting over high prices and against *seigneurs* and tax collectors. Two years later 500 Marseillais marched into the papal possession of Avignon to support those 'patriots' who wanted union with France. The city's National Guard took the law into its own hands in 1792 when, in the name of the Revolution, it disarmed an infantry regiment at Aix and drove alleged counter-revolutionaries out of Arles. Later in the year a battalion recruited in Marseilles to fight the invading armies of Austrians and Prussians gave its ferocious war song to France as a national anthem, and lent its military muscle to the Parisians who toppled the monarchy on 10 August.

However, the revolutionary zeal of the Marseilles 'patriots' went hand in hand with a suspicion of politicians in Paris. In the early months of the Revolution this suspicion had received a confirmation in the eyes of proud Marseilles when the much smaller city of Aix was nominated *chef-lieu* (literally 'chief place') of the new *département* of the Bouches-du-Rhône. Arguably this snub contributed to the Marseilles 'patriots' continued flouting of central government authority during the first three years of the Revolution. In the summer of 1793 this flouting of authority became full-scale insurrection as Marseilles joined with Bordeaux, Lyons, some smaller towns and a few rural districts in the Federalist Revolt.

Although, as noted above, there were ideas in the writings of some of the philosophers for a federated France of small, self-governing localities, and although these ideas had been developed by a few radical politicians in the early years of the Revolution, the Federalist Revolt was not the product of any such ideology. It was, rather, a protest about events in Paris, and particularly about the influence which the capital's radical Commune appeared to have over the deputies in the National Convention. The spark which fired the Revolt was the overthrow of the Girondin deputies. Generally speaking, spokesmen for the Federalist Revolt expressed loyalty to the Revolution and to the idea of the nation, one and indivisible.

The potential size and strength of the Federalist Revolt was extremely serious for the Jacobins in Paris, especially when the naval base of Toulon yielded itself to the British and Spanish fleets in August 1793. But it was difficult for the Federalist forces to form a united front. Not only did they draw support from a variety of political factions, bound only by their hostility to the Jacobins and the Commune in Paris, but it proved very difficult for them to link their forces. An uprising in Normandy was separated from the Federalists in and around Bordeaux by some 200 miles and by the savage war in La Vendée. Bordeaux was also an enormous distance from both Lyons and Marseilles, and the area between was not sympathetic. Troops from Paris were able to put down the revolts one at a time. The repression was fiercest in Lyons where the National Convention determined to make an example, as outlined in its decree of 12 October 1793:

> 'The city of Lyons shall be destroyed. Every habitation of the rich shall be demolished; there shall remain only the homes of the poor, the houses of patriots... the buildings employed in industry, and the monuments devoted to humanity and public instruction.

> The name of Lyons shall be effaced from the list of cities of the Republic. The collection of houses left standing shall henceforth bear the name of Ville-Affranchie [the Liberated City].'

The march of the Marseilles battalion and its involvement in the *journée* of 10 August 1792, together with the Federalist Revolt of 1793, mark the high spots of the three great cities' role in the Revolution. The repression of the Federalist

Revolt left them firmly subordinated to Paris. Lyons recovered from the repression and continued to be a thriving centre of the silk industry. The friction between the weavers and the merchants also continued, exploding in two massive insurrections in 1831 and 1834. War and revolution had a detrimental effect on the economy of Marseilles, but the effects were only temporary. This was not the case with Bordeaux: the war with Britain and the virtual destruction of France's empire in the West Indies had long-term serious effects on the city. Already in the revolutionary decade its population was recognised to be declining; it stagnated for the first third of the nineteenth century.

III The Revolution in rural France

Most of the population of France at the time of the Revolution were peasants; there were perhaps 20 million of them. The term 'peasant' can create problems of definition. Broadly speaking it can be used to refer to anyone engaged wholly, or partially, in agricultural pursuits. But there were enormous differentiations among the peasantry. Some owned and exploited their own land; others were landless labourers. It has been estimated that about two-thirds of the rural population had their own land, but the amount of land owned, or tenanted, varied considerably. Large-scale farming, generally the work of tenant farmers, was only to be found in the areas of major cereal production situated in the north. The land owned by peasants was often that of the poorest quality, and in the most remote regions; peasant holdings were often too small to feed even one family and consequently both men and women had to find wage labour elsewhere to eke out what they could grow for themselves. Some worked for larger farmers; some took industrial out-work from, particularly, clothiers in the small towns; the less fortunate were forced on to the roads to look for work, often in the large towns and cities, and to beg until they found it.

During the eighteenth century *seigneurs* had sought increasingly to maximise the profits from the lands which they owned, and from the feudal dues which they still claimed. The *seigneur* was not necessarily always a nobleman; he could be a wealthy cleric (monasteries had the rights to feudal dues in many areas); he could also be a wealthy bourgeois who had acquired the seigneurial rights to a piece of land. In many instances the collection of feudal dues was left to agents or collectors sometimes paid on a commission basis which encouraged them to raise the maximum sum possible. The increasing pressure of feudal dues, and especially the requirements that the peasant producer use the mill, the olive or wine press, and the oven of the *seigneur* infuriated the peasantry; many of their *Cahiers* drawn up in 1789 reflect this anger.

Some of the *Cahiers* also expressed concern about vagrants and brigands wandering on the roads, and stressed the need for improved policing. Anxiety over these issues had been mounting since the 1760s as the population increased faster than economic change could absorb and as, in consequence, more and more individuals were forced on to the roads to look for work.

The *Cahiers*, the elections, the meetings of the Estates-General, all provoked excitement in rural France. There was a belief that 'the good King Louis' was going to do something for his people. The excitement was gradually transformed into a nervous anxiety by a severe shortage of grain and then by apparent threats towards the Third Estate in general and the National Assembly in particular. Early in 1789 rumours had begun to circulate in provincial France of a plot by the nobles to starve the people into submission. In many areas peasants responded with attacks on *châteaux*. There was little personal violence in these attacks: what the peasants sought out, and destroyed, were the feudal rolls, believing that they thus destroyed the feudal dues. In July rumour was transformed into the Great Fear as the fear of a plot by the nobility, and the long-standing fear of brigands, coalesced into the belief that noble opponents of the Revolution and of the National Assembly were recruiting armies of brigands to destroy growing crops. The Great Fear swept across France in currents along the major roads prompting the rural population to arm itself, and leading to yet more attacks on *châteaux*. The first action seen by the new middle-class National Guard of many French towns was the restoration of order in the wake of these troubles.

The risings in peasant France contributed to the first noble emigrations of August and September 1789, and also prompted the National Assembly's theatrical abolition of feudalism in August. However, the departure of the more intransigent nobles and the boasted ending of feudalism did not ensure peace in the countryside. First and foremost, the abolition of feudalism was not as far reaching as it appeared and as was claimed: while the game laws, seigneurial justice, and many obligations imposed on the peasantry were abolished, the Assembly still intended that the peasants should find redemption payments to compensate the *seigneurs* for all feudal dues not derived directly from personal servitude. Attempts to enforce these payments led to further disorders. New legislation of August 1792 reduced the surviving vestiges of feudalism; finally, a decree of the Convention the following July completed its destruction, requiring, amongst other things, the public burning of all surviving feudal documents. In some respects the latter decree was ideological on the part of the Jacobins, though arguably it was also a logical continuation of the process begun in 1789. But since it had been almost impossible to enforce the remaining feudal payments, and since the Jacobins wanted to ensure peasant loyalty, given the problems of war and civil war, the decree can also be seen to have been prompted equally by pragmatism.

The National Assembly's decree of 2 November 1789 put all Church land 'at the disposal of the nation'. Following this decree large tracts of Church land were sold off as *biens nationaux* (literally 'national goods'). But the people who purchased the land were often wealthy urban bourgeois; in a few instances they were even middle men acting for *émigré* nobles. Such purchases essentially consolidated the existing agrarian structure of France and while some wealthy peasants were able to extend their holdings, the overwhelming majority could not afford land when it came on the market. Many peasants became resentful.

The peasantry had no qualms about the sequestration of Church land but when, in the west especially, their parish priests opposed the nationalisation of the clergy and refused to take the oath of allegiance to the State, peasant parishioners regularly stood by their old priest. Such peasants continued their loyalty to their priests and to their religion when de-Christianisation reached its peak in the winter of 1793-4. During their brief existence in 1793 and 1794 the *Armées Révolutionnaires* (People's Armies), units of citizen-soldiers recruited from among loyal, urban *sans-culottes* to ensure food supplies for the towns and cities, became notorious for bringing the campaign against religion into rural districts at bayonet point. The behaviour of these *Armées* reinforced the peasant's hostility to townsmen; and it did nothing to wean him away from the Church.

The requisitions of grain made by the *Armées Révolutionnaires* were but one of the demands which the revolutionary government made of the peasantry to meet the crises provoked by war and by food shortages resulting from bad harvests and a breakdown of the traditional system of supply. The war needed money, provisions, draught animals and, above all, young men for the army. It was the demand for conscripts which provoked the insurrection in the west in the spring of 1793.

Parts of Brittany and La Vendée were seething with discontent over the Revolution's hostile attitude to religion and because so few peasants had found themselves able to purchase former Church land when the authorities sold it off as *biens nationaux* in 1791. This discontent was coloured by the peasant's traditional dislike of the townsman; the latter always seemed to be profiting at the peasant's expense in the rural textile industry and now in the purchase of Church land. The townsmen in the west seemed generally more sympathetic to the Revolution, and when the urban-based local authorities sought to implement new recruiting legislation in February and March 1793, the situation exploded. In Brittany these insurrections took the name *Chouannerie,* and the form of guerrilla warfare. The *Chouans* controlled most of rural Brittany from the summer of 1794, until a significant army of *bleus* (the pejorative name given to the revolutionary troops because of their blue tunics) was deployed against them in the spring of 1796. But still conflict here spluttered on into the new century. South of Brittany, in La Vendée, the insurrection became full-scale war waged from March until December 1793, with the utmost savagery on both sides. To combat the insurrection the government in Paris was compelled to withdraw troops from Germany, and the organisation and discipline of trained soldiers began to tell over the peasants of the Vendéan army. The Vendéans were finally defeated shortly before Christmas 1793. However, this did not mean an end to the fighting. Guerrilla warfare continued and in the early months of 1794 columns of republican troops raged through La Vendée killing and destroying virtually at will. It has been estimated that nearly 15 per cent of the population of La Vendée died or was killed during the period of the war and perhaps 20 per cent of the dwellings were destroyed or rendered uninhabitable. Yet in spite of, and perhaps because of this, the Vendéans continued to resist.

The cruel, brutal war in La Vendée was the most dramatic manifestation of rural opposition to the demands of the Revolution on rural France. But the peasants did not necessarily have to look to Paris for their enemies: local enemies were more tangible and more traditional than the politicians in Paris. In this respect the Revolution perpetuated traditional hostilities between town and country under new political slogans. If the Vendéan war was the most dramatic manifestation, perhaps one of the most striking examples of long-standing traditional enmities taking new labels during the Revolution is to be found in the south, in the Vivarais region. Here the hostilities between town and country had a religious dimension: the peasants remained staunchly Catholic and hostile to the Revolution; the townsmen, loyal to the Revolution, were largely Protestant. In other areas squalid, small-town or village feuds assumed a more elevated level with the injection of revolutionary politics, and outsiders could be enlisted to assist in the struggle for dominance. Thus in the spring of 1794 troops from the Parisian *Armée Révolutionnaire* were ordered into the small town of Villeblevin near Sens to deal with counter-revolutionary fanaticism, unaware that they had been drawn into a long-standing feud between two factions, one led by the former *curé* and the other by a shoemaker who had now become a militant *sans-culotte.*

While the Revolution did not happen just in Paris, in the long run it confirmed and increased that city's dominance in national life. In rural France the Revolution largely confirmed the existing structure of agricultural exploitation; but it also freed the peasantry from the remaining burdens of feudalism and the interference of the *seigneur* or his representative. Through the administrative reforms enabling elections for, and participation in, local government, the Revolution also gave men in the provinces a taste of political rights and liberty. Often in the provinces revolutionary rhetoric was superimposed on traditional divisions and rivalries, yet this did not make the revolutionary language, and action, any less real or any less significant. Moreover the Revolution added another long-lasting layer to traditional rivalries. In Brittany, for example, at the time of the Popular Front during the 1930s political opponents were denouncing each other in language derived from the Revolution – *Chouans* on one side, *bleus* on the other.

Essay 2

IDEAS OF GOVERNMENT IN THE EARLY PHASE OF THE REVOLUTION

Noël Parker
Senior Counsellor
The Open University

In this essay we will look more closely at the political thinking behind the struggles that took place during the years 1787-91. The central issue that arose in the Revolution was the question of who had the best right to govern and how they ought to exercise that right. Most of the positions that we find expressed today on this issue were stated, or tried out, during this period of French history: from traditionalist royalism, through highly participative democracy, to rule by the military. The Revolution was a forge for a great many of our modern political ideas and practices.

The range of views in contention will already be evident from the divergence between different *Cahiers* described in Chapter 1 (pp.21-3). There were those who thought it proper merely to make humble suggestions for the monarch, with all his wisdom and justice, to take up. At the other extreme were those who thought everyone belonged on equal terms to the nation as a whole, a body which alone was entitled to come together and tell the King how to arrange public affairs, regardless of his private preferences. In due course this latter, more radical view took over, when kingly government was set aside altogether in late 1792 and a Republic officially founded. In this essay we will concentrate on the views of government espoused up to and including the completion of the constitutional monarchy in 1791.

It would be quite wrong to suppose that the issue in this period was a simple controversy between republicanism and old-fashioned monarchical government. Many other shades of opinion were expressed: those, for example, advocating reformist changes which would leave the monarchical set-up intact. Indeed, many of these would have claimed to be 'republican' in the sense given it at the time. For it merely meant a policy or form of government devoted to the public good. But who was entitled to decide what this public good was, and to carry it out?

Reformist ideas within the King's government

What one might call the established, official view of the monarchy was that the King had been granted, from God himself, an exclusive and unchallengeable right to power. The following baldly stated public pronouncements from Louis XV were quite usual:

> 'We hold our crown from God alone. The right to make laws, by which our subjects must be led and governed belongs to us alone, neither subject to others or shared with them....
>
> The whole of the public realm emanates from me, and the rights and interests of the nation are necessarily one with mine, and repose in my hands alone.'

Although such an uninhibited absolutist claim may suggest wilful conservatism in government, in fact the monarchy had often been a force for reform – in the second half of the eighteenth century more so than ever. The monarchy, like sections of the nobility, took on board enlightened ideas about the rational organisation of government and society. In 1779, for example, Louis XVI tried to take a lead in abolishing serfdom. And, when he had ascended the throne in 1774, Louis had appointed as controller-general of finances an Enlightenment thinker, Turgot, who then spent two years attempting to suppress tax privileges and restraints on trade. Turgot was only the first in a long line of ministers who held office as part of Louis's intermittent attempts to reform his government and its finances.

Reforms in the tax system were much needed from the government's point of view of course, simply to raise more money. But increasingly, such proposals were defended on the grounds that they were 'rational' improvements for 'the good of the country' as a whole. This is the language with which modern governments will defend – or disguise – their policies.

Let us look at how one of the royal servants proclaimed the view that the monarchy was a fit institution to act in the public interest. The King's controller of finances in 1786, Calonne, grappling with yet another crisis in the budget, (see Chapter 1, p.19) defended his proposals for reform in these terms:

> 'The disparity, the disaccord, the incoherence of the different parts of the body of the monarchy is the principal of the constitutional vices which enervate its strength and hamper all its organisation... the result is that general administration is excessively complicated, public contributions [i.e. taxes] unequally spread, trade hindered by countless restrictions, circulation [of goods] obstructed in all its branches, agriculture crushed by overwhelming burdens, the state's finances impoverished by excessive costs of recovery and by variations in their product. Finally, I shall prove that so many abuses, so visible to all eyes and so justly censured, have only till now resisted a public opinion which condemns them because nobody has attempted to extirpate their germ and to dry up the source of all obstacles by establishing a more uniform order.'

Implicit in this preamble are a number of claims about the proper authority of the monarchy, and its role. It appears, for example, that the interests of the monarch are very close to those of the country as a whole (just as Louis XV had claimed). The basis for this consensus is: shared interest in a prosperous economy (which will produce good tax revenues); an assumed preference for smoothly functioning, efficient systems over cumbersome ones; acceptance of necessary burdens, provided they are justly – that it to say, equally – distributed. One could say that Calonne was making a pitch for responsible people of good sense out there in society at large, the 'public opinion' to which he refers. Yet this entails a *major* amendment to the established view of the proper behaviour and the rights of the monarchy, as expressed by Louis XV. According to Calonne's vision, the King may still receive the right to rule from God Almighty, but to succeed he has to exercise power with due regard to the rational interests of the country as a whole. And, in doing so, he can appeal for support to a politically sensible public. Even if the King is never to be subject to re-election, there is something strikingly modern about this style of argument in favour of government policy.

Unfortunately for Calonne and his like, this kind of appeal to common sense was not received without opposition. As is often the case, statements advancing broad, rational principles with apparently universal benefits met with resistance as soon as it became clear that interests were at stake in the reforms. Calonne was faced by an aristocratic, ecclesiastical and legal establishment which regarded financially advantageous privileges as entirely normal pieces of property. For them, the concept of equally shared tax burdens was far from obvious good sense, and they put up forceful opposition to his plans. Moreover, he was employed by a monarch who, right to the end of his life on the scaffold, never made the very difficult choice for a hereditary monarch of whether to rely for support on the traditional privileged hierarchy to which he himself belonged, or to make a determined bid for the support of this new 'public'. After only a year, Calonne went the way of various other reformers in the royal administration: he was dismissed.

The traditional centres of authority

The claim that the monarch alone could represent the nation did not go unchallenged. Other sectors of society claimed to be essential to the constitution and the needs of the nation too.

As the Estates-General elections got under way in 1789 the senior nobility for example, viewed with alarm the changes being proposed in the Estates' procedures and make-up. Defending their political privileges in a warning to the King, they took the view that they were every bit as traditional and essential to stable government as the King himself. 'Supposedly sacred institutions,' they observed, 'are being put into question, or even decried as unjust.' Yet, without them, the 'constitution' would be 'corrupted and vacillating' and the 'nation... divided... weak and unhappy.' They were not opposed to fiscal reform. But they expressed the view, which was a corner-stone of the *ancien régime,* that 'the nation' consisted of distinct, well-established ranks, each with its own particular role and attendant privileges. Tinker with that, they suggested, and all authority may evaporate.

You will recall from the account given in Chapter 1 (pp.19-20) how in 1787 the King was induced to banish the *parlement* of Paris to Troyes. It did not work. The *parlement* was soon recalled, to public rejoicing – even though it was run exclusively by nobles. For, along with *parlements* in other provincial cities, the *parlement* of Paris was able, in the words of a contemporary noble, 'to constitute itself, on the model of the English Parliament, as the representative of the nation'.

In some ways, the *parlements* had a better claim to speak for their communities than the King or the senior aristocracy. They were long established: many dated back to the Middle Ages. Each was closely involved in the regulation of private and commercial life in its area, with considerable expertise in local law. Not infrequently they could pose as the defenders of legality and the life-style of ordinary people against the impositions of the King's officers. Compared to the monarch in Versailles, then, the *parlements* had tradition and roots in the community on their side.

It was on the basis of these strengths that the *parlement* of Paris threw down the gauntlet before the King in 1788. Invoking an alleged 'constitutional principle of the French monarchy' that taxes could only be levied where the taxpayers agreed, they spoke for the people in opposition to the latest fiscal proposals from the King's government. They then indicated – with due show of respect – that they would not levy 'illegal taxes'.

The case for tradition

There were really two kinds of argument available to the defenders of the traditional centres of power. First, there was the inherent value of tradition: to guarantee political stability. Second, there was the claim that liberty could best be preserved if political power was developed through a number of autonomous, traditional groups and institutions.

Even though, in the Revolution, traditions were soon being discounted, counter-revolutionary opponents continued to defend them from abroad, and rebels in the civil war fought in the provinces to reinstitute them. The period's most influential defence of tradition, the *Reflections on the Revolution in France* (1790), came from Edmund Burke, an Irish member of the British Parliament. This is still a classic of political thinking, and those who think that the modern world rejects tradition should note how contemporary arguments for the British monarchy and House of Lords rely upon it still. In a sense, indeed, tradition triumphed over the Revolution, for in 1815 the victorious European powers restored traditional monarchy and aristocracy in France.

The preference for devolved power – 'pluralism' as it is sometimes called – has fared even better. It was classically stated by Montesquieu, not only a crucial Enlightenment thinker but also at one time president of the *parlement* of Bordeaux, in his *Spirit of the Laws* (1748):

> 'Democracy and aristocracy are not free by their very nature.
> Political liberty is only found in limited governments.... To avoid the
> abuse of power, one power must limit another.'

Montesquieu initiated the study of how political institutions relate to the particular conditions of the nation and to each other. An admirer of the contemporary British political set-up, he advocated independent institutions, balanced against one another and operating within a framework of established laws, as a strategy to preserve freedom. This attitude was implicitly invoked by defenders of the political rights of the nobility and of the *parlements*. In due course, it made its appearance, too, in defence of the position of the King himself.

Monarchists in the National Assembly

When the National Assembly set about drawing up a new, written constitution in late 1789, some members looked for a model to the contemporary British constitution, where an assembly elected by the better-off enacted laws and was

116

asked to approve a government which the King appointed from amongst its members. In Britain, they thought, balance was ensured, and those who were responsible politically maintained the upper hand. This point of view was represented by the comte de Mirabeau, a uniquely forceful speaker, and by Pierre Malouet, with his 'Monarchical Club'. If such a balance was to be achieved in France, the monarchy would have to be given a crucial role.

Figure 23 The comte de Mirabeau, a leading orator in the Assembly, who was also in touch with the Court. *(Photo Bulloz)*

It was Mirabeau who best defended the status of the monarchy in crucial constitutional debates, and secretly urged the King to put himself forward as the friend and defender of the people. It is thus possible that Mirabeau's early death in 1791 changed the entire direction of the Revolution. In his view the monarchy ought to hold the ring, on behalf of stability and the voiceless mass of the people, between contending parties in the political process. This is a strategy, we may note, not unlike the populist appeals to the people made by modern presidents, as different as General de Gaulle and Ronald Reagan. But, in arguing in September 1789 that the King should be left a power of veto over new legislation, Mirabeau leaned heavily on the notion (which is found in Montesquieu) that there had to be checks and balances if freedom was to be maintained:

> 'The larger a nation is, the more it is vital that [the executive] is active; hence the necessity for a single and supreme head, for monarchical government in big nations.... It is striking that the executive power, exercised constantly over the people, is in a more

direct relationship with them; and that, given the task of maintaining equilibrium... it matters to those very people that [the executive]should always possess sure means to maintain itself.'

Radical claims for the Third Estate

So far, we have looked at claims made on behalf of the King or of established centres of authority, to govern – either alone or in some combination – in the interest of the nation as a whole. Yet, even in the late 1780s there was a strand of thinking fundamentally at odds with that view. According to this radical way of looking at the matter, the nation was not to be found in any combination of the old institutions or status groups. Obscured behind all those special interests was the true nation: a union of loyal, right-minded citizens which was perfectly capable of coming together in its own name to manage its own public affairs. Sketched out in theory by Enlightenment thinkers, in particular in Rousseau's *Social Contract* (1762), it was in the French Revolution that this conception took the stage politically.

The idea of the active, unitary nation came to dominate revolutionary politics by the time of the Jacobin Republic of the early 1790s. Yet it can be plainly seen already in the disputes around the election of the Estates-General. The members of the Third were, at least in principle, drawn from the people as a whole, rather than from the old privileged interests. In the context of the meeting of the Estates, then, the radical strand of thinking elevated the role of the Third Estate, demanding that the Third's vote should outweigh that of the other two orders. Claims for the right of the Third Estate to speak for the nation were different in kind, though, from claims from the traditional centres of power.

The most important statement of these claims came from the Abbé Sieyès (pronounced 'See-ez'), clerical administrator for the diocese of Chartres, who himself became a member of the Third Estate and an influential constitution writer in the National Assembly. Sieyès was rather like the Houdini of the Revolution. When asked what he did during the Terror that carried off so many of his colleagues, he is supposed to have said laconically: 'I lived'. Indeed, he did. He emerged again in 1799, after some years of obscurity, to share power and write the first of Napoleon's constitutions.

In a pamphlet called *What is the Third Estate?* (1789) Sieyès put forward his claim that the Third should have the exclusive right to resolve the crisis in the name of the public interest.

> 'In any free nation, and every nation must be free, there is only one way to end disputes about the constitution. It is not to the *notables* that we should turn, but to the nation itself. If we are without a constitution, we must create one: *only the nation has the right to do that.*'

In answer to his question 'What is the Third Estate?', Sieyès says that it is, in principle, 'the whole'. For, whereas the noble order is not acting for ordinary people, the Third Estate contains all those who truly belong to the nation. Yet, he asks, 'What has it been up to now in the political order? Nothing.'

There are three interesting and important aspects of the way that Sieyès supports his case on behalf of the Third Estate. First, he maintains that the political order must be settled by reference not to history and tradition, but solely to reason:

'the Revolution that is taking place bears no resemblance to any other... because it has as its first and true cause the progress of reason.'

Secondly, Sieyès sketches out the way in which the nation – any nation – can form, or *re*-form itself, ignoring its history and its different ranks. A nation is made up of a number of individuals who wish to be united, he asserts. Together they recognise that they have a common, or 'public' interest. They then appoint some from amongst their own number to look after the public interest, on behalf of the group as a whole. The last stage in this account of the construction of a nation suggested, in apparently abstract terms, a particular view of the formation of the Third Estate: individuals with nothing but a will to belong together electing some of their number to act on behalf of the whole nation. It gives a quite special status to the elected representatives of the unprivileged majority.

Figure 24 Abbé Sieyès, author of *What is the Third Estate? (Photo Bulloz)*

Thirdly, for the stage when the nation appoints representatives to govern, Sieyès lays great emphasis on the role of a constitution, which was to be the central concern of the National Assembly, and of its successor assemblies up until the mid-1790s.

> 'It is impossible to create a body for a given end, without according it an organisation, forms and laws such as to ensure that it fulfils the functions that it was conceived for.'

The constitution would enshrine the fundamental laws to regularise the actions of the government that the nation intended to act on its behalf.

This view of the intimate link binding the nation and the Estate drawn from the common people gave a powerful rejoinder to the claims of the rival institutions. For, according to this argument, the right to rule can only be derived from the body of the nation as a whole, and expressed by an elective assembly which represents it. The claims of God-given right, tradition, particular skills or an ingeniously balanced mechanism can only be subsidiary to the expressed will of the nation. This is a sea change in the nature of politics. Sieyès' radical claim in *What is the Third Estate?* that 'The nation exists before everything, it is the origin of everything' brings to the political arena a characteristically modern view of the State: the nation, which is a union of all citizens, can and must rule itself.

The Third Estate went on to capture the political initiative precisely by pursuing this claim to represent the nation. On 17 June 1789, at Sieyès' own suggestion, it decided that, given that it represented the vast majority of the nation, it should be renamed the 'National Assembly' and take on the job of national renewal, inviting the other orders to join it. In spite of the role it implies for the monarchy, this new spirit also imbued the Tennis Court Oath of 20 June 1789:

> 'We swear not to leave the National Assembly, and to meet wherever circumstances require it, until the constitution of the kingdom is established and settled on sound foundations.'

Liberties, laws, a constitution

The constitution agreed between King and Assembly in 1791 was a compromise between the various strands of thought that we have been looking at – adapted to suit the more or less undisguised interests of the better off. It set down in formal, coherent and (it was hoped) permanent terms, the underlying principles and organisation of the French State.

Before we consider its provisions, it is worth noting the significance of *writing* and *agreeing* a constitution in the first place. With the notable exception of the United States of America, it was almost unheard-of for a State, through its elected representatives, to draw up and acknowledge the terms of its own existence as a nation. This in itself was a major success for the radical view of the political crisis, and placed revolutionary France in the first rank of those many modern states who have since adopted written constitutions. The order of presentation of the constitution also represented a victory for the radical view.

At the head of the constitution, preceding even the definition of the French State, there was a Declaration of the Rights of Man and of the Citizen. This stipulated that all men are born free and equal, and guaranteed freedom from arbitrary arrest, unnecessary legal restrictions, taxation without due agreement by representatives, and interference with free speech or property. Many of us today would want to vary this list of fundamental rights – particularly its overriding emphasis on the right of property. But the point, again, is that the powers of the State were delimited by this declaration, and made subservient, in principle, to the interests of the individuals making up the nation. This is very much a constitution such as might be drawn up by a body of individuals coming together to form a nation, in the manner described by Sieyès.

The human rights of the citizens having been firmly stated, the constitution began in earnest with a radical definition of the State. 'Sovereignty,' it declared, 'is single, indivisible, inalienable and imprescriptible.' That is to say, the right to rule cannot be surrendered or contracted to someone else. What is more: 'It belongs to the nation, no section of the people, or any individual can claim the exercise of it.' Thus, ostensibly, the founding principles of the constitution are all borrowed from the radical view: they are derived from the rights of individuals, uniting together under the law to preserve their freedom.

The constitution then went on to stipulate that all are citizens, with full rights and equality before the law, a principle profoundly at odds with primacy of rank under the *ancien régime*. True, the small print somewhat undermined this impressive provision. A motion to include women, moved by Robespierre, had been rejected with vigour. And, at Sieyès' suggestion, those without a substantial income were defined as merely 'passive' citizens – that is, lacking the right to vote or stand for public office. None the less, in its historical context, citizenship is a remarkable innovation. It entrenched, for example, the abolition of 'feudal' rights over the persons of others. These, along with other 'seigneurial' dues, had first been declared illegal on the dramatic night of 4 August 1789 (though, again, the 'abolition' had been somewhat qualified thereafter, since it had been decided that many of those seigneurial rights, being property, would have to be bought out). The constitution also guaranteed to citizens a right to assemble and to petition the representative assembly. These rights, in themselves crucial to modern states, were greatly to impinge on the practice of politics in France in the subsequent years.

Only after it had determined the role and the rights of the citizens did the constitution go on to define the powers of the State: the National Assembly first, and finally the King. The Assembly, subject to re-election every two years, had supreme powers to legislate and to vote in taxes. The King had the task of enforcing such laws as the Assembly voted in (though he could delay doing so), via ministers he alone appointed. He could maintain a limited military force for his own protection or for the defence of the realm, but could neither declare war nor agree to a peace. Thus, his administration and his forces were subject to the law, and hence to the Assembly. In principle, the King had been reduced to an agent of the nation, as represented by the elected Legislative Assembly.

> 'In France, there is no authority above the law. The king rules only via the law, and can only demand obedience in its name.'
>
> Constitution, 1791

Yet the King's government could in practice enjoy considerable political freedom to act on behalf of the nation.

Even if it was not to survive for long, the constitution of 1791 gives us a snapshot of the ideas of government that had surfaced in the Revolution. The source of the right to govern had shifted fundamentally: from the will of God to that of the nation, expressing the public good through its own representative assembly. The status of the subject had been transformed to that of citizen. The mechanisms of government had been defined, for the first time, via the idea of law, and in terms of this new conception of the nature of the State.

Essay 3

IMAGES OF REVOLUTION

Lucille Kekewich and Noël Parker
The Open University

'The arts... are the imitation of nature in its most beautiful and its most perfect aspects; a sentiment natural to man attracts him towards the same object. It is not only by charming the eyes that the monuments of art have fulfilled this end; it is by penetrating the soul, it is by making on the mind a profound impression, similar to reality. It is thus that the traits of heroism, and of civic virtues offered to the regard of the people will electrify its soul and will cause to germinate in it, all the passions of glory, of devotion to the welfare of the fatherland.'

David to the Convention, 15 November 1793

The painter Jacques-Louis David, through his outstanding talent and unreserved commitment to the Revolution, played an important part in shaping its image in the period 1789-94. The arts, and their application in festivals and theatrical performances, had traditionally changed very slowly and had largely been dominated by conservative authorities such as the Church and the Royal Academy. This essay seeks to show how two kinds of imagery, pictures and festivals, were adapted during the Revolution to serve its changing needs, as they were defined by those in power. Art increasingly became an area of conflict, especially after the fall of the monarchy and the acceleration of de-Christianisation. It must also be recognised, however, that the authorities never exercised total control. Plenty of crucifixes and holy pictures remained on the walls of houses and even churches throughout. Traditional local festivals recalling victories over the Saracens or celebrating the grape harvest continued to be celebrated. Official and unofficial ceremonies continued to take place, arranged by both conservative and radical elements in society.

I Reaction against the art of the *ancien régime*

The reaction of European critical taste against the frivolities and indecencies of eighteenth-century court painters (as exemplified in Figure 25), pre-dated the Revolution by several decades. A revival of interest in the monuments of Greece and Rome and some knowledge of their paintings had been promoted by the excavations of Pompeii and Herculaneum in Italy. A preference for simpler styles of dress for both sexes and increased concern for personal hygiene was encouraged by the growing availability of relatively cheap cotton fabrics from America. The writings of Rousseau, which stressed the proper supremacy of the

General Will, would have been vehemently rejected by the English upper classes if they had bothered to read them. The eighteenth-century vogue for Nature, however, encouraged them to be painted wearing plain, harmonious clothes in rural settings surrounded by devoted animals and complacent children.

Figure 25 Boucher, *The Toilet (1742).* An example of the sensuous art of the *ancien régime. (Thyssen-Bornemisza Lugano/Switzerland)*

In France the coincidence of the cult of Nature, the rejection of the values of the *ancien régime* and the taste for antiquity produced a great enthusiasm for the neo-classical style most distinctively exemplified in the work of Jacques-Louis David. His formidable talent was combined with a commitment to the Revolution which did not waver until he was imprisoned after *Thermidor* 1794. His mastery of his art and strongly held views about how it should serve the Republic forged a powerful propaganda weapon. It has also left posterity with images such as the *Oath of the Tennis Court* (Figure 27, p.126) and *Marie-Antoinette on her way to execution* which have informed and, to some extent, conditioned our view of the Revolution. Classical times were revered by the radicals as they were uncontaminated by the monarchical and ecclesiastical dominance of the Middle Ages. The democracy of Greece and the republicanism of pre-Imperial Rome, and the noble histories and legends associated with them provided a kind of golden age which set the standard to which contemporary France could aspire. The reputed austerity of life-style and single-minded devotion to the public good, particularly that associated with Sparta, was very appealing. Not only were the designs for festivals and the subjects and style of paintings full of classical imagery and references: the speeches of revolutionary leaders from Mirabeau to Robespierre were too.

II The politics of imagery

Marianne and Hercules

We will now consider some specific examples of how visual images were used, by those who tried to form opinion during the Revolution, to introduce a new set of values. Large expensive paintings, such as the National Assembly's commission to David to commemorate the Oath of the Tennis Court, were beyond the means of most of the population. Even more intimate works like Boucher's *The Toilet* (Figure 25) could only be purchased by a tiny majority. Apart from the nobility and prosperous bourgeoisie, the experience of most people who lived away from Paris or the other cities would be confined to paintings in churches and prints and engravings. Almost as soon as printing was invented the Church had exploited the possibilities of circulating religious pictures on paper to the laity. For the first time ordinary people could possess their own portraits of Christ, the Virgin and the saints. Some of these were produced separately and were intended to be placed on walls, others appeared in books. European monarchs quickly realised the advantages of circulating images (usually rather flattering) of themselves and their families to promote loyalty amongst their subjects. The ecclesiastical and lay authorities, however, never enjoyed a monopoly of this invaluable propaganda device. The controversies over religion in the sixteenth and seventeenth centuries led to a lively underground commerce in illustrated pamphlets and broadsheets. The principal purpose of the pictures was to make opponents seem evil or ridiculous, or both. Many were scurrilous. National governments and even the Catholic and Protestant Churches could not afford to ignore these potent attacks and they too employed pamphleteers and cartoonists to defend them and to denigrate their adversaries.

The artists who produced prints for popular consumption were able to respond readily to the needs of the Revolution, for they already had a tradition of adapting promptly to changing political circumstances. They had two principal tasks. One was to continue the traditional supply of cartoons and caricatures with which unacceptable policies and unpopular personalities had always been lampooned. The cartoon of the three Estates (Figure 2, p.7) is a good example of this type of work. No alteration of style was required although the underlying assumptions were transformed. The common people who, if they figured at all in such pictures under the *ancien régime* were portrayed as stupid and brutish, now assumed a certain strength and purpose. The other task of the print makers was to substitute new symbols of national authority and virtue for the old icons of Church and State.

The figure of Liberty, a beautiful young woman in classical garb, often wearing a cap of liberty (a classical phrygian-style cap) and popularly named 'Marianne', fulfilled this function admirably. The *ancien régime* had been intensely patriarchal: the Church was dominated by the Pope, cardinals, bishops and priests; government was directed by the King, the nobility and male civil servants. Women were traditionally revered as mothers, comforters, sustainers and peace-makers. The Catholic Church accorded these attributes to the female saints, and particularly to the Virgin Mary. Marianne became, therefore, not only a symbol of a regenerated political system, but also of national unity. By cultivating the feminine virtues, all the groups in society could be reconciled and sink their differences in harmonious agreement to pursue the common good irrespective of personal interests: Marianne took her place on the seal of the Republic and ousted Louis XVI from the coinage. Yet during the emergency of 1792-4 she was too pacific a figure, even when she carried a pike, to embody all the national aspirations. Some women had even taken her political role too literally and were agitating for some measure of emancipation for their sex!

Figure 26 *The People, Destroyer of Kings.* This contemporary engraving shows a *sans-culotte* in the traditional pose of the classical hero Hercules. *(Cliché: Musées de la Ville de Paris, © by SPADEM 1989)*

Hercules was a traditional symbol of the French nation, and had appeared in public festivals and in court art for several centuries. As Lynn Hunt (1984) says, he 'recaptured and rehabilitated a distinctly virile representation of sovereignty, a concept that had connotations of domination and supremacy'. Other advantages of the figure were that he was of respectable classical status yet not burdened with too princely a character. He could also be adapted easily into a rumbustious figure of a *sans-culotte*. Figure 26 shows a male figure, half naked, muscular and carrying a club, all signs that we are seeing a representation of Hercules. Yet his cap of liberty, rolled up trousers and moustache identify him as a man of the people, an image with which the *sans-culottes* could proudly identify. Hunt believes, however, that this blatant recognition of the power of the people was too threatening to governmental authority, even for the Jacobins. Before *Thermidor* 1794, more conventional classical models were being substituted, and under the Directory the representations of both Marianne and Hercules were used to reinforce ideals of order and stability rather than insurrection and change. They were joined by pictures of soldiers and generals as the government increasingly sought to divert popular patriotic fervour towards the war in Europe and away from the unsatisfactory situation in France.

Civic virtue

The style of popular prints could only reflect spasmodically the predominant taste in educated circles for neo-classicism. Despite the apparent destruction of the old élite, the taste for high art continued to encourage David and his followers. Some of the factors which had enabled the patronage of painting to flourish under the *ancien régime* changed and led to a decline. The Court and the majority of the nobility were in no position to commission works of art, and the revolutionary governments could hardly fill the vacuum. On the other hand, a number of painters, especially those of low status, welcomed the chance to challenge the rigid control the Academy had exercised over style and subjects. David was reasonably successful by 1789, but he had been irked by the Academy's stultifying influence and, together with some other radical artists, he founded the 'Popular and Republican Society of the Arts'. It petitioned the Assembly to withdraw the privileges of the Academy and to encourage commissions for the production of paintings which portrayed civic virtue to instruct the public. By 1794 David exercised supreme power in the art world, dominating a 'Commune', a national jury of artists which awarded prizes annually, a conservatory which supervised teaching and a 'Commission' which granted honours and co-ordinated policy on art. Cynics might claim that painters had gained little freedom in the transfer from the predominant values of the *ancien régime* to those of the Jacobin Republic.

Within the range of what was considered acceptable art after 1789, some scope for individual initiative was allowed. Quatremère de Quincy for example, a critic and designer, was a moderate member of the Legislative Assembly. He sat on the Committee of Public Instruction with David and was responsible for the refurbishment and secularisation of the *Panthéon* to receive the remains of heroes of the nation. More controversially he organised a festival in honour of the bourgeois mayor of Étampes who had been murdered by a mob. That event showed how the prosperous and stable bourgeoisie could appreciate the uses of artistic propaganda as well as the revolutionary leaders. On the other hand, some artists were even more radical than David; two ended up on trial for a republican conspiracy during the rule of Napoleon.

Figure 27 David, *The Oath of the Tennis Court*, 20 June 1789. This cartoon or large sketch was mostly drawn in 1791 to celebrate the beginning of the Revolution. Bailly stands on the table administering the oath; Mirabeau, to the far right, strikes a dramatic pose; Barère sits, legs crossed, taking notes; Robespierre stands looking upwards with both hands on his chest. *(Versailles. Lauros-Giraudon)*

David's great design for the *Oath of the Tennis Court* (Figure 27) can furnish an example of a painting produced for a political purpose at a stage when the Revolution was still embracing a constitutional monarchy. Despite this, no symbols of kingship clearly appear in the picture. Neither is it obviously classical. Yet the uncompromising austerity of the setting, the sober dignity of the figures, their statuesque grouping and the noble sentiment informing the scene link it closely to David's great pictures of antiquity such as the *Brutus* (Figure 12, p.62)and the *Oath of the Horatii*. It should be noted that the figures he chose to portray prominently reflected the date of composition, between 1790 and 1791. Bailly would hardly have been shown administering the oath so heroically after the Massacre of the *Champ de Mars*, nor Mirabeau striking such a noble pose after the discovery of the incriminating contents of the iron cupboard. No clerics, even reformers, would have been tolerated in their cassocks and habits after the outbreak of civil war. Later Marat (shown scribbling his paper up against a wall by the window – he was not a deputy), Barère and Robespierre would surely have been given even greater importance in the composition.

One of the most vital functions of art during the Revolution was to provide new models for virtuous citizens. This was important because the civic responsibility, or virtue, of the citizens was essential if the Republic was to prosper. Brutus was all very well but he was a remote and rather severe figure. The violence of life in revolutionary Paris and the provinces affected by civil war was to keep the Republic regularly supplied with martyrs who could fulfil this function. For example, Lepeletier de Saint-Fargeau was a friend of Robespierre, a Jacobin ex-noble who had voted for the death of the King. He was fatally stabbed by an ex-member of the Royal Guard on the eve of the royal execution whilst dining at the *Palais Royal*. The painting David made of his dead body has not survived but the remaining sketches show that he managed to turn the classically draped figure of this very ugly man into an image of touching nobility. His funeral bier was the centre of a great procession. At one point deputies of the Convention filed past and kissed his brow.

The assassination of Marat the following July provided an even better opportunity for propaganda, as he was such a famous and controversial member of the Jacobins. The stark simplicity of David's picture of his dead body (Figure 17, p.81), still holding Corday's letter testifying to his benevolence towards those in trouble, makes an almost irresistible impact. Devoid of any specifically classical detail, except perhaps the turban and drapery on the bath, it is nevertheless pervaded by that style and spirit.

These actual pictures would only have been seen by a limited number of people. The Committee of Public Safety ensured that prints of the martyrdoms of revolutionary heroes should be widely circulated. In this manner three obscure people, a teenager killed by the royalists in La Vendée, a representative of the government with the army of the Pyrenees and a thuggish Jacobin mayor of Lyons, all entered popular mythology. Their pictures were circulated and displayed in official buildings, songs and poems were performed recounting their sacrifices, and streets and districts were named after them. As David said to the Convention on 15 November 1793 (see p.122), the intention was to arouse virtuous and patriotic sentiments in people or, putting it less politely, to influence them by government propaganda.

III Festivals

The legacy of the past

The change in values which increasingly stressed civic virtue above mere ornament and which was affecting art, also determined a change in the view of the purpose of festivals and how they should be celebrated. Many of the greatest public processions and ceremonies had traditionally been associated with the monarchy and the Church. An outstanding example is the coronation of Louis

XVI in 1774 at Rheims, where the largely medieval pageantry emphasised the divine origin of kingship. Festivals served the purposes of the Revolution uniquely well and carried with them the blessing of the philosophers. After attempting to demonstrate unity and harmony in earlier festivals, such as the Festival of Federation in 1790, the revolutionary government rejected the authorities which had survived from the *ancien régime* and the kind of rituals and images that had formerly accompanied their public demonstrations of power. Processions and celebrations commemorating saints or feasts of the Virgin were, after the Civil Constitution of the Clergy in 1790, condemned as archaic and superstitious practices. Once he had been forced to take up residence in Paris, the King only appeared in public at the will of the Legislative Assembly, participating in occasions that they had planned. Theatres had been condemned on ideological grounds by Diderot:

> 'a place in which social hierarchy and an intoxicating display of social stratification had reached their apogee. The theatre was a "dark little place" that Diderot judged incapable of "holding the attention of an entire nation".'

Ozouf, 1988

Rousseau reacted with pleasure to an outdoor festival he had witnessed and hoped that 'these patriotic celebrations, which accord with morality and virtue, which we enjoy with rapture and recall with delight, [will] be revived among us'.

There were several aspects of festivals that gave them this strong appeal. The first is implied by Diderot: outdoor events could be staged in practically limitless space, so both those who were actively participating in the festival and the spectators could be accommodated without any particular preference being given to the rich or powerful. The vogue for Nature lent ceremonies which took place out of doors a particular appeal. For example, after Marat was murdered, his body was exposed for the public to grieve over in a garden by the Cordeliers Club. Surrounded by rocks and trees the intention was to emphasise his simplicity and virtue and, perhaps, anticipate some republican paradise to which he had ascended.

Figure 28 A print showing the murdered Marat lying in state in a garden amid the purity of the natural world. *(Editions Pierre Horay)*

Another advantage of festivals, and this is clearly demonstrated in the illustrations of Marat 'lying in state' (Figure 28) and of the Parisian Festival of Federation (Figure 29), was that the public could, in some measure, participate as well as watch. They were actively encouraged to do this: weeping at funerals, cheering and throwing flowers for soldiers, oath-taking, even dancing and moderate feasting at patriotic banquets were part of the programmes designed by the authorities.

The 1790 Festival of Federation marked a transition from the traditional kind of military parade of the *ancien régime,* firmly dominated by Church and monarch, to the more romantic, emotional and spontaneous popular manifestations that characterised some revolutionary festivals. It was a genuine reaffirmation of national harmony and an acceptance of the new order. Divisive elements such as floats portraying the destruction of aristocratic enemies had been deliberately excluded. Religion had a role in the ceremonial and proved reassuring to moderates and conservatives. The values proclaimed in the oath, however, could engage the support of the reformers.

It is hard for us to realise today how potent a part was played by rituals and festivals in the life of ordinary people in early modern Europe. The poverty and monotony of life, the dependence on the changing seasons and the whims of the representatives of Church and State could, to some extent, be alleviated by means of ceremonies concentrating on powerful folk symbols such as the May tree. Sutherland gives an example of an ancient practice that became associated with revolutionary ideology. Long before 1789 there seem to have been elements in the May tree ceremonies that were pagan and anti-establishment (see also Figure 11, p.58):

> 'in the Dordogne... the folkloric element was prominent, although here it took the distinctive feature of planting what were called "May trees". These were trees planted in the village square decorated with flowers, laurel leaves, and blue, white and red ribbons and topped with a crown. They did not differ from the thousands of liberty trees which were springing up all over the country. But, like any powerful symbol, May trees had more ancient levels of meaning in the south-west. They certainly came to symbolize regeneration and deliverance and may have related to a customary belief that if they were kept standing for a year and a day, vassals would be free of seigneurial dues. They also symbolized the joy of spring and rebirth, and villages traditionally marched them throughout the countryside and planted them in the lord's courtyard. By suspending measures, small sacks of grain, chicken feathers or weather vanes (a sign of the lord's right to give justice) from them, the villages informed the lord symbolically that they considered his collection of dues abusive. Planting May trees, therefore, was a symbol of freedom and a provocation to the lords... villages blended traditional and new symbolism to express their aspirations to be rid of the seigneurial system entirely'.

> Sutherland,1985

We should remember that during this period the dividing line between performers and spectators in most kinds of performance was less clearly drawn than it is today. In theatres people talked to each other and even to the actors and frequently interrupted with applause or jeers. A higher proportion of the population, at all levels, was prepared to recite, tell stories, sing or play an instrument in public, since these activities were often their only form of entertainment. Large numbers of ordinary citizens, often grouped by age or sex (virtuous old men, for example, or pure young virgins) frequently took part in revolutionary festivals singing, dancing, declaiming or carrying symbolic objects, and there is no indication that most of them had any prior professional training.

There were also the traditions of popular activism such as feasts at harvest time and celebrations of past French victories which the revolutionary governments, and particularly the Jacobin Committees, could try to harness. Danger existed, however, in the deep-rooted and potentially violent nature of some such practices. There was no guarantee that anti-authoritarian displays could not be redirected by disgust at shortages, or by the skilful machinations of refractory priests against the new regime. This fear seems to have increased over the years as the capacity of the urban *sans-culottes* and disaffected rural peasantry to take political action was constantly reaffirmed. One possible device that could be adopted by the government was to exploit the long-standing popularity of holidays, merry-making and shows to its advantage and to organise festivals to celebrate great anniversaries in the history of the Revolution and proclaim allegiance to republican virtues. The considerable political importance of festivals as well as their changing nature in response to official requirements can be demonstrated by briefly considering some of the best known.

Figure 29 The Festival of Federation on the *Champ de Mars* in Paris, 14 July 1790. This huge public spectacle celebrated the first anniversary of the Fall of the Bastille. *(Bibliothèque Nationale, Paris)*

The Festival of Federation in Paris on the anniversary of the storming of the Bastille, 14 July 1790, was partly spontaneous, partly sponsored by the municipality. There seems to have been a movement from all over the country to send representatives of the National Guards and regular soldiers to the capital to swear their loyalty to the new constitution before the King. A strong religious element remained in the programme, a huge altar of the nation was raised in the *Champ de Mars*, a large area used for military exercises on the edge of Paris. At the same time as the oath was taken there, local festivals were celebrated all over the country. In many, priests officiated at outdoor altars surrounded by orderly ranks of guards and civilians. Other unofficial rejoicing, banquets and dancing were less dignified. The principal feature of the Parisian ceremony was its martial character. Five hundred women had offered to participate but they were rejected, although groups of children and old men were included. Apart from the deputies from the National Assembly no other civilians were allowed. As up to 300,000 guards and soldiers participated, it is not surprising that it took over two hours for the members of the huge procession to take up their positions. Desmoulins drily remarked: 'It was not by the procession that this festival surpassed those of antiquity, for curiosity soon tires of a procession.' The King, who arrived late, seemed rather bored by the proceedings and was upstaged by the, at the time, immensely popular La Fayette, commander of the Parisian National Guard.

Republican models

De-Christianisation policies attempted to turn deep-rooted habits of participation in religious festivals upside-down. The popular society at Tulle arranged a procession and the farandole was danced; a coffin was carried ornamented with donkeys' ears, a service book and a clerical hat as well as various stolen church ornaments. The most notorious anti-Christian demonstration was the Festival of Reason at the cathedral of Notre-Dame on 10 November 1793. This was arranged by the Commune and the journalist Hébert was one of the principal organisers. A temple on a small mountain was erected in the middle of the cathedral, adorned by two rows of young girls. An actress portraying Liberty emerged from the temple and sat on a throne. Whilst republican hymns were sung she received the homage of those present. The show was then taken to the Convention – where some deputies, including Robespierre, were not amused – and was repeated at Notre-Dame later in the day. Hunt (1984) considers this to have been a truly spontaneous production by the people of Paris. Nevertheless, as the journal *The Revolutions of Paris* commented, there was a serious ideological point to be made in the choice of a living woman to represent Liberty:

> 'One wanted from the first moment to break the habit of every species of idolatry; we avoided putting in the place of a holy sacrament an inanimate image of liberty because vulgar minds might have misunderstood and substituted in place of the god of bread a god of stone... and this living woman, despite all the charms that embellished her, could not be deified by the ignorant, as would a statue of stone'.

This festival served to confirm the fears of the Great Committees that the *sans-culotte* campaign of blasphemy and de-Christianisation had gone too far. A number of measures curbed their power, and the programme announced by Robespierre in March 1794 of government-organised festivals in honour of various republican virtues also represented a reaction. Official control of at least the large urban celebrations was reasserted, and deism rather than atheism was substituted as the prevailing inspiration. Robespierre, a few weeks after his initial announcement of the programme of festivals, fostered a project close to his heart, which emphasised the cult of the Supreme Being. This was the most spectacular and best recorded of these new carefully programmed, intensely moral festivals and it took place on 8 June 1794. Music was provided by the composer Gossec who had produced a hymn in honour of the Supreme Being. Groups from each of the Paris Sections were formed according to sex and age: young girls carried baskets of flowers, matrons roses, men oak branches, and deputies of the Convention had bouquets. An uplifting discourse on the growth of republican virtue was delivered by the president of the Convention, Robespierre, who then set light to a large statue of atheism. As it was consumed, it revealed the figure of wisdom. The participants then went in procession to the *Champ de Mars*, accompanied by a float which bore a statue of liberty and an oak tree with objects symbolising industry and agriculture. It was parked by an artificial mountain surmounted by a liberty tree. Near by, a statue of Hercules surmounted a column. He represented the might of the people, which was now confined again to the decorum of a graceful classical pose. The wild *sans-culotte* figure of the previous year had been tamed, just as anti-religious sentiment had been subdued by this national reaffirmation of the existence of the Supreme Being.

Figure 30 The Festival of the Supreme Being in Paris, 8 June 1794. This marked the high point of Robespierre's campaign to introduce natural religion to the French. *(Cliché: Musées de la Ville de Paris, © by SPADEM 1989)*

Festivals continued to feature as part of government policy after *Thermidor* 1794, but their celebration had lost the old enthusiasm and patriotic fervour. This was increasingly diverted to the purely military triumphs of the Republic's generals and, especially, of Bonaparte. As religious persecution diminished and the civil wars came to an end, many of the traditional religious feasts were tacitly tolerated. The Directory knew only too well how the power of popular feelings aroused for political purposes could, if unchecked, browbeat or overthrow governments. Purged of innovatory and radical contents, festivals were reduced in importance and given back to the people.

Essay 4

THE WAR AND THE REVOLUTION

Clive Emsley
Professor of History
The Open University

The Revolution began with an emphasis on the fraternity of mankind, but within three years of the Fall of the Bastille, France was plunged into a war in which she was to conquer vast areas of Europe and which was to continue, with the occasional truce and two brief respites, for 23 years. The early stages of the war prompted profound shifts of direction in the process of the Revolution: military defeat contributed significantly to the 'Second Revolution' of August 1792; the opportunities for confident and successful young soldiers produced Napoleon Bonaparte and many of his marshals. The aim of this essay is to give a brief chronological survey of the Revolution and the war, and to give an introduction to the inter-relationship between the two.

I The origins of the war

Although the French Revolution began on a note which was, at the same time pacific, humanitarian and internationalist, warning clouds were perceptible. The promise of liberty for all men inspired the political dissidents and reformers in other countries. Both this, and the first wave of emigration involving die-hard reactionaries like Louis XVI's brother, the comte d'Artois, unsettled European monarchs, princelings, and their governments. The *émigrés* found ready sympathisers in the nobles of western Germany, some of whom were directly affected by the abolition of feudalism by the National Assembly in August 1789, because they owned property in France. But the period from the summer of 1789 to the spring of 1792 was not one of steady, inexorable progress to war. There was no immediate united front among the monarchs of Europe to oppose the Revolution. They had no intention of going to war with France over the loss of some feudal rights in Alsace or the occupation of the Papal enclaves of Avignon and the Comtat Venaissin. Europe's monarchs remained wary of one another, and were more concerned with events in eastern Europe than those in France; indeed, in many respects, they saw the Revolution as working to their advantage in that it had dramatically reduced French power and influence. It was only in the summer of 1791 that the relations between France and the monarchs of Europe began to deteriorate seriously and dramatically.

The initial event in the deterioration of relations was the French royal family's abortive flight to Varennes in June 1791. The arrest of the royal family at Varennes prompted the Declaration of Pillnitz (27 August 1791) by the Emperor of Austria and the King of Prussia. The declaration, on the surface, appeared to threaten the Revolution with joint action by the two monarchs to restore order in France; but it made co-operation between the crowned heads of Europe a prerequisite for any action, and the Austrians, at least, thought that there was no chance of British co-operation. The Declaration of Pillnitz raised little comment in France, yet in the autumn of 1791 the Girondin faction in the Assembly began increasingly to advocate war as a solution to France's problems. The Girondins believed that the Revolution was only half accomplished. They were not happy with the new constitution and they were determined to prove the King's lack of sympathy for it; this led them to harry the King into using his veto. The Girondins made much of the supposed 'Austrian Committee' which existed at the Court, and exploited the unpopularity of the Austrian-born Marie-Antoinette; they also stressed the potential threat from the *émigrés* who were assembled at Coblentz, and they played upon every slight to France, real or imagined, which emanated from a foreign Court. 'War', declared Jacques-Pierre Brissot to the Assembly in December 1791:

> 'is necessary for France in every respect. It is necessary for her external security; for she will be thoroughly compromised, if we await peacefully by our hearths the iron and flame which threatens us.... It is necessary for her internal security, for the malcontents... are insolent only because Coblentz exists. This is the centre where all the relations of the fanatics and the privileged succeed; it is therefore Coblentz which must be sacked, if you wish to destroy both nobility and fanaticism. This war is necessary to re-establish our finances; for it is Coblentz which throws us into extraordinary expense, which absorbs the precious resources of our *assignats*. It is necessary to establish our public credit; for this credit values the opinion that strangers and citizens can have of the stability of our Revolution; and they cannot believe in this stability when twenty-five million men hesitate to punish a few rebels. Finally, it is necessary to put an end to terrors, treasons and anarchy, for there will not be any more terror if the home of counter-revolution is destroyed, and there will not be any more treasons if there no longer exists a place for them to lean on. I am not going to compare here our military forces with those of our open and secret enemies: we must, if we wish to stay free, ask, like the Spartans, where our enemies are and not how many they are.'

While the Girondins were the most vocal advocates of war, other factions were equally sympathetic to the idea. Some liberal noblemen like La Fayette and Narbonne believed that war would provide the opportunity for a revival of aristocratic leadership and silence extremists at both ends of the political spectrum. At the same time there were counter-revolutionary elements at Court, as the Girondins feared, who hoped that war would destroy the Revolution and restore the monarchy to its former power and glory.

The bombast of the Girondins in turn drove the Austrians and Prussians closer together and their alliance, again in turn, strengthened the advocates of war in France. On 20 April 1792 the French Assembly declared war on the Emperor of Austria (addressing him as 'the King of Hungary and Bohemia'). Significantly the declaration of war was couched in terms of a free, sovereign people, against a monarch.

Figure 31 Brissot, leader of the Girondin faction in the National Convention. *(Hulton-Deutsch Collection)*

II Reorganising for war

In the spring of 1792 the combatant powers on both sides expected a short war and an easy victory. The Girondins believed in their own rhetoric about the superiority of the French Revolutionary Army – an army of citizen-soldiers fighting for liberty. Unfortunately the French Army was anything but that when the war commenced. It had been severely weakened by the emigration of large numbers of its officers, and morale was low. Defeat followed defeat as the combined armies of Austrians, Prussians and *émigrés* pushed towards Paris. Suspicions about the French monarchy's loyalty to the nation increased, and these were aggravated by the publication of the Brunswick manifesto at the end of July 1792. The Duke of Brunswick, the commander of the allied armies, allowed an inflammatory declaration, drafted by an *émigré*, to be published over his signature. The document was designed to cow the population of Paris, threatening 'exemplary vengeance, forever memorable' on the city if any action was taken against Louis XVI and Marie-Antoinette. Its effect was precisely the opposite of that which was intended: rather than overawing, it encouraged the radicals in Paris, backed by the armed might of the *sans-culottes* and the provincial battalions which had hurried to the city's defence, to storm the Tuileries Palace and to suspend the monarchy on 10 August.

The new regime in Paris, drawing its inspiration from the powerful oratory of Georges Danton, began to organise France totally for war. On 2 September Danton instructed the Assembly:

> 'one part of the people will march to the frontiers, another will dig trenches, the third, with pikes if that's all we've got, will defend the towns. Commissioners will proclaim solemnly, an invitation to all citizens to arm themselves and to march for the defence of the

Country. The National Assembly will become a committee of war. We demand that you join with us to assist this sublime movement of the people. We demand that whoever refuses to serve in person or to give up any arms, be punished with death. The tocsin that we are going to sound is no alarm signal, it is the charge, the charge against the enemies of the Fatherland. To beat them citizens, we need daring, more daring, always daring, and France is saved.'

On the same day, apparently fearful of a potential fifth column in their midst, gangs of *sans-culottes* moved round the Paris prisons beginning the five days of slaughter known as the September Massacres.

The surge of patriotism, which brought volunteers from all over France to the army, and the participation of thousands of men and women in preparing defences and making clothes and equipment, was crowned with military success. On 20 September the French checked the Prussians at Valmy and forced them to withdraw. On 6 November the French defeated the Austrians at Jemappes and proceeded to occupy the Austrian Netherlands (Belgium). Success went to the Convention's head. On 16 November it decreed the Scheldt to be a free and open river, provoking the hostility of the United Provinces (The Netherlands) and her ally Great Britain. The same decree announced that 'the glory of the French Republic requires, that wherever the protection of her arms extends, liberty should be established, and tyranny overthrown.' The latter declaration was extended on 19 November, when the Convention promised 'fraternity and assistance to all people who wish to recover their liberty.' This decree prompted suspicion in London, as well as in other capitals. Convinced of the superiority in its armies and the rightness of its cause, the Convention proceeded to enforce the opening of the river Scheldt, which ran partly through the territory of the United Provinces. This action aggravated the worsening relations with Britain, a guarantor of Dutch sovereignty. The execution of Louis XVI on 21 January 1793 heightened the tension, but it did not provide the British government with a cause for war in the way that the occupation of Belgium and the threat to Holland did. However, in the event it was the National Convention which declared war on both Britain and the United Provinces on 1 February. The Convention believed that the United Provinces would be an easy conquest, and it was right; but it also believed, quite wrongly, that British radicals who had sent congratulatory addresses to the Convention in the preceding November, were prepared for insurrection. On 7 February the Convention completed its catalogue of enemies by declaring war on Spain.

Again the hopes and expectations of the Assembly in Paris outstripped the abilities of its armies in the field. The successes of the autumn and winter of 1792 turned into disaster: Belgium rose in revolt; the Netherlands had to be evacuated. The demands for 300,000 men for the military, to be recruited voluntarily if possible but by ballot if necessary, was the spark which set off the revolt in La Vendée early in 1793. The military situation continued to deteriorate in the spring and early summer. On 2 June 1793 the purging of the Girondin faction in the Convention by the Jacobins and their street allies from the Paris Sections provoked more internal unrest in France. But this action also led to the installation of the Jacobin dictatorship whose draconian measures were to turn the tide of the war once again in France's favour.

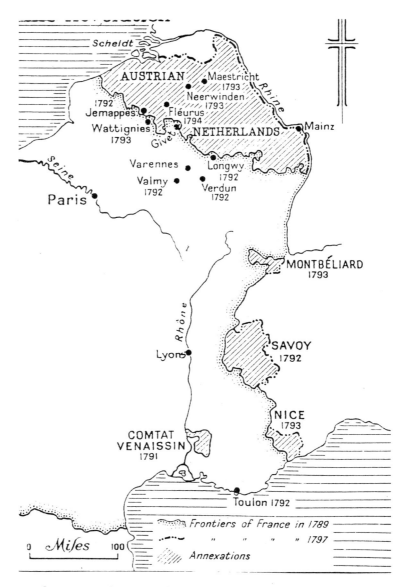

Figure 32 The eastern frontier of France during the revolutionary war, 1792-5. *(A. Cobban, A History of Modern France, Volume 1, 1963, Harmondsworth, p.205. Reproduced by permission of Penguin Books Ltd)*

On 23 August 1793 Bertrand Barère introduced the celebrated decree of the *Levée en Masse* into the Convention. The decree sought to legislate along the lines of Danton's clarion calls of 12 months before. France was to be mobilised totally for war. In the words of the decree:

> 'The young men shall go to battle; husbands shall forge and transport provisions; women shall make clothes and tents, and serve in the hospitals; children shall turn old linen into bandages, and old men shall go out into the public squares to rouse the courage of the combatants, and to preach the unity of the Republic and the hatred of Kings.'

The legislation enabled France to field an army of about three-quarters of a million men at the end of 1793 and in 1794. It provided the means by which these men were to be armed and equipped, though the organising abilities of two deputies, Prieur de la Côte d'Or and, in particular, Lazare Carnot were essential to ensuring that the means achieved the desired ends and that troops received the necessary arms and ammunition. New munitions factories were set up and produced at unprecedented levels. Prieur and Carnot supervised military recruitment as well as the requisitioning of animals and foodstuffs. There was no military effort comparable with that of Jacobin France until the total wars of the twentieth century. Political representatives from the Convention (*représentants en mission*) were sent to the armies to ensure the correct sentiments in the troops, and to keep an eye on the generals. The shadow of the guillotine hung over everything. Military defeat, or failure to follow up a victory, became a political crime: 17 generals were executed in 1793, and 67 in the following year.

III The war after *Thermidor*

The war effort of the Jacobin dictatorship did not survive *Thermidor*. However, war did continue creating both benefits and problems for the Thermidoreans and for the Directory.

Not every young man had gone off to war fired with patriotic enthusiasm. The increase in marriages during the Year II suggests that some young men got married at an earlier age than was usual so as to avoid the draft. But after the patriotic fervour and passion of the Jacobin dictatorship, many of the men who had been recruited during 1793 and 1794 deserted. Some of these deserters supported themselves on their way back to their native towns and villages by petty crime and brigandage; some took to the life of brigands permanently, thus contributing to the breakdown in the internal order of France under the Directory. Many of the men who remained in the armies of the Republic clearly did so because they enjoyed military life; while unquestionably patriotic and proud of their Revolution, they became professional soldiers, different from the enthusiastic part-trained levies of 1793-4. The soldiers were strongly attached to their commanders. The leaders of the Revolutionary Army after *Thermidor* were increasingly young generals who had risen through their military ability, and who owed everything to the Revolution. Many of them had been born into the lower orders of French society and would never have risen above non-commissioned rank in the army of the *ancien régime*. Lazare Hoche, the son of a keeper of the royal hounds, was a general at 27; Jean-Baptiste Jourdan, who had been a draper in Limoges, became a general at 31; and, of course, Napoleon Bonaparte, the son of a petty Corsican noble, who in 1796, aged only 26, became commander of the French army in Italy.

The professional army of the Directory fought its battles outside French territory. While it drew its pay, munitions, and equipment from France, it lived off the land which it occupied and fought over. This land was of considerable benefit to France while she was in economic and financial difficulties, especially during the famine years of 1795 and 1796. Moreover the success of the French armies brought back profit to the depleted treasury in the form of both plunder and tributes from 'liberated' nations. But the success of the young generals had disadvantages for the Directory, since these capable, confident young men – General Bonaparte in particular – were quite capable of conducting their own foreign policy regardless of directives from Paris. Bonaparte concluded the preliminaries of peace with Austria at Leoben in April 1797, acquiring territory in Italy in contradiction of the Directory's policy; and his peace treaty with Austria (Campo Formio in October 1797) was concluded with no reference to his political masters. The generals did not become a praetorian guard, making and unmaking governments at will, but they were deeply involved with civilian politicians in the coups and counter-coups of the post-*Thermidor* period, which culminated in the coup of 18 *Brumaire* (9 November 1799) and General Bonaparte's appointment as Consul.

IV A new kind of war?

War was nothing exceptional to eighteenth-century Europe, but the kind of war unleashed by the French Revolution was qualitatively and quantitively different. The wars of the eighteenth century had been fought by professional soldiers. Since battles were exceedingly costly, generals had concentrated on manoeuvre, only engaging the enemy in battle when they felt the situation was strongly in their favour, or when it was unavoidable. Generally speaking too, eighteenth-century armies were small. Theorists and tacticians had long debated the role of improved artillery, of light infantry deployed as skirmishers, and the possibility of raising citizen armies. But it was the Revolution which provided the opportunity, and the impetus, for change.

Eighteenth-century monarchs and their professional armies did not fight wars about ideas. While ideology may not have been the key element in starting the wars of the French Revolution – arguably governments declare war because they think they have sufficient advantage over their enemies to win – nevertheless ideology became a motivating force behind many of the combatants. As noted earlier, the initial declaration of war was couched significantly in terms of the French nation declaring war on the King of Hungary and Bohemia. For many, especially in France, the war was seen as a struggle of Kings (representing the *ancien régime*) against a free people or people seeking their freedom (representatives of a new order). French soldiers fought for *their* nation, *their* Republic, as opposed to fighting as the subjects of the King of France; and every Frenchman owed a military duty to his nation, his Republic. In the words of the chorus of one of the most popular patriotic songs of 1793, *Le chant du départ* (*The Song of Departure*):

> 'The Republic calls us,
> We will conquer, or we will die.
> A Frenchman must live for her,
> And for her, a Frenchman will die.'

Such sentiments can be found reflected in some citizen-soldiers' letters home. 'Sooner die than yield an inch' wrote trooper Bourgognonaux on the fifth anniversary of the storming of the Bastille. 'Our cause is just, and we will uphold it as we have always done, to the last drop of our blood.' Drummer Corney explained that he had slept in the open for four months in bad weather, 'but in serving the Motherland, pain turns to pleasure and convinces me that I will remain at my post to complete the extermination of our enemies.'

The recruitment practices of the Revolution also helped to create an army which was more 'French' than its predecessors. Some foreign 'legions' did fight under the tricolour, but the foreign regiments which had served the monarchy were disbanded; the Swiss Guards Regiment which served as part of the royal bodyguard was massacred on 10 August 1792. The traditional recruiting areas for the army of the *ancien régime* were the north and the east; the various calls for volunteers and levies during the Revolution brought far more recruits from the south and the west, and they also brought a greater proportion of peasants. While the precise impact of this would be difficult to assess, it probably contributed to a much greater perception of the entity of France and thus contributed to greater national unity.

The *Levée en Masse* and the idea that every Frenchman was a soldier and a defender of *his* nation gave the Revolutionary Armies a vast reservoir of soldiers. Rather than seeking to out-manoeuvre the enemy, the new French armies endeavoured to bring the enemy to battle at every opportunity, and the aim of

139

the battle was the annihilation of the enemy. Battles became far more common; in consequence, losses became much heavier. The citizen army of the French nation could bear such losses better than the small professional armies of absolute monarchs. The citizen-soldiers lacked training, which militated against the rigid formations used in traditional eighteenth-century warfare; but the independence and initiative of the citizen-soldier, together with his dedication to his cause, meant that he could be depended upon to act on his own as a skirmisher. The rigid lines of eighteenth-century armies found themselves decimated by scores of skirmishers from the Revolutionary Armies before the two sides clashed at close quarters.

It could be argued that civil wars have a special kind of barbarity which sets them apart from most international conflicts. Certainly the fighting in La Vendée and against the *Chouans* in Brittany was marked by appalling savagery. Both sides took reprisals, and one historian (Reynald Secher, 1986) has recently described the Convention's policy in La Vendée as the first example of genocide in modern war. Similarly the suppression of the Federalist Revolt in Lyons was undertaken with great ferocity, and the aftermath was marked by mass executions. The National Convention made one move to bring a new kind of barbarism on to the international battlefield by decreeing, in May 1794, that no prisoners were to be taken in battles against British or Hanoverian troops. However, save for the killing of the crew of a British merchantman taken in the Mediterranean, the Revolutionary Armies, and Navy, appear to have ignored the order. Nor do British and Hanoverian prisoners of war appear to have been treated with any greater severity than the prisoners of any other state.

Even though Great Britain came into the revolutionary wars relatively late, she was to become the principal opponent of revolutionary, and later Napoleonic France. In some respects the Anglo-French aspect of the war was a continuation of the struggles which the two countries had waged since the end of the seventeenth century on the seas, in the Americas and the Indies, as well as in Europe. These struggles had always had an economic aspect, but during the Revolution this became more marked as both sides forbade trade with the other (something not always enforced during the eighteenth-century conflicts fought, as they were, by the professional armies of monarchs) and began the process which was to lead to the blockade policies of the Napoleonic period. Britain, with its dynamic new industrialising economy, became the paymaster for European coalitions as they came together against France. *Sans-culotte* propagandists commonly fumed against the English Prime Minister's military subsidies, 'Pitt's gold', which they tended to see everywhere (and in far greater quantities than actually existed) financing counter-revolution and enemy armies. It suited Britain to pay for European armies rather than to field her own: her wealth allowed it, her population was much smaller than that of France, and she saw herself primarily as a sea power. Subsidising European armies allowed Britain to concentrate her own military efforts on her navy. It is significant that the two great exponents of the new kind of war, in which the aim was bringing the enemy to battle and destroying him totally, were a Frenchman, Napoleon, on land, and an Englishman, Nelson, on the sea.

Essay 5

JACOBINISM

Gwynne Lewis
Professor of History
University of Warwick

'Jacobins' frightened the social and political élites of Europe in the nineteenth century just as 'Communists' have done throughout the twentieth. The many definitions of a 'Jacobin' underline the fear they inspired in the corridors of privilege and power. Terrorists, atheists, idealists, socialists, anarchists – these are just some of the terms used to isolate the nineteenth-century Jacobin from decent, God-fearing liberals and conservatives. It is certainly true that Jacobins belonged to a 'broad church', whose membership becomes even broader when we include British, German, American, Italian, Hungarian and Swiss 'Jacobins'. Little wonder that historians continue to disagree over their political and social philosophy. Were they nationalists, centralisers, theists, proto-socialists, totalitarian democrats, or were they quite simply pragmatists, members of a club thrust into power by the peculiar circumstances of revolution and war? This essay does not pretend to provide definitive answers – the ultimate arrogance of the historian – to these questions; it seeks rather to discover how a movement which began with a few deputies arriving at Versailles for the meeting of the Estates-General in the summer of 1789 came to dominate the history of the Revolution and to bequeath their name to posterity.

I The history of the Jacobin Club

The history of the Jacobin Club begins in 1789 with a handful of Bretons, soon to be joined and outnumbered by like-minded deputies, exchanging ideas in a café around the corner from the National Assembly at Versailles. After the October Days they followed the royal family back to Paris where they rented a room from the monks of a Jacobin convent in the rue Saint-Honoré, hence the name now hallowed by history. Their official title remained 'Society of the Friends of the Constitution'. Ignoring the dangers of over-simplification, the rise and fall of this society may be compared to a drama in five acts: the first would cover the formation of the Club to the split with the Feuillants (the supporters of Barnave, Lameth and Duport) in the late summer of 1791; the second, the period of the Legislative Assembly from September 1791 to the downfall of the monarchy on 10 August 1792; the third would relate to the 'Girondin' Convention, from September 1792 to the expulsion of the Girondins after the insurrection of 2 June 1793; the fourth, and by far the most important, would concentrate upon the period of the Revolutionary, or Jacobin, Government of the Year II, ending with the execution of the Robespierrists on 10 *Thermidor* (28 July 1794); the last act would deal with the degeneration of Jacobinism from 1794 to the advent of Napoleon Bonaparte in 1799. Like all good plays, there would, of course, be a prologue and an epilogue.

Figure 33 *Club des Jacobins.* The interior of the Jacobin Club, whose members met in the former monastery of St James (in Latin, Jacobus), in the rue Saint-Honoré, Paris. Here many of the most radical of the revolutionaries made their reputations. *(Roger-Viollet, Paris)*

The prologue would take us back at least to the mid-eighteenth century, to the heyday of the French Enlightenment. Most historians insist upon the intellectual apprenticeship served by the Jacobins – Robespierre, Brissot, Danton and their respective followers – although it is important to add that, during the first two years of the Revolution, the Jacobins also included influential and wealthy figures like the comte de Mirabeau and Joseph Barnave, as well as a thin sprinkling of priests. The narrow definition of Jacobinism which identifies the movement with Robespierre and his colleagues was the result of a long and painful revolutionary process, and it is worth remembering that, even during the Terror, not all Jacobins were unqualified supporters of Robespierre. During the second half of the eighteenth century, literary societies (*sociétés de pensée*), masonic lodges and provincial academies often turned their attention to politics. Many literary societies in the provinces simply transformed themselves in 1789 into 'Societies of the Friends of the Constitution'; some societies were formed in imitation of the action taken by the Breton deputies in Paris whose 'Jacobin Club' in the rue Saint-Honoré soon became known affectionately as the *société-mère* (the mother-society).

The first act proper of the drama of Jacobinism coincided with the life of the Constituent Assembly from 1789 to the summer of 1791. It was during this period that the Jacobins began to shape their ideology and refine their institutions, particularly their 'Correspondence Committee' which proved to be the administrative powerhouse of the Jacobin Club. Letters and petitions were received from, and despatched to, the four corners of the known world. It was also during this period that the Jacobins began to implement their policy of 'affiliation', creating a network of sympathetic societies, officially associated with the 'mother-society' in Paris, throughout the provinces and even outside France. Even before the split with the Feuillants in 1791, over 400 provincial 'Societies of the Friends of the Constitution' had affiliated to the Paris Jacobin Club. So great was the demand for affiliation that the Club was forced to take its vetting procedures far more seriously. It also decided to delegate the responsibility for keeping in touch with the smaller town and village societies to affiliated clubs in the major provincial cities like Marseilles, Bordeaux, and Strasbourg. 'Correspondence' and 'affiliation' proved to be the twin pillars of the administrative structure of Jacobinism throughout its existence. They served to distinguish the Jacobin Club from its many competitors, transforming it into a national, indeed, international organisation.

The split within the Club in the summer of 1791, provoked by the King's flight to Varennes and the related Massacre of the *Champ de Mars*, heralded in the most troubled and relatively obscure period in the history of Jacobinism. Joseph Barnave and his friends took half the members of the Jacobin Club with them to create the Feuillant Club. It should also be noted that, partly as a result of the self-denying ordinance passed by the deputies of the Constituent Assembly preventing them from standing in the next elections, the Jacobins probably represented less than a quarter of the membership of the Legislative Assembly. Those months of the summer and autumn of 1791 represented one of the decisive turning-points in the history of the Revolution. Fortunately for the more radical members who stayed in the rue Saint-Honoré, only 72 out of around 400 affiliated societies in the provinces decided to support the Feuillants. In addition, the intellectual and oratorical skills of politicians such as Robespierre, Danton, Brissot and Vergniaud continued to attract influential people to the Jacobin Club. Jacobinism was in the process of being reborn.

It was the overthrow of the monarchy on 10 August 1792, in which the Jacobins played an important if shadowy role, and the inauguration of the First French Republic the following month which provided the Jacobins with their new point of departure. On 28 August the Society of the Friends of the Constitution in Chablis sent a letter to the *société-mère* in Paris which began: 'Jacobins! Henceforth, you will be our rallying-point'. Many – certainly not all – of the provincial clubs followed suit, and from the summer of 1792 to the expulsion of the Girondins from the National Convention following the insurrection of 2 June 1793, we see a steady if gradual increase in the popularity and influence of the Jacobins. They had swept the board in the elections to the National Convention in Paris whilst the bloody September Massacres, associated with the widely-loathed Jean-Paul Marat and the Insurrectionary Commune of Paris, had opened up an unbridgeable political chasm between the followers of Brissot and Roland, now collectively known as the Girondins, and those who preferred to cluster around Robespierre, Couthon and Saint-Just in the rue Saint-Honoré.

It was the failure of the Girondin ministry to deal with the mounting internal and external crisis – inflation, unemployment, rising prices, the outbreak of counter-revolution in La Vendée coupled with war against the Allied Powers – which gave the radical Jacobins their chance to convert speechifying into political practice. The popular Parisian insurrections of 31 May – 2 June 1793 ended the tripartite division of power which had hitherto characterised the history of the Revolution: National Assembly – Paris Commune – Jacobin Club. For one year, the history of the Revolution and the history of Jacobinism were to become almost synonymous. It was the experience of the Revolutionary Government of the Year II which finally shaped the ideology of Jacobinism; it was the need for a national war-time leader that propelled Maximilien Robespierre on to the centre of the historical stage, that enabled this intelligent and prissy lawyer from Arras to impose his personal philosophy upon the movement. It should never be forgotten, however, that it was the Parisian *sans-culottes* who had helped the Jacobins to triumph over their political enemies, and that ultimate power remained with the National Convention.

The degeneration of Jacobinism during the late 1790s failed to eradicate the image of Jacobinism as the most significant revolutionary movement of the late eighteenth century. Indeed, the 'martyrdom' of Robespierre and his reluctant disciple, Gracchus Babeuf, probably added a few cubits to the historical stature of the Jacobins. It would be appropriate to leave this epilogue until the end of our essay.

II The structure of the Jacobin Club

It is relatively simple to periodise the history of Jacobinism, far more difficult to be precise about its institutional structure. Clearly, at its apex stood the Jacobin Club of Paris. Dominated during its formative years by great orators representing a wide political spectrum, it attracted the propertied, professional, and educated élite of France, acolytes of the Enlightenment to a man. Through the quality of its membership, its *comité de correspondance*, and its journals – the first issue of the *Journal des Amis de la Constitution* appeared on 21 November 1790 – the Jacobin Club rapidly acquired international stature. Radiating out from the *société-mère* were the hundreds of affiliated clubs in the provinces. Crane Brinton (1957) has estimated that there were almost 7,000 'Jacobin' societies in France at the height of their influence. This may well be an exaggeration. However, Michael Kennedy, author of an extensive study of the Jacobin clubs, does not disagree with Brinton's estimate that around 2 per cent of the French population (approximately 500,000 people) were captured by the movement, although he adds that 'the percentage of militants was far smaller' (Kennedy, 1988). What would be misleading is to conclude that all the provincial clubs supported the radical 'Robespierrist' wing of Jacobinism. Many of the early Societies of the Friends of the Constitution supported the Feuillants, and later on the Girondins, alienated by the 'extremism' of the Robespierrists. The vast majority of 'Jacobins' in the first two or three years of the Revolution were loyal supporters of the monarchy; some towns boasted 'aristocratic' Jacobin societies. Finally, there were powerful rivals to the Jacobin Club in Paris, like the Cordeliers, who attracted a far more 'popular' clientele. The identification of Jacobinism with the Revolution was the product of the Year II.

Most of the major cities in the provinces had more than one Jacobin society, a fact which was bound to create rivalry and jealousy. Five societies were operating in Bordeaux by 1792; Nantes had three, Nîmes two. Membership varied: the influential and wealthy Récollets society in Bordeaux had 1,533 members on its books in December 1791; the oddly-named *Club des Anti-Politiques* in Aix, around 1,000. The great majority of societies, however, recorded a far smaller membership. As one might expect, societies in the countryside, particularly in the more remote regions, were not common, and even if they had been founded they were rarely very active. The society at Arre in the department of the Gard, for example, kept no register for 17 months and, according to its secretary, 'dealt with nothing of significance' throughout the Terror! We need to recall that, for the vast majority of French men and women, the Revolution only impinged upon their daily lives in a fitful, oblique, occasionally frightening manner. However, one should also beware of dismissing altogether the degree to which the French countryside was 'politicised' during the 1790s. Peter Jones (1988) reminds us that 'squabbles over pews became part of a nation-wide campaign of anti-seigneurialism; on-going quarrels over the commons acquired strange new ideological reference points'. 'Village Jacobinism' did exist.

In the capital, the *sans-culotte* societies attached to the 48 Sections into which Paris had been divided for administrative and electoral purposes looked to the Jacobin Club for guidance and inspiration, particularly after the foundation of the Republic in 1792. Once again, however, it would be misleading to describe the Parisian *sans-culottes* as servile creatures of the Jacobins. Albert Soboul (1989) has illustrated the degree to which the social, economic, and political ideas of the sans-culotterie differed from those of the Jacobins, thus helping to explain the downfall of the Robespierrists on the night of 9 *Thermidor*. The Sections, and the popular societies they created after September 1793, were very jealous of their independence even if, in the final analysis, they recognised that 'the sovereignty of the people' was vested in the National Convention. The same cautionary note must be sounded when dealing with the Sections in Lyons, Marseilles, or Bordeaux, divided as they were in 1793 between Girondin and Jacobin factions.

III Who were the Jacobins?

It is much easier to say who the Jacobins were than to describe their institutional structure. Brinton (1957) concluded that they were 'neither noble nor beggar... representing a complete cross-section of their community'. Kennedy's detailed study (1988) confirms the predominantly bourgeois composition of the Jacobin clubs. The Paris Club demanded a relatively high entry fee of 24 *livres;* provincial societies usually asked for less, between 12 and 3 *livres*. The Caussade club decided on a sliding scale, relating the fee to personal income. In general, one can say that the Jacobin clubs became more middle class and lower middle class as the Revolution progressed. Up to 1791 the Jacobin Club in Paris, as well as a good percentage of those in the provinces, were staffed 'almost exclusively from the middle and upper strata of the bourgeoisie' (Kennedy, 1988), professional men, lawyers, doctors, merchants and property-owners, with the odd sprinkling of priests and liberal nobles. The Society of the Friends of the Constitution in Nîmes was the preserve of very wealthy textile merchants, lawyers and landowners; 73 per cent of the Jacobin Club in Toulouse could be described as 'well off'. Following the crisis of the Revolution in the summer of 1791 initiated by the King's flight and the continued economic depression, 'Popular Societies of the Friends of the Revolution' began to open their doors to a far less favoured clientele. In Nîmes, for example, among the 24 founder-members of the popular society in 1791 we find two relatively poor merchants, 12 textile workers, and a cobbler. The radicalisation of the Revolution attracted more petty bourgeois shopkeeper and artisan 'Jacobins', although, as Donald Sutherland (1985) insists, in even 'the most democratic societies... the leaders were still likely to be lawyers, doctors, teachers, priests and small merchants'.

IV The ideology of the Jacobins

Does the ideology of Jacobinism reflect its middle-class clientele? In many ways it does, although the metal of Jacobinism, quarried from the Enlightenment, was to be refined in the crucible of revolution and war. This fusion of theory and practice was to produce the peculiar and often paradoxical brand of French Jacobinism. Kennedy, for example, believes that the first few months of 1793 were possibly the most important months in the history of the Revolution: in February, war between Britain and France; the following month, the outbreak of the counter-revolution in La Vendée and, in response to the mounting crisis, increased powers conferred upon the representatives-on-mission to the provinces, coupled with the establishment, on 10 March, of the Revolutionary Tribunal. A few months later, the Jacobins were in charge of the machinery which would eventually create the Terror. It is no exaggeration to claim – and this is one of the main threads running through this essay – that the Revolution shaped the ideology of Jacobinism more than Jacobinism determined the destiny of the Revolution.

Let us begin with the economic ideas of the Jacobins. Few historians, if any, would disagree that the Jacobins were in favour of free trade, at least within the boundaries of France. They associated themselves with the ideas of the Physiocrats, whose most influential advocate had been Turgot, controller-general of finances during the first years of the reign of Louis XVI. Turgot's failure to implement his ideas on free trade, a land tax, and the abolition of the guilds had aggravated the crisis of the *ancien régime*. During the early years of the Revolution the Jacobins raised no serious objections to the introduction of free trade in grain, nor to the abolition of the guilds in 1791, nor, indeed, to the Chapelier Law, passed in the same year, which forbade combinations of workers (and employers in theory) seeking higher wages or better working conditions. If the Jacobins moved gradually and grudgingly towards an acceptance of the need for a controlled economy, the explanation lies in the problems posed by war, inflation, and counter-revolution, and even then, controls had to be forced upon them by the Popular Movement in Paris and the provinces. Political realism (the essential factor distinguishing the Jacobins from their enemies) convinced Robespierre and his colleagues that the failure of the Girondins lay in their refusal to swallow the unpalatable lessons of war and counter-revolution, the most important lesson being that some alliance would have to be forged with the *sans-culottes* in the cities, and the peasantry in the countryside. As early as 12 February 1793 the 48 Sections of Paris had asked for a ceiling to be fixed on the price of grain. Kennedy (1988) stresses that by the spring of 1793 the majority of societies in the provinces had become convinced that 'economic liberalism had not worked'. The response of the Girondin ministry had been extremely half-hearted; the Jacobins themselves took a few months after seizing power, to agree to the famous General Maximum of Prices, which placed a price ceiling on 39 basic commodities. It is doubtful whether the law would have been passed at all on 29 September 1793 had it not been for an invasion of the Convention three weeks earlier by the Sections of Paris, aided and abetted by a few radical Jacobins.

The Law of the General Maximum was never in the Jacobin manifesto: it was imposed upon them. In more general terms, Jacobin economic theory – as it had evolved by the time of the Terror – hovered uneasily between eighteenth-century liberalism and nineteenth-century socialism. Ferenc Fehér in his essay on Jacobinism (1987) argues that the Jacobins can only be understood if one sees them manning the bridge between a pre-industrial and an industrial age. The confusion between 'liberal individualism' and 'socialist collectivism' can be illustrated by looking at the response to the economic crisis of the Popular Society of the Friends of the Constitution in the town of Chablis which, on 2 *Germinal,* Year II (13 April 1794), decided that all grain should be stored in a municipal warehouse to be distributed equally among the town's inhabitants, only to rescind its decision two days later!

The Jacobins were less uncertain of their stance on property: they were for it. However – and with all aspects of Jacobin ideology there is a 'however' – their ideal was a society of property-owners in which the extremes of wealth and poverty would be eradicated. This was not far removed from the *sans-culotte* ideal that each man and woman should own just one farm, or one shop, or one workshop: the ideal of an eighteenth-century small property-owning, artisan economy. It was the Jacobin society in Chablis again which revealed the dilemna confronting revolutionaries who were desperately seeking to square the circle which joined political liberty to social and economic equality. The ultimate aim of their members, they said, was a fair measure of equality so far as property and income were concerned, but the less fortunate townspeople were told that 'whilst awaiting that happy epoch, the poor man should respect the heritage of the rich'. No doubt many of the poor in Chablis today are still awaiting the dawn of this 'happy epoch'.

Figure 34 Twin engravings, from a sympathetic source, of a male and female *sans-culotte. (Bibliothèque Nationale, Paris)*

On social policy the Jacobins gave little proof of anything but solid, respectable middle-class virtues. Modest, powdered wigs and breeches were favoured over *sans-culotte* coiffures and the working man's trousers. If it is possible to spot a 'revolutionary' by his dress or manner of speech then Robespierre was not one: a rather synthetic and intellectual regard for the poor certainly did not entail living or talking like them. The real issue was how to narrow the gap between the bourgeois ideal of morality and civic virtue, and the ghastlier circumstances of the poor. Or, as Robespierre himself put it: 'It is far more a question of lending dignity to poverty than of making war on wealth', a dictum shared by liberals ever since. The State's function was to iron out the disparities which arose from the evils inherent in man's nature (or rather in his social being) and the historic development of property. Education would be one method of doing so, a top priority for all Jacobins and many *sans-culottes*. The most obvious link in the chain binding the Jacobins to the Enlightenment was the belief that the perfectibility of man might be achieved through the application of Reason.

Jacobin ideology, then, was based upon an amalgam of Enlightenment thought and revolutionary practice, with all the confusions and paradoxes this involved. What really distinguished the Jacobin from his peers in the Revolution, however, was what he *did* rather than what he thought. The Jacobins were, first and foremost, political animals, men of action – hence their success, brief as it was, and their place in the history of nineteenth-century revolutions. One of the many paradoxes about Jacobinism is the fact that if its revolutionary theory (such as it was) looked to the future, its political practice drew inspiration from the classical past, which prompted Marx to accuse the Jacobins of 'false consciousness', bourgeois acting out a modern drama in the ancient costume of Greece and Rome. Jacobins indulged in endless talk of 'a new Athens' or 'a new

147

Sparta'. David, neo-classical painter and 'pageant-master of the Republic', also a member of the Committee of General Security, had drawn deep of the classical well in order to come up with his moral and republican message. 'Republicanism' became one of the most cherished words in the Jacobin dictionary; a republicanism founded upon a strict moral and civic *vertu* which, it was hoped, might help to square the circle between political freedom and social equality. It should be stressed, however, that the Jacobin was a relatively late convert to republicanism. Rousseau had argued that republics did not work in large states. The vast majority of Jacobin club members throughout France remained loyal to the monarchy up to 1791, albeit of the constitutional variety. Even Robespierre had not campaigned openly for a republic at the time of the King's flight to Varennes.

'Centralisation' was another keyword in the Jacobin dictionary, but one which was also coined from the circumstances of war and counter-revolution after 1792. Again, early Jacobinism favoured a considerable measure of decentralisation and popular democracy, including local elections of mayors and departmental councils. There is little insistence before 1792 on the need for a centralised State. This is Robespierre *On Revolutionary Government*:

> 'The principal concern of constitutional government is civil liberty; that of revolutionary government, public liberty. Under a constitutional government little more is required than to protect the individual against abuses by the state, whereas revolutionary government is obliged to defend the state itself against the factions that assail it from every quarter'.

The need for centralisation arose out of the widespread resistance to the Revolution; it was nothing to do with the constitutional theory of Jacobinism. It was to be a temporary measure. Unlike Trotsky, Robespierre did not toy with the notion of 'permanent revolution'.

'Action' was the word which separated the Jacobin from the Girondin. Action over the introduction of price mechanisms; action over the fate of the King; action in forging a temporary alliance with the Popular Movement in order to achieve victory over the factions which assailed the infant Republic from every quarter. The Jacobins 'got things done'. Claude Mazauric's detailed knowledge of western France during the period of the Revolution led him to the conclusion that:

> 'One of the main impressions to arise out of my research in Rouen is this practical capacity of the Jacobins to decide, to take the initiative and force others to push forward more quickly and more effectively'.

Mazauric, 1984

From the beginning of the Revolution, but particularly after the fall of the monarchy in 1792, it was the action taken by the Jacobin Club in Paris to prepare the agenda for the debates in the Assembly which explains its political ascendancy. It became a clearing-house for ideas and projects, exerting a powerful influence upon the deliberations of the government. The Club also vetted the names of prospective deputies and leading government officials.

One should, of course, be careful not to exaggerate: the Jacobin Club was not 'a rival parliament'; it was more like a 'party headquarters'. The fact that Robespierre was applauded in the Jacobin Club the evening before he was arrested in the Convention serves as a useful corrective to the notion that the Jacobin Club master-minded every act in the Revolution. In the last analysis, as the *sans-*

culottes realised full well, the Convention was the ultimate repository of the people's sovereignty. One should also recall that the Jacobins did not believe in 'factions' or 'opposition parties': it was the 'General Will' which had to be obeyed. The resolution to this dilemma was found in the concept of the 'Revolutionary State', in the bureaucratisation of the clubs throughout France, whose function changes from one of stimulating debate and radicalising the Revolution to that of serving as administrative and repressive cogs in the machinery of the Terror. Local and revolutionary administration were fused as the *sociétés populaires* exercised their influence over the appointment of municipalities and revolutionary committees, over the organisation of food supplies and volunteers for the armies, and as they became liaison committees for representatives-on-mission from the Convention and *commissaires* from the Sections in Paris. As opposition 'factions' were despatched to the guillotine during the Great Terror of the spring and early summer of 1794, debate in the clubs was stifled, and conformity triumphed over the healthy clash of contrary opinions. As the local newspaper in Besançon, writing of the Jacobin Club, put it: 'For a long time now the meetings of our society have been cursed with the kind of sterility which alarms good citizens'. In Paris, the popular societies of the Sections closed down under pressure from Robespierre and the Jacobin Club. The most revealing and poignant reflection of the bureaucratisation of the Revolution may be found in the record of the debate in the *société populaire* in Nîmes just after the execution of the Robespierrists. Having learned from the secretary of the bad news from Paris, one brave, not to say foolhardy, soul named Bourdon stood up and declared his loyalty to Robespierre's memory. He was immediately shouted down by colleagues who were more concerned with personal survival than political philosophy, whereupon Bourdon shot himself declaring that he 'was dying for his country'. The facts were recorded by the society's secretary who then wrote: 'At this point the discussion ended'. A stunning example of bureaucratic sang-froid!

It was indeed the end of the discussion so far as the majority of Jacobin clubs were concerned, or almost the end. Before writing *finis*, however, we should emphasise the fact that the Jacobins achieved a remarkable degree of success during their brief spell in power. When they took over the two great Committees in the summer of 1793, the paper currency of the Revolution, the *assignats*, were tumbling in value, the war was going badly, the Federalist Revolt had broken out in the south and west, whilst the Vendéan counter-revolution was threatening the very survival of the Revolution. By the time Robespierre had made his fatal speech in the Convention on 8 *Thermidor*, the fall in the value of the *assignat* had been halted, the French armies had moved into Belgium, and the Federalist and Vendéan insurrections had been crushed. The territorial integrity of France had been saved, as indeed had the Revolution. The Jacobins may have been short on theory but they were long on action.

V The Jacobin legacy

It is the image of the Jacobin as a man of revolutionary action which the Robespierrists bequeathed to posterity. It is this aspect of the legend which fascinated Lenin, even more than Marx. As François Furet (1988) has written:

> 'Rather than a concept, or a tradition, or a political system, the word Jacobinism evokes the history of a club whose *action*, from the outset, was essential to the history of the Revolution.'

The closure of the Paris Jacobin Club in November 1794 signifies the end of a very important chapter in that drama. From 1794 to the advent of Napoleon Bonaparte, Jacobinism was increasingly relegated to the sidelines of the Revolution, invading the pitch occasionally, such as during the mutiny on 10 *Floréal*, Year IV (29 April 1796) of the Police Legion which guarded the deputies in Paris, or the far more significant 'Conspiracy of the Equals' led by Gracchus Babeuf in the spring of 1796. Following the failure of these 'neo-Jacobin' uprisings, Jacobinism increasingly became involved in trying to influence the result of the annual elections which the Directory unwisely foisted upon itself – not always without a measure of success, as the results of the 1798 elections indicate, when an embarrassingly large number of radicals were chosen as deputies. Most survivors satisfied themselves with recalling the 'good old days' over a glass of wine in their local café, or quarrelling with their neighbours over the memory of Robespierre. The image of the Jacobin as a romantic revolutionary was created out of his failure during the Directory, as much as his success during the Year II.

It was Babeuf's fellow conspirator, Filipo Buonarotti, who did more than anyone else to improve the image of Robespierre and the Jacobins as the harbingers of socialism and democracy. His account of Babeuf's abortive coup published 30 years after the event bridged the gap between the actuality of Jacobinism during the Revolution and the development of socialism in the 1820s and 30s. Many of the followers of Saint-Simon, even more of Louis Blanc, saw themselves as latter-day Jacobins. Nineteenth-century French Republicanism, with its emphasis upon universal suffrage, liberating the oppressed peoples of Europe, its romantic attachment to the tradition of the barricades, embraced the Jacobin legend, at least until 1848, when a popular movement in Paris helped to overthrow the King, Louis Philippe. Republicanism and revolutionary Jacobinism finally parted company in the bloody Paris Commune in 1871. After this date, bourgeois liberals and Marxist-socialists went their separate ways, leaving 'romantic' Jacobinism suspended in a political void. It could be, and has been, argued that a hybrid version of Jacobinism was bred in Russia, with Lenin as the new Robespierre. Certainly the French Communist Party after 1936 consciously adopted the Jacobin mantle to prove their nationalist credentials. Many leading French socialist historians, such as Albert Soboul, have been accused of being Jacobins in Marxist clothing. Some faint stirrings of the Jacobin ghost may even be detected in France 200 years after the Revolution. Confronted by the threat, as opponents view it, of a resurgence in 'provincialism', many French intellectuals and politicians – not all of them on the Left – invoke the idea of a secularised, centralised France which they associate with Jacobinism.

Twentieth-century historians vary in their assessment of Jacobinism. For Brinton (1957) Jacobinism also included a semi-mystical, idealist element, proving that 'Man cannot live by bread alone', as he somewhat cryptically comments at the end of his classic study. For J. L. Talmon (1952), Jacobinism was the precursor of 'Totalitarian Democracy', founded upon the utopian and dangerous elevation of social equality above political freedom. For Marxists, or Marxist-Leninists, like Soboul, they were saviours of the Revolution, pushing it towards more radical, if not socialist, perspectives, though by doing so they became the architects of their own downfall. A more recent interpreter of Jacobinism, Ferenc Fehér, dismisses the idea of Jacobinism as a 'proto-socialist' movement, although he adds that 'It had remained at the threshold, caught, as it were, between two worlds' (Fehér, 1987). This last quotation helps to explain the many paradoxes of Jacobinism, and also its attraction for the historian.

PART THREE

APPENDICES 1-3

Appendix 1

WHO'S WHO

Aelders, Etta Palm, baronne d' (1743-99) A Dutch woman who made several eloquent pleas for women's rights. She was also anxious that women should actively participate in the fight for liberty.

Aiguillon, Armand-Désirée, duc d' (1761-1800) Member of a very prominent and wealthy family. Father was Governor of Brittany and a minister to Louis XV. Elected a noble deputy for Agen in 1789 and involved in arranging the events of 4 August. Emigrated to London 10 August 1792; later lived with Lameth in Hamburg.

Alembert, Jean le Rond d' (1717-83) A foundling later educated by his father, a general in the artillery. A mathematician popular in the Paris *salons* who was associated with the *Encyclopédistes* and who corresponded with foreign rulers.

Arkwright, Richard (1732-92) Came from a poor Lancashire family but became involved in the development of the cotton industry in England, setting up one of the first mills at Cromford in Derbyshire. Died a wealthy and respected man.

Artois, Charles-Philippe, comte d' (1757-1836) Brother of the King, known as a rake and womaniser. Inspired *Memorandum of the Princes of the Blood,* the manifesto of the most reactionary nobles, in 1788. Left Versailles 16 July 1789 for the Austrian Netherlands and became leader of the *émigrés*. Finally became King as Charles X in 1824. Overthrown in 1830. Died in exile in Austria.

Austria, Emperor of
a) **Joseph II** (1741-90) Marie-Antoinette's eldest brother who was greatly influenced by Enlightenment ideas.
b) **Leopold II** (1747-92) Also a brother of Marie-Antoinette and concerned for her safety. Issued the Declaration of Pillnitz but died before war broke out.
c) **Francis II** (1768-1835) A relentless enemy of revolutionary France whose daughter married Napoleon to seal the temporary alliance between the Empires of France and Austria.

Babeuf, Gracchus (François Noel) (1760-97) Extreme radical journalist and agitator, frequently prosecuted. Convicted of plot to restore the constitution of 1793 he was guillotined in 1797. Became socialist hero in the nineteenth century.

Bailly, Jean-Sylvain (1736-93) An astronomer and scientist; elected to the Estates-General for the Third Estate for Paris, 1789. Presided over taking of Oath of the Tennis Court, then became Mayor of Paris. By November 1791 seen as too moderate (he was held to be responsible for the Massacre of the *Champ de Mars* with La Fayette), and replaced. Executed 1793 despite his retirement to Nantes.

Barère, Bertrand (1755-1841) Lawyer at Toulouse, also freemason; deputy in 1789 for the Third Estate of Bigorre. In favour of moderate constitutional reform, but nevertheless elected to the Convention in 1792 and became a member of the Committee of Public Safety where he was an eloquent speaker. Survived Danton's fall and later was involved in the events of *Thermidor* 1794. Napoleon used his services and he returned from exile in Belgium after 1832 to die in his bed.

Barnave, Antoine-Pierre (1761-93) Lawyer and deputy, 1789. Frequent speaker with radical reputation; colleague of Lameth brothers and Duport; became more favourable to the King after Varennes. Executed November 1793.

Barras, Paul François, vicomte de (1755-1829) Followed a military career until he became a deputy in the Convention. Behaved in a very ferocious way as a representative-on-mission. Among leaders of the coup of *Thermidor* 1794. Later used his friend Bonaparte to suppress the rising of *Vendémiaire*. Director until Bonaparte became dictator in 1799, then retired from public life.

Barre, Chevalier de la (1747-66) A young French nobleman executed for blasphemy in 1766.

Beccaria, Cesare, Marchese de (1735 or 38 -94) An Italian political theorist who lived in Milan. His major work, *On Crime and Punishment*, argued fiercely against capital punishment and judicial torture.

Billaud-Varenne, Jacques Nicolas (1756-1819) Unsuccessful lawyer and writer. Joined Cordelier and Jacobin clubs in Paris. Deputy to the Convention in 1792 and soon identified with extremist supporters of the *sans-culottes*. On Committee of Public Safety in September 1793, involved in 1794 coups against Danton and Robespierre. Later exiled to Cayenne.

Blanc, Louis (1811-82) French radical journalist advocating establishment of workshops run by the common people. Put his ideas into operation in revolutionary government of 1848 with little success. Later in exile in England, but returned to France after 1870.

Boissy d'Anglas, François-Antoine (1756-1826) *Parlementaire* lawyer in Paris and elected to Estates-General in 1789. Hardly spoke because of stammer, but opposed execution of the King and arrest of the Girondins. Later helped dismantle Jacobin regime and establish the Directory. Ennobled by Napoleon and in favour also after the Restoration.

Bonaparte, Napoléon (1769-1821) Born in Corsica, trained for the army. From 1789 friendly with the Jacobins. In 1793 came to the fore by retaking Toulon from the English. His friendship with Robespierre the Younger then led to his disgrace after *Thermidor* 1794. In 1795 he regained his credit by helping Barras suppress the royalist rising of *Vendémiaire*. As general of the army of the interior he then won a series of dazzling victories and, in 1799, at the instigation of Sieyès he overthrew the Directory and established the Consulate, soon becoming dictator. He took the title of Emperor in 1804. His success in war finally deserted him and he was forced into exile by the European powers in 1814. His brief restoration in 1815 was ended by the battle of Waterloo, and a final exile to St Helena.

Bouillé, François, marquis de (1739-1800) Soldier, fought in West Indies against England. Member of Assembly of Notables 1787-88. Waiting for King at Montmédy June 1791 with loyal troops. Emigrated 1791. Died in London.

Brezé, Henri, marquis de (1766-1829) Only 22 in 1789 when given task of organising the meetings of the Estates-General as hereditary Grand Master of Ceremonies. Remained with the royal family until 1792 and then retired to his estates until the restoration, when he resumed his duties for Louis XVIII.

Brienne – see **Loménie**

Brissot, Jacques-Pierre (1754-93) Aspiring writer and *philosophe,* forced into being police spy by lack of money; member of the Parisian communal Assembly in 1789, also writing for various journals. Elected to the Legislative Assembly in 1791 where led the pro-war party, known as the Girondins, but lost influence following the King's trial. Fled in May 1793 but captured and executed.

Broglié, maréchal de (1718-1804) A member of a very distinguished military and noble family, he had fought in the Seven Years War and other recent actions. By 1789 he was military adviser to the King and became Minister of War when Necker fell in July. He left France after the Fall of the Bastille and fought with the *émigré* forces in 1792. He died in Munster in 1804.

Brunswick, Duke of (1735-1806) Commander of the Austrian and Prussian armies against France. His manifesto, threatening reprisals against Paris if the royal family were harmed, precipitated the September Massacres. Defeated at Valmy 1792. Died of wounds sustained in battle of Auerstadt against Napoleon.

Buffon, Georges, comte de (1707-88) Scientist and philosopher, best known for his *Histoire Naturelle*.

Burke, Edmund (1729-97) MP, English orator and political theorist whose writings against the Revolution were very influential, especially the *Reflections on the French Revolution*.

Calonne, Charles-Alexandre de (1734-1802) Lawyer from 'robe' family. *Intendant* of Flanders 1778. Controller-General of Finances 1781 on fall of Necker. Reform programme of 1787 aroused much hostility. In exile in England but then joined *émigrés* in 1789. Died in Paris 1802.

Carnot, Lazare (1753-1823) Originally a military engineer, he was elected to the Legislative Assembly for the Pas de Calais. Soon involved in the organisation of supplies for the army with great success. Politically sat with the Mountain but survived the various troubles to become a Director and to serve Napoleon. Died in exile.

Chabot, François (1756-94) A Capuchin monk who had been disciplined for scepticism before the Revolution. A deputy to the Legislative Assembly and the Convention, he became prominent for extreme views. He also became involved with Fabre d'Englantine and various unsavoury foreigners in the Company of the Indies which led to his arrest for corruption in November 1793. He was executed with the Dantonists the following year.

Cloots, Jean-Baptiste, baron (1755-94) A rich German nobleman who came to Paris to join in the Revolution, taking the name of Anacharsis. He represented the Oise in the Convention and was full of plans for international revolution. Was soon suspected of being a spy and was guillotined with his friend Hébert in March 1794.

Coke, Mary, Lady (1726-1811) A much-travelled lady who visited France frequently, especially after the death of her husband in 1764.

Collot d'Herbois, Jean-Marie (1749-96) An actor-manager from Paris who adopted very radical views. Was a member of the Commune and the Convention. He fell out with Robespierre over the severity used to suppress the Federalist Revolt in Lyons (1793). He presided over the Convention on 9 *Thermidor* when the Robespierrists were impeached. He himself was then exiled to Cayenne for his Terrorist activities, where he died of fever.

Condorcet, Jean Antoine-Nicolas de Caritat, marquis de (1743-94) A leading mathematician and philosopher in Enlightenment circles in Paris and later a deputy to the Convention. He helped draw up the Girondin version of the constitution of 1793, superseded by the similar Jacobin version. Denounced after the fall of the Girondins he poisoned himself in prison.

Corday, Marie Anne Charlotte (1768-93) Came from a devout royalist family in Normandy – two of her brothers had joined the army of *émigrés*. She got into Marat's house on 13 July 1793 and stabbed him to death. She was guillotined a few days later.

Corneille, Pierre (1606-84) Forsook a legal career in order to write plays: at first comedies, later tragedies on Roman themes which were widely acclaimed. At the end of his life his reputation suffered in comparison with Racine.

Couthon, Georges Auguste (1755-94) A lawyer and member of the Legislative Assembly and the Convention, his disabilities finally confined him to a wheelchair. He behaved with moderation in putting down the revolt in Lyons and was recalled by the Committee of Public Safety. He also introduced the Law of *Prairial* in June 1794 which accelerated the Terror. He was executed with Robespierre on 28 July.

Custine, Adam-Philippe, comte de (1740-93) Served with the Americans during the War of Independence. In 1789 was elected as a liberal noble to the Estates-General. Commanded the Army of the Rhine in 1792 with some success, but also wrote to the Convention suggesting a military dictatorship. The following year he was accused of corresponding with Austria and Prussia and was tried and guillotined.

Danton, Georges (1759-94) Educated by the Oratorians for the priesthood, but became a lawyer and student of Enlightenment writers. Involved with the Paris Commune and the Cordelier club; elected to the Legislative Assembly in 1792, when also organised the resistance to the invasion of France. Later on the Committee of Public Safety, but suspected of corruption and leniency and fell out with Robespierre. Arrested and executed in 1794.

Dauch, Martin (b.1741) A lawyer and deputy in 1789 who never spoke in the Assembly but who refused to swear the Tennis Court Oath and who alone removed his hat in respect when Louis appeared in the Assembly on his return from Varennes.

David, Jacques-Louis (1748-1825) Member of the Royal Academy of Painting and already a successful artist before 1789. He supported radical policies, and was commissioned to paint the *Oath of the Tennis Court*. He also designed several state funerals and *fêtes* for the Republic including the Festival of the Supreme Being. As a supporter of Robespierre he was imprisoned for a time after *Thermidor*, but enjoyed further success under Napoleon. In exile after the Restoration, he died in Brussels.

Desmoulins, Camille (1760-94) Attended *lycée* of Louis le Grand with Robespierre. Lawyer at Paris *parlement*. Active in politics in Paris from July 1789 and brilliant radical journalist. Deputy to Convention 1792, *Montagnard* voting for the King's death but later called for a diminution of the Terror in his paper *The Old Cordelier*. Arrested with Danton March 1794; executed in April.

Diderot, Denis (1713-84) Originally intended for the Church but scraped living as a writer. Was the originator of the *Encyclopédie,* which became a great success, and the friend of all the leading intellectuals in Paris.

Dorset, Duke of (1745-99) British Ambassador Extraordinary to France 1783-9.

Dumouriez, Charles-François (1739-1823) A professional soldier and diplomat before 1789, he was made a general in 1792 and won the victories of Valmy and Jemappes. He allied himself with the Girondins but, hoping for a moderate settlement, also negotiated with the Austrians. His armies refused to support

156

him in his plan to evacuate Belgium, make peace, and march on Paris to subdue the Convention. He himself fled into comfortable exile in England but his fall helped to discredit the Girondins.

Duport, Adrien Jean (1759-98) A Parisian lawyer and freemason heavily involved in the opposition to the Calonne reforms. Noble deputy for Paris in 1789, leading 'patriot' group with Barnave and the Lameth brothers. Closer to the Court and La Fayette in 1791; arrested in 1792 but released and left for Switzerland.

Fabre d'Eglantine, Philippe François Nazaire (1750-94) An actor and playwright who promoted radical ideas in his plays which were frequently performed in Paris during the Revolution. He became a deputy to the Convention and promoted the new calendar with its months poetically named after the seasons. His involvement with the Company of the Indies with Chabot and others led to his execution for corruption in April 1794.

Fare, Anne-Louis, duc de and **Bishop of Nancy** (1753-1829) A clerical deputy in 1789 and very hostile to any idea of reform. He left France in 1791 and joined Louis XVIII in exile. He returned at the Restoration and eventually crowned Charles X in 1825.

Ferrières, Charles Elie, marquis de (1741-1804) Nobleman, educated by the Jesuits but strongly influenced by Enlightenment ideas. Wrote on Deism. Noble deputy for Saumur in 1789 and favoured moderate reform; lived quietly in retirement during Terror but took part in public affairs under the Consulate.

Fitzgerald, Lord Robert Chargé d'affaires at the British Embassy in Paris from October 1789 to June 1790.

Fouché, Joseph (1759-1820) A priest who taught mathematics and science but who married after the Revolution and voted for the King's death in the Convention. Frequently sent on missions for the Committee of General Security, he was involved with the atrocities in Lyons and expelled from the Jacobins. Deadly enemy of Robespierre, he organised the coup of *Thermidor* but managed to survive the subsequent reaction. He eventually became Napoleon's Chief of Police and Prince of Otranto. At the Restoration he went into exile in Trieste.

Fréron, Stanislaus Louis Marie (1754-1802) A rabidly revolutionary Parisian journalist, he was elected to the Convention. He was responsible with Barras for the atrocities in Toulon and Marseilles following the Federalist Revolt, thus incurring Robespierre's censure. He therefore supported the coup of *Thermidor* and his paper became the mouthpiece of the 'gilded youth'. He managed to survive unharmed through both the Directory and the early Napoleonic period, finally dying of yellow fever in St Domingo where he had been posted as Under-Prefect.

Gossec, François-Joseph (1734-1829) A composer who was trained as a musician in the Cathedral at Anjou, having some success before the Revolution. In 1789, he founded a National Conservatoire and became the official composer for revolutionary celebrations, being responsible for the music at the 1790 *fête*, Voltaire's reburial in the *Panthéon* etc. He also composed hymns to Liberty, Nature, the Supreme Being etc.

Grégoire, Henri, abbé (1750-1831) Elected as a clerical deputy to the Estates-General in 1789 and soon known as a reformer. He was the first cleric to take the oath prescribed under the Civil Constitution and was elected a 'constitutional' bishop. However at the Festival of Reason he refused to renounce Christianity publicly. When Napoleon came to an agreement with the Pope he was forced to resign his bishopric.

Hébert, Jacques-René (1757-94) Radical Parisian journalist, editor of *Le Père Duchesne,* a scurrilous and racy paper named after a character in popular folklore. He was behind the people's rising of 1793, and also supported the Law of the General Maximum and de-Christianisation. This brought him into conflict with the Committee of Public Safety and the Dantonists; he was arrested, tried and executed with 17 associates in March 1794.

Hoche, Lazare (1768-97) Joined the army at 16 and was a corporal in the French Guards in 1789. Then was very rapidly promoted, being a general by the age of 26. Defeated the British in La Vendée in 1795. Died of illness in 1797.

Holbach, Paul d' (1723-89) German-born philosopher who lived in Paris and was connected with the *Encyclopédie.*

Jourdan, Jean-Baptiste (1762-1833) Professional soldier from the time of the American War of Independence and in command at the battle of Fleurus. Later a deputy under the Directory and devised the method of conscription. Became a Marshal in Napoleon's army and also served the Bourbons after the Restoration.

Lacombe, Claire (1765-98) An actress who used her talents to rouse the crowd to attack the Tuileries on 10 August 1792. She was a founder of the 'Society of Revolutionary Republican Women', which was a radical body associated with the Hébertists and which quarrelled with the more moderate Jacobin market women. The society was closed down by the Committee of Public Safety on 30 October 1793. She was briefly imprisoned and then resumed her stage career.

La Fayette, marquis de (1757-1832) Served in America with great distinction. Member of the Assembly of Notables 1788 and identified with reform. Noble deputy for Riom in 1789; became commander of the Paris National Guard after the Fall of the Bastille. In 1791 became closer to the Court and was accused of responsibility for the *Champ de Mars* Massacre. Emigrated following the fall of the monarchy but was imprisoned in Austria; released in 1797 and returned to France under Napoleon.

Lameth, Alexandre, comte de (1760-1829) Elected a noble deputy for Péronne in 1789 and urged the abolition of feudal privileges on 4 August. Worked very effectively in committees of the Assembly as a Feuillant. Joined the Army of the North in 1792 and fled with La Fayette; also arrested. Returned in 1800 and became a prefect until his final retirement.

Lamoignon de Basville, Chrétien (1735-89) A lawyer from a family of lawyers; became Keeper of the Seals on the fall of Calonne and helped devise the system of plenary courts which was intended to replace the *parlements.* Resigned in 1788 because of a lack of royal support and died in 1789.

Launay, Bernard-René, marquis de (1740-89) Commander of the Bastille in July 1789. Despite his surrender of the fortress, the crowd seized him and lynched him parading his head through the streets on a pike.

Lebas, Philippe François Joseph (1746-94) A deputy to the Convention for the Pas-de-Calais, he sat on the Committee of General Security going on missions to the Armies of the Rhine and the North. He joined Robespierre voluntarily when he was impeached and later shot himself to avoid arrest.

Le Chapelier, Isaac René Guy (1754-94) He joined the Breton, later the Jacobin, Club in 1789 when elected to the National Assembly. In 1791 he left to join the more moderate Feuillants; in the same year he was responsible for a law which in effect made trade unions illegal. He was guillotined as a moderate in 1794.

Lepeletier de Saint-Fargeau, Louis-Michel (1760-93) From a 'robe' family in Paris, he was a distinguished radical in the National Assembly and the Convention. He devised a system of national elementary education supported later by Robespierre and Barère. He was assassinated by a royal guard on the eve of the King's execution; his funeral in the *Panthéon* became an occasion of anti-royalist ceremonial.

Lindet, Jean-Baptiste Robert (1746-1825) A lawyer and deputy to the Legislative Assembly and Convention, he did much work on finance, supply and correspondence as a member of the Committee of Public Safety. He refused either to condemn Danton or to support Robespierre at *Thermidor*. He left public life under Napoleon and returned to his practice as a lawyer in Bernay.

Locke, John (1632-1704) An English philosopher and writer whose ideas on government had great influence on events in America at the time of the War of Independence as well as in Enlightenment circles in France. He laid emphasis on the need of the ruler to have the consent of the governed if he was to rule justly; also on the inviolability of property rights.

Loménie de Brienne, Etienne-Charles de (1727-94) Younger son of a noble family, consecrated Archbishop of Toulouse in 1763. Generally had reputation of an Enlightened reformer. Appointed Controller-General of Finances on the dismissal of Calonne in 1788 and attempted to replace the power of the *parlements* by a new plenary court. Resigned when royal credit seemed exhausted. Arrested 1793, and executed in 1794.

Louis XIV (1638-1715) King of France from the age of 5, he pursued a policy of enhancing France's European position by all possible means when he finally achieved personal power in 1661. He also reformed French internal government so that it became highly centralised on the King and his advisers at Versailles.

Louis XV (1710-74) Great-grandson of Louis XIV he too followed a European policy which led to France being involved in almost continuous war. This also extended to French colonies where France was involved in bitter rivalry with England. He was greatly influenced by his mistresses, Madame de Pompadour and Madame du Barry. He left enormous financial problems for his successor.

Louis XVI (1754-93) Grandson of Louis XV, married Marie-Antoinette at the age of 16, crowned in 1774. A kindly man but very indecisive and apt to seem stiff with strangers; quite unable to handle the crisis of his reign. Executed in 1793.

Louis XVII (1785-95) Became Dauphin on the death of his brother in June 1789. He spent his last three years in the Temple prison losing his father, mother and aunt to the guillotine. Although not intentionally ill-treated, conditions were unhealthy and he died of tuberculosis.

Malouet, Pierre (1740-1814) A lawyer and government servant who was elected to the Estates-General in 1789 adopting a moderate monarchist position. He left France in August 1792 but returned in 1801 to enter Bonaparte's naval administration.

Marat, Jean-Paul (1743-93) Originally qualified as a doctor but from 1789 best known as a radical editor and journalist (editor of *L'Ami du Peuple*). Strong supporter of the Mountain, assassinated in his bath by Charlotte Corday in 1793.

Marie-Antoinette (1755-93) Daughter of the Emperor Francis I of Austria and Maria-Teresa. Married Louis XVI at the age of 15. Unpopular with French people and generally thought of as frivolous and insensitive. In touch with foreign princes after the Revolution and accused of treason in October 1793, found guilty and executed.

Mirabeau, Honoré-Gabriel, comte de (1749-91) Member of old noble family whose father kept him in prison for eight years under a *lettre de cachet* in his youth. Elected for Third Estate of Aix-en-Provence in 1789, he soon became renowned for his rousing oratory in favour of reform. At first hostile to the Court but by 1790 seen as an ally of the King. Deeply mistrusted by most of his contemporaries.

Molière (stage name of **Jean-Baptiste Poquelin**) (1622-73) An actor and playwright at the court of Louis XIV; wrote many highly successful comedies which satirised social trends.

Montesquieu, Charles (1689-1755) A member of a noble family from Bordeaux, he at first practised as a lawyer but took up writing, largely on political subjects, after a prolonged visit to England. His book *De l'esprit des lois* was very influential in Enlightenment circles.

Morris, Gouverneur (1752-1816) A wealthy American, he became Ambassador to France for the United States in 1791. His obvious sympathy for the royalists alienated the Jacobins and he was recalled in 1793. He remained in Europe, working as an English spy for some of the time.

Mounier, Jean-Joseph (1758-1806) A lawyer from Dauphiné, active in the provincial Estates of 1788, the Estates-General and the Constituent Assembly. He proposed the Tennis Court Oath and drafted the first three articles of the Declaration of the Rights of Man. He left Paris after the October Days for his home, eventually fleeing to Switzerland in May 1790.

Nancy, Bishop of – see **Fare.**

Napoleon – see **Bonaparte.**

Narbonne, Louis, comte de (1755-1813) Rumoured to be the illegitimate child of Louis XV he was trained as a soldier and was very close to the King. However he became a Marshal after the Flight to Varennes and was very much involved in preparations for war. Emigrated in 1792, but returned under Napoleon and became his trusted servant.

Necker, Jacques (1732-1804) Born in Geneva he first became Controller-General of Finances for Louis XVI in 1776-81 when he gained the reputation of being a financial genius by his success in arranging loans to pay for French involvement in the American War of Independence. Great expectations were aroused by his return in 1788 but he was unable to stave off the coming Revolution. His final resignation in 1790 was almost unnoticed.

Newton, Isaac (1642-1727) An English scientist and mathematician whose work had an enormous influence on his successors. This work seemed to presuppose an almost clockwork universe acting on fixed and knowable laws. His emphasis on the experimental method helped to create a new attitude to the external world.

Noailles, Louis-Marie, vicomte de (1756-1804) A noble deputy to the Estates-General but with progressive opinions; very involved in the events of 4 August 1789. He fought in the French Army during the Revolutionary Wars and died of wounds in the West Indies.

Orléans, Louis Philippe Joseph, duc d' (1747-93) Louis XVI's cousin, but because of his debauched lifestyle he was on bad terms with him. He began to support the reformers in France, particularly Abbé Sieyès, from 1787. He was one of the first nobles to join the Third Estate in the National Assembly. When titles were abolished in 1792 he took the name of Philippe Égalité. By 1793 he had become disillusioned with the Revolution and was arrested and guillotined after his son had fled to the Austrians with General Dumouriez.

Paine, Thomas (1737-1809) An English Deist and political radical who spent time in both America and France during the Revolution; elected a deputy to the Convention for the Pas-de-Calais as a Girondin sympathiser. He was arrested during the Terror but was released unharmed. His *Rights of Man* was one of the most radical political statements of the period.

Parisot, Jean (1757-1838) A member of a legal family and deputy for Bar-sur-Seine in 1789.

Pétion de Villeneuve, Jérôme (1756-94) A lawyer and deputy to the Estates-General who soon gained the reputation of a radical. He was elected Mayor of Paris in 1791 and the following year took the lead in demanding Louis's removal. However he did not favour the King's execution and was identified with his Girondin adversaries by Robespierre. He fled from Paris to the west of France and was found dead in 1794.

Prieur de la Côte d'Or, Claude-Antoine (1763-1832) Elected to the Legislative Assembly in 1791 and was soon identified with the radicals. When war broke out he was active in assuring the supply of armaments. He was not directly affected by the Terror or the fall of Robespierre and remained in public life, eventually founding the *École Polytechnique*. During the Napoleonic era he became a successful manufacturer.

Provence, Louis Stanislas Xavier, comte de (1756-1824) Louis XVI's brother, little interested in public life before the Revolution. He emigrated in 1791, on the same day as Louis's abortive flight to Varennes. He became officially Louis XVIII on the death of the young Louis XVII in 1795. He only managed to regain the throne in 1815 with the help of the European allies.

Prussia, King of, Frederick William II (1744-97) Succeeded Frederick the Great in 1786 but did not possess the ability of his predecessor; was the ally of Austria in the war against revolutionary France.

Quatremère de Quincy, Antoine-Chrysostome (1755-1849) A Parisian critic and designer and a deputy in the Legislative Assembly; he was a colleague of David on the Committee of Public Instruction, and planned the conservative festival for Simoneau. He also refurbished the *Panthéon* as the burial place of the 'heroes of the nation'.

Racine, Jean (1639-99) A good friend of Molière, who also enjoyed royal favour for most of his life. Wrote mainly tragedies on elevated classical themes in elegant verse.

Réveillon (?) A wealthy wallpaper manufacturer in Paris whose premises were attacked by rioters on 28 April 1789. He was rumoured to have suggested a wage cut for his employees. The real reason for the violence was probably the acute food shortage in Paris and the high price of bread.

Robert, Pierre François Joseph (1762-1826) First a lawyer then a wholesale grocer, finally a journalist, editor of the radical paper *Le Mercure National*. Narrowly escaped injury during the so-called Massacre of the *Champ de Mars;* was elected to the Convention in 1792 and accused of being a hoarder during the Terror but survived. In 1815 went into exile in Belgium.

161

Robespierre, Maximilien François de (1758-94) A lawyer in Arras who was elected to the Estates-General as deputy for the town; he joined the Jacobin Club and was soon seen as a radical and gained the nickname 'the Incorruptible'. He opposed the declaration of war. In July 1793 he joined the Committee of Public Safety and was soon heavily involved in using his powers of oratory to defend the Terror. By the summer of 1794 he had lost much of his support and was himself arrested and executed.

Robespierre the Younger, Augustin Bon Joseph de (1763-94) Younger brother of Maximilien and also a lawyer. He was a deputy to the Convention and went on a mission to the south during the Federalist Revolt. He voluntarily joined Robespierre when he had been condemned and was executed with him the next day.

Roland de la Platière, Jean-Marie (1734-93) Originally a government inspector of manufactures with an interest in science. He married Marie-Jeanne Phlipon who, when her husband had become involved in radical politics in Paris, held a *salon* attended by the Girondin deputies. He was twice Minister of the Interior, but resigned the post in order to remain a deputy. He fled when proscribed on 2 June 1793 but committed suicide on hearing of his wife's execution.

Rousseau, Jean-Jacques (1712-78) A political philosopher and writer who wrote for the *Encyclopédie* but who later quarrelled with his colleagues. He put forward the ideas of the General Will and of the natural goodness of man in his works including *Emile* and *The Social Contract*. He was eventually buried in the *Panthéon* beside Voltaire.

Saint-André, Jeanbon (1749-1813) A Protestant pastor and deputy in the Convention. Soon known as an ardent republican and became a member of the Committee of Public Safety. He went on several missions, notably to restore order in the navy. Absent from Paris on 9 *Thermidor,* he was imprisoned as a Terrorist but survived to hold office and became a baron in Napoleonic France.

Saint-Just, Louis Antoine de (1767-94) From a farming family but educated as a lawyer. Became a lieutenant-colonel in the National Guard and was then elected to the Convention where he joined in the anti-Girondin campaign of the Mountain. As a close associate of Robespierre on the Committee of Public Safety he helped develop his ideas on social and religious matters. After 9 *Thermidor* he shared the fate of Robespierre and 20 others: execution.

Saint-Simon, Claude-Henri de Rouvray, comte de (1760-1825) Played no significant part in the Revolution though he was briefly in prison. After the Restoration he developed a political theory which combined Christianity and socialism, foreseeing many of the consequences of industrialisation. This was very influential on later thinkers including John Stuart Mill, Engels and Carlyle.

Sieyès, Emmanuel-Joseph, abbé (1748-1836) A very influential political writer and deputy to the Constituent Assembly responsible for drafting the Tennis Court Oath. He was also a member of the Convention and of all subsequent governments up to the defeat of Napoleon. He was then exiled in Brussels until 1830.

Target, Guy (1733-1806) A lawyer and counsellor of the Paris *parlement,* he was elected to the Estates-General in 1789. He was largely responsible for the legal reforms of the Constituent Assembly and also helped draft the Napoleonic Codes of Laws.

Terrier de Monciel, Antoine René, marquis de (1757-1831) Already in politics at the time of the Revolution, he was loyal to the King, being Minister of the

Interior after Roland in 1792. On the fall of the monarchy he went into exile but returned in 1806 and later welcomed the Restoration.

Turgot, Anne-Robert-Jacques (1727-81) A lawyer and economist who was responsible for the early attempts to reform French government and the system of taxes. He spent thirteen years as *Intendant* of Limoges under Louis XV and then became Controller-General of Finances in 1774. His plans for reform aroused great opposition and he was forced to resign in 1776, living the rest of his life in retirement.

Vadier, Marc Guillaume Alexis (1736-1828) Member of the Committee of General Security from September 1793: he was a remorseless Terrorist. As one of the leaders of the coup against Robespierre (9 *Thermidor* 1794) he managed to survive the ensuing reaction, and lived quietly under Napoleon.

Vergniaud, Pierre (1753-93) One of the most eloquent orators of the Girondin faction. He was arrested and imprisoned on 2 June 1793, and was guillotined with a number of his colleagues on 31 October 1793.

Voltaire, François-Marie Arouet de (1694-1778) The most celebrated of French eighteenth-century writers, responsible for many satires, poems, novels and other works, all putting forward Enlightened reforming ideas. He visited England which he admired, and also Prussia where he stayed some time with the King, Frederick the Great. He was particularly hostile to the French Church, calling it *'l'infâme'*. In 1791, some thirteen years after his death, he was reinterred in the *Panthéon* in Paris to a wave of revolutionary enthusiasm a few days before the Massacre of the *Champ de Mars*.

Young, Arthur (1741-1820) Very prominent English writer on agriculture and related topics. Founded the *Annals of Agriculture* in 1784. Visited France at the invitation of the comte de la Rochefoucauld. *Travels in France* was first published in 1794.

THE REVOLUTIONARY CALENDAR

Vendémiaire	22 September	–	21 October
Brumaire	22 October	–	20 November
Frimaire	21 November	–	20 December
Nivôse	21 December	–	19 January
Pluviôse	20 January	–	18 February
Ventôse	19 February	–	20 March
Germinal	21 March	–	19 April
Floréal	20 April	–	19 May
Prairial	20 May	–	18 June
Messidor	19 June	–	18 July
Thermidor	19 July	–	17 August
Fructidor	18 August	–	21 September

The revolutionary calendar was established by the Convention on 5 October 1793. It had been planned by a commission which included Fabre d'Eglantine, who was responsible for giving the twelve months new, poetic names evoking nature, such as *Vendémiaire,* 'the time of vintage', and *Brumaire,* 'the time of mists'. The intention was to break with the superstitions of the past and to substitute the wholesome imagery of nature in people's minds. Year I had been proclaimed on 22 September 1792 to mark the overthrow of the monarchy and the inauguration of the Republic. Succeeding years commenced on that date and were divided into twelve months, each of thirty days. Every tenth day, called logically a *decadi,* was to be a holiday, replacing the traditional Sunday rest. The five days left over every year would be known as *sans-culottides* and would be kept as national festivals in honour of patriotic virtues such as 'industry' and 'heroic deeds'.

Figure 35 The revolutionary calendar vanquishing the traditional Gregorian calendar. The print is full of neo-classical imagery. *(By permission of the Houghton Library, Harvard University)*

165

CHRONOLOGY

1786

August — Calonne warns King of looming royal bankruptcy and suggests reforms.

1787

February – May — Meeting of the Assembly of Notables.

May 25 — Calonne dismissed and replaced by Loménie de Brienne.

August 15 — *Parlement* of Paris exiled to Troyes for opposition to royal plan of reform.

1788

May 3 — *Parlement* declares fundamental laws of the kingdom.

May 8 — King uses his absolute power to override *parlement* and set up new courts.

August 8 — Brienne resigns.

August 25 — Necker appointed as Controller of Finances.

September 25 — *Parlement* of Paris decrees that customs of 1614 must be used in forthcoming Estates-General.

1788-9

Winter — Controversy over voting method in forthcoming Estates and election campaign in Paris and the provinces.

1789

May 4 — Opening mass at Versailles for deputies to the Estates-General.

May 5 — Opening session of the Estates-General.

June 17 — Sieyès proclaims that Third Estate constitutes National Assembly.

June 20 — Oath of the Tennis Court.

June 23 — Royal Session.

July 11 — Dismissal of Necker by the King.

July 14 — Fall of the Bastille.

July 17 — The King visits Paris.

Late July–August — The Great Fear.

August 4 — The abolition of feudal privileges.

August 20-26 — Discussion and Declaration of the Rights of Man.

September 11 — Motion to grant King a suspensive veto passed.

October 1 — Banquet for the Flanders Regiment at Versailles.

October 5 — March of the women to Versailles.

October 6 — The royal family move to Paris.

November 2 — The nationalisation of Church property.

December 14-22 — Reorganisation of local government.

December 19	First issue of *assignats*.

1790

May 22	Decree abolishing King's right to declare war.
June 19	Abolition of the nobility.
July 12	Civil Constitution of the Clergy.
July 14	First *Fête de la Fédération*.
November 27	Clerical oath imposed.

1791

April 2	Death of Mirabeau.
April 18	The royal family prevented from going to Saint-Cloud.
May 16	Self-denying ordinance passed by the National Assembly.
June 20-21	Royal flight to Varennes.
June 25	Return of royal family to Paris, humiliated.
July 17	Massacre on the *Champ de Mars*.
August 27	Declaration of Pillnitz.
September 14	The King accepts the constitution.
September 30	Final session of the Constituent (National) Assembly.
October 1	First session of the Legislative Assembly.
November 12	King vetoes decree on *émigrés*.
November 16	Pétion mayor of Paris.
November 29	Refractory priests are declared suspect.
December 19	King vetoes decree on clergy.

1792

End January	100 *livres assignats* = 63 *livres* in coins.
March 1	Francis II succeeds as Emperor of Austria.
April 20	France declares war on Austria.
April 27	Banishment of refractory priests.
June 8	Camp of *fédérés* established by decree outside Paris.
June 11	King vetoes decrees of 27 April and 8 June.
June 12	King dismisses Girondin ministry.
June 20	People invade the Tuileries.
June 30	Arrival of Marseilles *fédérés;* the *Marseillaise* sung.
July 11	Call to people to defend France.
July 25	Brunswick manifesto.
July 27	*Emigrés'* property confiscated.
August 10	Revolutionary Commune set up in Paris. Tuileries captured. Convention summoned.
August 14	Sale of *émigrés'* properties.
August 17	Court established to try crimes of 10 August.
August 23	Surrender of Longwy to the Austrians.
September 2-5	Massacres in prisons of Paris.
September 20	Victory at Valmy. End of Legislative Assembly.
September 21	Abolition of the monarchy. Opening of the Convention.
September 22	**Year 1** of the Republic
November 6	Victory at Jemappes.
November 20	Iron chest found in the Tuileries.

December 10	Opening of the trial of the King.

1793

January 17-20	Louis XVI condemned.
January 21	Louis XVI executed.
February 1	War declared on Great Britain and Holland.
February 23	Mass conscription of 300,000 men.
March 7	War declared on Spain.
March 11	Rising in the Vendée.
March 18	Defeat at Neerwinden.
April 1	Treachery of Dumouriez.
April 6	Creation of Committee of Public Safety.
May 4	Maximum prices for grain and flour.
May 31 – June 2	Rising against the Girondins; arrest and exclusion of deputies.
Early June	Federalist risings in the west, south-west, and east of France.
June 24	New constitution adopted.
July 10	Danton resigns; Committee of Public Safety reorganised.
July 13	Assassination of Marat.
July 27	Robespierre joins Committee of Public Safety.
August 1	Destruction of La Vendée ordered.
August 14	Carnot and Prieur de la Côte d'Or join Committee.
August 23	Mass conscription ordered.
September 5	Demonstration of *sans-culottes*.
September 9	Creation of the Revolutionary Army.
September 17	Law of suspects.
September 29	General Maximum on food and wages.
October 5	Adoption of the revolutionary calendar.
October 15	Trial of the Girondins.

Year II of the Republic

Vendémiaire 19	(October 10)	Declaration of revolutionary government in France.
Vendémiaire 26	(October 16)	Execution of Marie-Antoinette. Victory at Wattignies.
Brumaire 10	(October 31)	Execution of Girondins.
Brumaire 20	(November 10)	Festival of Liberty and Reason in Notre-Dame.
December		100 *livres assignats* = 48 *livres* in coins.

1794

Pluviôse 10	(February 4)	Abolition of slavery in the colonies.
Germinal 1-4	(March 21-24)	Trial and execution of the Hébertists.
Germinal 13-16	(April 2-5)	Trial and execution of the Dantonists.
Prairial 20	(June 8)	Festival of the Supreme Being.
Prairial 22	(June 10)	Law of *Prairial* (of suspects).
Messidor 8	(June 26)	Victory at Fleurus.
Thermidor 8	(July 26)	Robespierre's speech to the Convention.
Thermidor 9	(July 27)	Saint-Just shouted down in the Convention; arrest of Robespierre and his associates.
Thermidor 10	(July 28)	Execution of Robespierre, Saint-Just and 20 supporters.
Thermidor 13	(July 31)	Reorganisation of committees.
Thermidor 14	(August 1)	Law of *Prairial* revoked.

Thermidor 18	(August 5)	Many prisoners released.

Year III of the Republic

October		100 *livres assignats* = 20 *livres* in coins.
Brumaire 22	(November 12)	Closure of the Jacobin Club in Paris.
Frimaire 18	(December 8)	Return of excluded Girondin deputies.
Nivôse 4	(December 24)	Abolition of the Maximum.

1795

Pluviôse 29	(February 17)	Agreement between the Republic and the leaders of the *Chouans*.
Ventôse 3	(February 21)	Decree on freedom of worship and separation of Church and State.
Germinal 16	(April 5)	Peace between France and Prussia.
Floréal 15	(May 4)	Massacre of imprisoned Jacobins at Lyons.
Floréal 27	(May 16)	Treaty between France and Holland.
Prairial 12	(May 31)	Suppression of the Revolutionary Tribunal.
Prairial 20	(June 8)	Death of Louis XVII in the Temple.
Messidor 6	(June 24)	Manifesto of Verona issued by Louis XVIII.
July		100 *livres assignats* = 8 *livres* in coins.
Thermidor 3	(July 21)	Hoche's victory at Quiberon Bay.
Thermidor 4	(July 22)	Peace with Spain.

Year IV of the Republic

Vendémiaire 1	(September 23)	Annexation of Belgium. The Convention adopts the new constitution.
October		100 *livres assignats* = 1.4 *livres* in coins.
Vendémiaire 13	(October 5)	Royalist rising in Paris crushed by Barras and Bonaparte.
Vendémiaire 24	(October 16)	Bonaparte a Major-General.
Brumaire 3	(October 25)	Law excludes relatives of *émigrés* from office. Also laws passed against priests.
Brumaire 4	(October 26)	Convention is dissolved. Napoleon Commander-in-Chief of the Army of the Interior.
Brumaire 9	(October 31)	Election of the Directory.

Glossary

Academy
In provincial France, a club which met to discuss intellectual and political questions of the day.

Active citizen
A Frenchman who paid sufficiently high taxes to have the right to vote for the Legislative Assembly.

Ancien régime
The pre-revolutionary government of France.

Aristocrats
A term of abuse aimed by revolutionaries against nobles and other opponents.

Armées révolutionnaires
Units of citizen soldiers recruited from among loyal, urban *sans-culottes* to ensure food supplies for French towns in 1793-4.

Assignats
A form of paper money originally secured against the value of Church lands, used after November 1789 in France.

Bastille
A fortress used as a state prison, with cannon in the towers which could be used to bombard the city of Paris itself if a rebellion broke out. In 1789 it contained 7 prisoners, 30 Swiss Guards and 80 veterans of the French Army.

Biens nationaux
The nationalised property of the Church which was sold for the national benefit after November 1789.

Bleus
Government troops, so-called by counter-revolutionaries because of their blue tunics.

Bourbons
Family name of the French royal family.

Bourgeoisie, bourgeois
Used loosely to mean 'middle-class'; the richer elements of non-noble French society. Strictly speaking means 'town-dweller'.

Cahiers de doléances
Lists of grievances prepared by the Electors in each electoral district for the meeting of the Estates-General in 1789.

Champ de Mars
Large open space on the edge of Paris where the *Fête de la Fédération* was held. Previously used for military drill.

Châteaux
Large country houses belonging to the nobility.

Chouans
Counter-revolutionary rebels in Brittany.

Cockade
Badge usually of coloured ribbon worn in a hat to show allegiance to a group, cause or country.

Commune	The smallest administrative unit in French society, a community.
Communes	In the National Assembly, these were the deputies from the former Third Estate.
Constituent Assembly	The title taken by the National Assembly by a resolution of 9 July 1789. This body met from that date until 30 September 1791. It had its origin in the assembly of the Third Estate which met at Versailles in May 1789 and which voted itself the title of National Assembly on 17 June 1789. The King ordered the other Estates to join the National Assembly on 27 June 1789.
Consulate	The form of government in France from the fall of the Directory (November 1799) until Napoleon made himself Emperor in 1804.
Convention	A national assembly summoned without the authority of the King or by any other traditional legal method.
Cordelier	A radical club, taking its name from the convent in which it met. Power base for demagogues such as Danton.
Corvée royale, or ***corvée***	Either forced labour for the King on the roads or, more generally, unpaid labour for a feudal lord.
Counter-revolutionary	Somebody actively hostile to the aims of the Revolution.
Curés	Parish priests.
Deism	A philosophical theory which accepted a benevolent Creator but rejected any revealed religion (e.g. Christianity).
Département	Basic local government division of post-revolutionary France.
Directory	The government of France by an executive of five members between 1795 and 1799.
Émigré	A Frenchman or -woman, usually of noble birth, who fled from France during the Revolution.
Enlightenment	Term used to describe the intellectual climate of the eighteenth century.
Enragés	Very extreme radical urban revolutionaries.
Estates-General	Body representing all the elements in French society, which met in May 1789 for the first time since 1614.

Estates – First – Second – Third	The Church. The nobility. The remainder of the community. These were the customary and legal divisions of French pre-revolutionary society.
Factions	Divisions between political groups caused by policy differences. Usually used with a derogatory implication.
Federalist Revolt	The revolt of moderate, provincial supporters of the Revolution against the political dominance of Jacobin Paris in the summer of 1793.
Fédérés	National Guards from the provinces who came to Paris to celebrate and defend the Revolution.
Feudal dues	Payments in money or in kind due to a feudal lord.
Feuillants	Name given to moderate revolutionary leaders and their Club, founded after the Massacre of the *Champ de Mars*.
Free trade	International trade unimpeded by customs duties.
Gabelle	Salt tax. In some areas of France everyone was compelled to buy a certain large quantity of salt at a high price every year.
Généralités	The major administrative divisions of pre-revolutionary France.
Girondins	Deputies in the Legislative Assembly who came from the Bordeaux area, and their supporters. In favour of the declaration of war but not of the extension of political rights to the urban *sans-culottes*.
Gouvernements	Provinces or military districts of pre-revolutionary France.
Indulgents	Jacobins such as Danton who were accused of wishing to be lenient or 'indulgent' towards counter-revolutionaries.
Intendant	The royal official in charge of a *généralité*.
Invalides	The building storing arms and housing retired veterans of the royal army, whose chapel became a national shrine.
Jacobin	Supporter of the Parisian Club which met in the former Jacobin convent, or one of its provincial branches.

Journée	Literally 'day'. Used for the important days of action by the *sans-culottes* during the Revolution.
Laboureurs	The wealthiest group of peasant farmers.
Law of *Frimaire*	The suppression of most of the People's Armies on 4 December 1793.
Law of *Prairial*	Simplified and speeded-up trials during the Terror from 10 June 1794.
Legislative Assembly	The second elected Assembly to rule during the Revolution from 1 October 1791 to 20 September 1792.
Lettre de cachet	A pre-revolutionary order committing a person to prison without trial indefinitely.
Lit de justice	A ceremony at which royal decrees were registered despite the objections of the *parlement* (see below).
Livre	A unit of account, not a coin. Valued at 10½d (rather less than 5p) in 1789.
Manifesto	A public declaration of policy by a person or body.
Maximum	A series of laws which attempted, with varying success, to fix the maximum price of essential commodities.
Métayers	Peasants who owed half of their produce for the year to their landlord who provided all tools, seed, animals and buildings.
Mountain	Jacobin deputies in the Convention who supported the radical policies of Robespierre and who sat on high benches in the Convention.
Muscadins	Thuggish, dandified young men of the Thermidorean reaction.
National Guard	Part-time local militia formed in 1789 by local communities as a reaction to widespread disorder in Paris and in the provinces.
Notables	The members, all of high social standing, of the first assembly summoned by the King in 1787.
Noblesse de la robe	Nobles who had acquired their title by the purchase of high legal or royal office.
Noblesse de l'épée	The old military nobility.

Panthéon	The church of Sainte-Geneviève in Paris, converted into a mausoleum for the heroes of the Revolution.
Paris Commune	The municipal government of Paris 1789-95.
Parlements, parlementaires	The sovereign courts of France and their principal officials; these had the power to object to royal decrees.
Parricides	Those who killed their own fathers. Often used as a term of abuse against counter-revolutionaries.
Passive citizen	A Frenchman who did not pay sufficiently high taxes to have the right to vote for the Legislative Assembly.
Patriot	Usually a description of a supporter of the Revolution, but counter-revolutionaries could also use this term to refer to themselves.
Philosophe	An intellectual imbued with Enlightenment ideas.
Physiocrats	Group of French intellectuals who believed that land was the only source of wealth and that landowners should therefore pay the bulk of the taxes.
Plain	The majority in the Convention who were not committed to extreme radical policies.
Radicals	Those in favour of fundamental changes in the nature of French government and society.
Refractories	Catholic priests who had refused to take the oath of civil obedience established by the Civil Constitution of the Clergy.
Regicide	A deputy in the Convention who voted for the execution of Louis XVI in January 1793.
Restoration	Louis XVI's brother, the comte de Provence, was restored to the throne of France in 1814 following the defeat of Napoleon. He fled from Paris when Napoleon escaped from exile on the island of Elba, but returned again after the battle of Waterloo in 1815. He died in 1824.
Sans-culottes	Literally 'those who do not wear knee breeches'. Urban artisans and lower-middle-class supporters of the Revolution.
Sections	The electoral districts in Paris and other large towns set up by the reform of local government undertaken in 1790-91.
Seigneur	A feudal lord.

Société-mère	The original Jacobin Club in Paris.
Sous	Copper coins. 20 *sous* = 1 *livre*.
Taille	Tax paid by non-noble individuals on the annual value of their landholding.
Terror	The period in late 1793-4 when the Jacobin government used harsh measures varying from summary imprisonment to mass executions, creating an atmosphere of fear and intimidation to repress their opponents.
Thermidor **9-10**	The downfall and execution of Robespierre and his followers.
Tyrannicide	The destruction of an unjust ruler by virtuous citizens.
Vendéans	Royalist counter-revolutionary fighters in La Vendée, in south-west France.
Vendémiaire **12-13**	Counter-revolutionary rising in Paris on 4-5 October 1795, suppressed with the help of Bonaparte.
Versailles	The huge and splendid palace built originally by Louis XIV 12 miles outside Paris where the royal family lived until October 1789, and which was also the centre of French pre-revolutionary government.

Specimen A level questions

1. Why did the Revolution not end with the promulgation of the Constitution in September 1791?

2. Did anything more than personal animosity divide Girondins and Jacobins?

3. 'In the last analysis, a passion for equality appears to be the distinctive characteristic of the *sansculotte*'. Do you agree?

4. Do you agree with the view of R. C. Cobb that 'The events of the Revolution constantly accentuated the economic, religious and political gulf between town and country'?

5. What do you consider to have been the greatest achievements of the Revolutionaries in the period from 1789 to 1795?

Northern Ireland Schools Examinations Council
1987

6. Why did the authority of the crown collapse so quickly in 1789?

7. What, if anything, united the Thermidorians?

8. 'The War moulded the Revolution far more than the Revolution moulded the War.' How far do you agree with this view?

9. Was the French Revolution down to 1795 primarily a triumph for the bourgeoisie?

10. How close to success did the Counter-Revolutionaries come between 1789 and 1795?

11. Answer ALL the questions relating to the following sources:

Source—No. 1.

Jacques-Louis David *Oath of the Tennis Court,* 20 June 1789

Source—No. 2.

'"M. Mounier supported by MM. Target, Chapelier, and Barnave, presented a motion which declared that it was unprecedented for the Chamber of the Estates-General to be occupied by armed men; that another meeting place should be offered to the National Assembly;... that wounded in their rights and dignity,... the representatives of the nation bind themselves to the preservation and interests of the country by a solemn oath." This motion was approved to general applause.'

Account of Debate in the *Moniteur,* I.89.

Source—No. 4.

(*a*) Roland to Louis XVI, 10 June 1792.

'The French people have given themselves a Constitution; it has engendered malcontents and rebels; the majority of the nation wishes to maintain it; it has sworn to defend it at the price of its blood, and it has greeted with joy the war which offered a great opportunity to guarantee it. The minority, however, sustained by hope, has united all its efforts to gain advantage. Hence this internal struggle against the laws, this anarchy which good citizens lament and of which malevolent persons take good care to avail themselves in order to slander the new regime.'

(*b*) Despatch from the British Embassy, Paris, Earl Gower to Lord Grenville, 6 July 1792.

'Mr. de la Fayette's conduct during his stay in Paris was not sufficiently bold and energetic to affect the Jacobins with that degree of fear which it was intended to have produced, and it has only served to make them more active in sending for the assistance of their friends from all parts of the kingdom. Those friends are accordingly arriving from all quarters, from Marseilles, from Bordeaux, from Brest, and their arrival is legalized by a decree of the National Assembly which has received royal sanction'.

(*c*) Speech by Robespierre at the Jacobin club, 11 July 1792.

'*La Patrie* is in danger. These words say everything to warm hearts, truly enamoured of liberty and of our country. This message does not teach us any new facts. Before this declaration, we knew that a treacherous general led our armies, we knew that a corrupt court plotted without cease against our country and our constitution.'

Source—No. 3.

'Executions by département, 1792-93'.

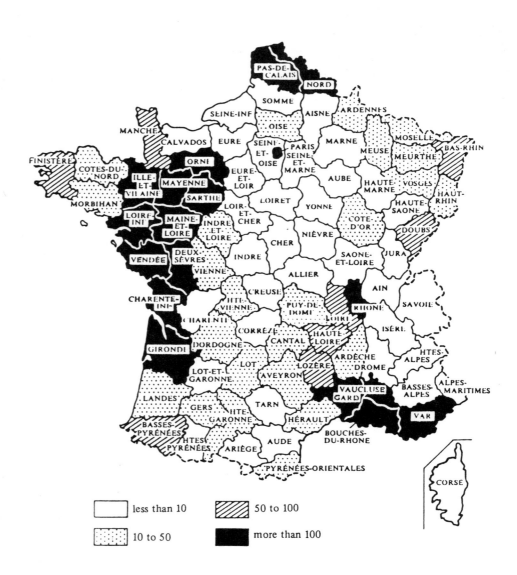

Distribution of Executions by Département, 1793-4.

(i)   What does the map in source 3 tell you about the impact and incidence of the Terror?   [5 marks]

(ii)   What interpretation of the Revolution is presented in David's painting in source 1?   [10 marks]

(iii)   To what extent is David's depiction of the Tennis Court Oath, source 1, consistent with the report given in the *Moniteur*, source 2?   [10 marks]

(iv)   What light do the documents in source 4 throw on the political climate in France during the summer of 1792?   [10 marks]

(v)   Assess the nature and value to the historian of the different types of sources used above.   [15 marks]

Northern Ireland Schools Examinations Council
1988

---

12. How far was Louis XVI personally responsible for the decline and fall of the French monarchy in 1792?

University of Oxford Delegacy of Local Examinations
Summer 1987

---

13. Why was the French Estates General summoned in 1789?

University of Oxford Delegacy of Local Examinations
Summer 1988

---

14. Who in France benefited most from the French Revolution?

University of Oxford Delegacy of Local Examinations
Summer 1989

---

15. 'It was the inability of the *ancien régime* to understand the needs of the times that finally provoked revolution.' How accurately does this explain the French Revolution?

Southern Universities' Joint Board
Summer 1988

---

16. 'The "Declaration of the Rights of Man" was the first sign that the French Revolution had developed beyond the satisfaction of local grievances.' How far do you agree?

17. Examine the process by which the Revolution became Parisian rather than national during the years 1789-1791.

18. How radically did the Constituent Assembly reshape the administrative and judicial institutions of France?

19. What bearing had the royal flight to Varennes upon the outbreak of war against foreign powers in 1792?

20. 'Directed originally against the enemies of the Revolution at home and abroad, the Terror developed its own momentum, and ended by consuming its originators.' Examine the truth of this statement.

21. FINANCIAL PROBLEMS OF THE FRENCH CROWN ON THE EVE OF THE REVOLUTION

Study Documents I, II, III and IV below and then answer questions (*a*) to (*e*) which follow:

DOCUMENT I

One cannot take a step in this vast kingdom without encountering different laws, conflicting customs, privileges, exemptions,... rights and claims of all kinds... His Majesty therefore proposes:

1.   To suppress the two *vingtièmes* and the four *sous pour livre* as from 1 January of this year...

2.   As it is unjust that land devoted to pleasure should be more favourably taxed than that employed in useful cultivation, chateaux, parkland, closes, houses and all kinds of land shall be subject to the tax but only in respect of the surface area they occupy; they will be assessed at the rate of the best land in the parish.

(*A memorandum by Calonne*, 1787)

DOCUMENT II

The King does not have the competence to institute a percentage tax but only to ask for a fixed sum to meet specific requirements. Such a tax could not be accepted by the *parlements*, who possess only a subsidiary and fiduciary power in the absence of the Estates-General. Accordingly, only the Estates-General could give the necessary consent to such a tax. An Assembly of Notables which gave its blessing to the institution of such a tax would be exceeding its powers and would be dishonoured in the eyes of the nation.

(*Le Blanc de Castillon, Procurator-General of the Parlement of Provence, speaking in a committee of the Assembly of Notables, February* 1787)

DOCUMENT III

We are about to make *great changes* in the *parlements*. For several months the King's orders and replies have displayed unswerving consistency and firmness of principle. The *parlements* are stunned and worried but persist nonetheless with seditious resolutions and remonstrances. The idea is to confine them to the function of judges and to create another assembly which will have the right to register taxes and general laws for the kingdom.... It is very irksome to be obliged to institute changes of this nature, but it is clear from the state of affairs that delay would diminish the resources for preserving and consolidating the King's authority.

(*Marie Antoinette to Joseph II, 24 April* 1788)

DOCUMENT IV

The Revolution in France is attended with many novel circumstances, not only in the political sphere, but in the circle of money transactions. Among others, it shows that *a Government may be in a state of insolvency, and a Nation rich.* So far as the fact is confined to the late Government of France, it was insolvent; because the nation would not longer support its extravagance, and therefore it could no longer support itself—but with respect to the Nation, all the means existed....

The French Nation, in effect, endeavoured to render the late Government insolvent, for the purpose of taking Government into its own hands; and it reserved its means for the support of the new Government.

(*Thomas Paine, 'The Rights of Man'*, 1791)

(Maximum marks)

(*a*) What were the '*parlements*' (lines 13, 18 and 20)? What 'great changes' (line 18) were now envisaged for them, and for what reasons? **(4)**

(*b*) 'A Government may be in a state of insolvency, and a Nation rich, (line 29). How accurately does this statement reflect the actual economic situation of France and its monarchy in 1787? **(4)**

(*c*) What is revealed by Document I (lines 1-10) concerning the obstacles likely to be encountered in any attempt to reform the French tax system in 1787? **(4)**

(*d*) Summarise the constitutional theories put forward in Document II (lines 11-17). What political consequences would be likely to follow from the full adoption of such theories in 1787? **(5)**

(*e*) Using both your own knowledge and the evidence presented in Documents I, II and IV, consider what value may be placed upon Paine's views on the role played by royal insolvency in bringing about the French Revolution in the years 1787-1789. **(8)**

University of London School Examinations Board
Summer 1988

---

 22. Why did the bankruptcy of the French Crown lead to a revolutionary situation in France by 1789?

23. 'The surrender of feudal rights marked for some the end of the Revolution, for others the start of a counter-revolution.' Discuss.

24. Assess the strengths and weaknesses of the Constitution of 1791.

25. How important were the outbreak and continuance of war in bringing about the fall of the Girondins?

26. Why was Robespierre unable to preserve either his political power or his life?

27. How important was religion in sustaining provincial opposition to the Revolution?

University of London School Examinations Board
January 1989

---

28. What were the obstacles to financial reform which made orderly constitutional change in France in the years before 1789 impossible?

29. 'Too much thinking, too little action': how far do you agree with this view of the work of the Constituent Assembly in the period from its meeting in June 1789 to the end of 1790?

 30. Why did the experiment in constitutional monarchy end in the deposition and execution of Louis XVI?

31. How far did the outbreak of war, and the development of the war up to the

Thermidorian Reaction, create a new sense of national unity and a new social structure within France?

University of London School Examinations Board
Summer 1989

Bibliography

Entries in bold type are especially recommended for further reading.

Ascherson, N. (ed.), *The Times reports of the French Revolution*, Times Books, 1975.

Bertaud, J-P., *La Révolution Armée: les soldats-citoyens et la Révolution Française*, Paris, Laffont, 1979.

Blanning, T.C.W., *The Origins of the French Revolutionary Wars*, Longman, 1986.

Blanning, T.C.W., *The French Revolution: aristocrats versus bourgeois?*, Macmillan, 1987.

Brinton, C., *The Jacobins: an Essay in the New History*, Macmillan, 1930.

Carré, H. (ed.), *Correspondance inédite du marquis de Ferrières*, Paris, Armand Colin, 1932.

Cobb, R., *The People's Armies*, Yale University Press, 1987.

Cobban, A., *The Social Interpretation of the French Revolution*, Cambridge University Press, 1964.

Davenport, B.C. (ed.), *A Diary of the French Revolution by Gouverneur Morris, 1782-1816*, Greenwood Paris, 1972.

Dickens, C., *A Tale of Two Cities*, Chapman and Hall, 1890.

Dowd, D.L., *Pageant-Master of the Republic: Jacques-Louis David and the French Revolution*, Books for Libraries Press, 1948.

Doyle, W., *The Ancien Regime*, Macmillan, 1986.

Doyle, W., *The Origins of the French Revolution*, Oxford University Press, 1980.

Egret, J., *La Révolution des Notables*, Paris, Armand Colin, 1950.

Emsley, C., *British Society and the French Wars, 1793-1815*, Macmillan, 1979.

Favier, J. (ed.), *The Chronicle of the French Revolution*, Longman, 1989.

Fehér, F., *The Frozen Revolution: an Essay on Jacobinism*, Cambridge University Press, 1987.

Ford, F. L., *Europe, 1780-1830*, Longman, 1989.

Forsyth, M., *Reason and Revolution: the Political Thought of the Abbé Sieyès*, Leicester University Press, 1987.

Furet, F., 'La Révolution Française et la tradition jacobine', in Lucas, C. (ed.), *The Political Culture of the French Revolution*, Vol. 2, Pergamon Press, 1988.

Gilchrist, J. and Murray, W. J., *The Press in the French Revolution*, Cheshire, Ginn, 1971.

Godechot, J., *La Pensée Révolutionnaire 1780-1799*, Paris, Armand Colin, 1964.

Godechot, J., *Les Institutions de la France sous la Révolution et l'Empire*, Paris, Presses Universitaires de France, 1968.

Godechot, J., *The Taking of the Bastille, July 14, 1789*, Faber, 1970.

Greer, D., *The incidence of Terror during the French Revolution*, Harvard University Press, 1935.

Hampson, N., *Prelude to Terror: The Constituent Assembly and the Failure of Consensus, 1789-1791*, Blackwell, 1988.

Hampson, N., *Social History of the French Revolution*, Routledge and Kegan Paul, 1963.

Hampson, N., *Will and Circumstance: Montesquieu, Rousseau and the French Revolution*, Duckworth, 1983.

Hardman, J., *The French Revolution. The Fall of the Ancient Régime to the Thermidorean Reaction 1785-1795*. Documents of Modern History, Edward Arnold, 1981.

Hardman, J. (ed.), *French Revolution Documents*, Vol. 2, Blackwell, 1973.

Hunt, L., *Politics, Culture and Class in the French Revolution*, University of California Press, 1984.

Jones, P. M., *The Peasantry in the French Revolution*, Cambridge University Press, 1988.

Jordan, D. P., *The Revolutionary Career of Maximilien Robespierre*, The Free Press, 1985.

Kekewich, L. and Rose, S. (eds.), *Hyperbook French Revolution*, Longman Logotron, 1990.

Kelly, L., *Women of the French Revolution*, Hamilton, 1987.

Kennedy, M., *The Jacobin Clubs in the French Revolution: the Early Years*, Princeton University Press, 1981.

Kennedy, M., *The Jacobin Clubs in the French Revolution: the Middle Years*, Princeton University Press, 1988.

Lefebvre, G, *The Coming of the French Revolution*, Princeton University Press, 1947.

Lefebvre, G., *The Great Fear of 1789*, New Left Books, 1973.

Lefebvre, G., *The French Revolution*, Vol. 1, Routledge and Kegan Paul, 1965.

Lefebvre, G., *The French Revolution*, Vol. 2, Routledge and Kegan Paul, 1967.

Levy, D. G., Applewhite, H. B. and Johnson, M. D. (eds.), *Women in Revolutionary Paris*, University of Illinois Press, 1979.

Lewis, G., *The Second Vendée: the Continuity of Counter-revolution in the Department of the Gard, 1789-1815,* Clarendon Press, 1978.

Lough, J., *An Introduction to Eighteenth Century France*, Longman, 1980.

Lough, J., *France on the Eve of Revolution: British Travellers' Observations,* Croom Helm, 1987.

Macdonald, J., *Rousseau and the French Revolution 1762-91,* Athlone Press, 1965.

Maxwell, C. (ed.): Young, Travels in France during the years 1787, 1788, 1789, Cambridge University Press, 1929.

Mazauric, C., *Jacobinisme et Révolution*, Paris, Editions Souches, 1984.

McManners, J., *The French Revolution and the Church*, SPCK, 1969.

Morley, H. (ed.): Voltaire, *Letters on England*, Cassell's National Library, 1889.

Orczy, Baroness, *The Scarlet Pimpernel,* Hodder and Stoughton, 1960, (1st published 1905).

Ozouf, M., *Festivals and the French Revolution*, Harvard University Press, 1988.

Palmer, R. R., *Twelve Who Ruled: The Year of the Terror in the French Revolution*, Princeton University Press, 1941.

Parker, N., *Portrayals of Revolution: Images, Debates and Patterns of Thought in Representing the French Revolution,* Harvester, to appear 1990.

Prichard, J. V. (ed.): Montesquieu, *The Spirit of Laws*, Bohn's Standard Library, 1914.

Roberts, J. M., *French Revolution documents,* Vol. 1, Blackwell, 1966.

Rudé, G., *Great Lives Observed,* Prentice Hall, 1967.

Rudé, G., *The Crowd in the French Revolution*, Oxford University Press, 1959.

Rudé, G., *The French Revolution*, Weidenfeld and Nicolson, 1988.

Rudé, G. (ed.), *Robespierre,* Prentice Hall, 1967.

Schama, S., *Citizens: a Chronicle of the French Revolution*, Viking, 1989.

Secher, R., *Le Génocide franco-français: la Vendée-vengé,* Paris, Presses Universitaires de France, 1986.

Slavin, M., *The Making of an Insurrection: Parisian Sections and the Gironde,* Harvard University Press, 1986.

Soboul, A., *A Short History of the French Revolution, 1789-99,* University of California Press, 1977.

Soboul, A., *The French Revolution*, University of California Press, 1977.

Soboul, A., *The Parisian Sans-Culottes and the French Revolution, 1793-4,* Oxford University Press, 1964.

Sutherland, D., *France 1789-1815: Revolution and Counter-revolution*, Fontana Press, 1985.

Sydenham, M. J., *The Girondins,* Athlone Press, 1961.

Talmon, J. L., *The Origins of Totalitarian Dictatorship*, Secker and Warburg, 1952.

Thompson, J. M., *The French Revolution*, Oxford University Press, 1985.

Thompson, J. M. (ed.), *English Eye Witnesses of the French Revolution*, Blackwell, 1938.

Thompson, J. M. (ed.), *French Revolution Documents 1789-94,* Blackwell, 1933.

Wickham Legg, L. G. (ed.), *Select Documents Illustrative of the History of the French Revolution,* Vol. 1, Clarendon Press, 1905.

Wordsworth, W., *The Prelude,* Macmillan Educational Press, 1988, (1st published 1850).

Wright, D. G., *Revolution and Terror in France 1789-1795,* Seminar Studies in History, Longman, 1974.

Index

References including illustrations are shown in italic.